THE
INARTICULATE
SOCIETY

BOOKS BY TOM SHACHTMAN

The Day America Crashed (1979)
Edith and Woodrow (1981)
The Phony War, 1939–1940 (1982)
Decade of Shocks, 1963–1974 (1983)
Skyscraper Dreams (1991)
The Inarticulate Society (1995)

COLLABORATIVE BOOKS

The FBI–KGB War by Robert J. Lamphere and Tom Shachtman (1986)
The Gilded Leaf by Patrick Reynolds and Tom Shachtman (1989)
Straight to the Top by Paul G. Stern and Tom Shachtman (1990)
Image By Design by Clive Chajet and Tom Shachtman (1991)
Whoever Fights Monsters by Robert K. Ressler and Tom Shachtman (1992)
Justice Is Served by Robert K. Ressler and Tom Shachtman (1994)

FOR CHILDREN

Novels
Beachmaster (1988)
Wavebender (1989)
Driftwhistler (1991)

Non-fiction
Growing Up Masai (1981)
The Birdman of St. Petersburg (1982)
Parade! (1985)
America's Birthday (1987)
Video Power by Tom Shachtman and Harriet Shelare (1988)
The President Builds a House (1989)

THE INARTICULATE SOCIETY

Eloquence and Culture in America

TOM SHACHTMAN

THE FREE PRESS

New York   London   Toronto   Sydney   Tokyo   Singapore

The Free Press
A Division of Simon & Schuster Inc.
866 Third Avenue, New York, N.Y. 10022

Printed in the United States of America

printing number

1 2 3 4 5 6 7 8 9 10

Text design by Carla Bolte

Library of Congress Cataloging-in-Publication Data
Shachtman, Tom
    The inarticulate society : eloquence and culture in America/Tom Shachtman.
        p.   cm.
    Includes bibliographical references (p.   ) and index.

    1. Oral communication—United States.   2. Eloquence.   I. Title.
P95.S49   1995   95–13611
302.2'242—dc20   CIP

    ISBN-10: 1-4165-7679-7
    ISBN-13: 978-1-4165-7679-2

To some friends who were exemplars and champions of articulate behavior.

BOB BROWN, 1928–1994

JOHN LORD, 1924–1994

NANCY K. ROBINSON, 1942–1994

CONTENTS

Introduction

THE CRISIS IN ELOQUENCE

"Talking and eloquence are not the same: to speak, and to speak well, are two things. A fool may talk, but a wise man speaks," Ben Jonson wrote, rather neatly drawing the distinction between two functions of speech.[1] People talk incessantly these days—on television and radio news and talk shows, on the telephone, at social gatherings—but they say little that is memorable and less that can be called eloquent. Within our families, though we may keep in touch through pagers and beepers, we cannot find the time and show no inclination for conversation. At all educational levels, from kindergarten to graduate school, our institutions produce students who seem not to care about the words that emerge from their mouths or that they spill onto paper or computer screens. On the job, while as often as not enmeshed in our own specialized dialect, we scoff at other groups' private language and chafe at the obfuscations and bureaucratic discourse of government. Eloquence has almost entirely vanished from its historic habitat, the political arena. Those elected to speak for us do so mostly through television, with seconds-long sound bites instead of hour-long explorations of an issue. We are shown a thousand pictures rather than offered a single insightful word. The direction and emphasis of these changes are in all cases the same: away from precise, reasoned, thoughtfully argued, verbally adroit, idea-laden communication. If we have not yet reached the point of becoming an inarticulate society, we are

1

at a crisis in eloquence. Unless we are able to resolve this crisis, the dystopia of an inarticulate society will become increasingly real.

As Ben Jonson suggests, ease of utterance does not mean speaking well, or even effectively, but his remarks imply that we all intuitively understand what constitutes articulate expression, even if we seldom stop to consider its elements. This book will consider those elements, will try to determine what and who in our society is creating and exacerbating the crisis in eloquence, and what can be done about countering it.

Such analysis requires that the distinction between talking and eloquence be made clearer. If we imagine speech as something that occurs along a continuum of structured situations, the differences between the situations become apparent: each occupies a separate level of concentrated thought.

The great bulk of speech consists of relaxed interpersonal conversation, casual verbal interchange among a few friends on subjects of no great importance. Such talk depends heavily for comprehension on the clues available in the immediate environment of both speaker and listener.

FRED: Where's he going?
GEORGE: Around the corner.
FRED: Can't get that done there.

To an outsider, this snippet of conversation is virtually impenetrable, but it is meaningful to Fred and George, because they know the context and the antecedents. The meaning: A third friend who needs to have a tire repaired has taken the tire to the local hardware store in the next block, but Fred tells George that he believes the store will not be able to fix it. How Fred and George express themselves in this fragment is *not* inarticulate; rather, it is ordinary conversation in which the level of articulation is adequate and appropriate to the circumstances. The level may be low, but it accomplishes the task of information exchange.

Conversations that take place in more structured situations require and reward slightly more formal speech. Verbal exchanges between employee and supervisor, parent and child, teacher and individual student, or doctor and patient exhibit a slightly higher degree of thoughtfulness. There is a sense from both parties of needing to prepare what is to be said. The speaker—especially the senior speaker in these situations—makes an effort to achieve clarity of expression, and some characteristics associated with performance enter into the conversational equation.* A requirement for articulate expression begins to emerge, though such expression may appear infrequently. Were Fred and George to go beyond their informational exchanges to discuss mechanical aptitude in general, or were there to be an outsider present who does not know the antecedents, their conversation would adjust itself accordingly and would display some of the signifiers of this second category.

Next we come to somewhat more formal situations in which one person speaks to a small group: the teacher working with a classroom of pupils, a business person addressing associates in the conference room, a government official responding to questions from the press. Most of us take part in such situations regularly, and it is in them that articulateness or the lack of it becomes an issue. When addressing one child, one colleague, one student, speakers tend to use specifics and to be deliberately conversational. When speaking to several people at once, as on this third level, we tend to use more general, more widely applicable terms. That is because greater expectations of the speaker exist in this small-group situation than in the first two situations. Here, both speaker and audience have heightened anticipation of performance, and there is also a higher need for comprehensibility. In this third situation, to a greater degree than in the previous two, the speaker's words must stand on their own and be understood even when listeners or hearers know relatively little about the antecedents. Despite those expectations and needs, listeners still assume that the speaker's words will not be tightly scripted, even while they also expect a fair amount of thought to have gone into the preparation of what is being said. In third-level situations, articulate expression is mandated if not always achieved. Eloquence, however, is not really expected.

The most structured situations are the occasions of formal and prepared speeches, whether toasts at a banquet or addresses of public officials at important gatherings. In this category also are the meticulously prepared dialogue of the stage and its counterparts in film and television—speeches that have clearly been written out in advance of being spoken. When the occasion is special, so must be the speeches to mark it. Audiences in these situations confidently expect what is addressed to

---

*Cicero recommended that "ordinary talk" be easygoing and free from passion. He said that it ought to include everyone in the group and allow each to take his or her turn.

them to reflect substantial forethought and to be exceptionally comprehensible even beyond the immediate context. In such formal situations the audience demands articulate expression and listens in hope of hearing eloquence.

These four levels allow clarification of Ben Jonson's distinction between talking and speaking: Although articulate expression is a necessity for good communication, eloquence is not. Eloquence is a glory and a goal of human speech, and as such is not easily or readily attained. Perhaps we cannot all achieve eloquence, yet we can, and must, be articulate in most situations, or else communication itself is likely to fail.

Eloquence was once a synonym for excellence, and it retains many of the same connotations today. Some people narrowly construe excellence by attaching it to the championing of certain standards. Excellence in that sense is lovingly referred to in such business books as *The Pursuit of Excellence*, wherein excellence is confused with winning. Others insist that excellence must be synonymous with products or personas that eschew evaluation by the marketplace. This cult of esotericism, too, is off the mark. Commercial success and excellence can and do coexist: Shakespeare's plays, the most majestic, most eloquent portrayals of human experience we have in English, were popular successes in his lifetime, and the same can be said of almost any playwright whose reputation has survived. We all know what excellence is: a mixture of high quality and uniqueness; to excel is to stand out from the crowd, to lead, to radiate goodness and virtue, to shine so brightly that others seem by contrast to dwell in the shade. Eloquence has similar attributes. The opposite of excellence is less easy to pinpoint. Dictionaries and thesauruses suggest that it has to do with conformity, mediocrity, anonymity in a crowd, being a follower, possessing neither distinguishing virtue nor particular goodness. We also know that excellence does not exist in a vacuum; it requires an appreciative audience.

Eloquence and excellence are sometimes derided as elitist concepts. In many ways they are, but so are any concepts that incorporate the idea of leadership. Excellence and eloquence are desirable in part precisely because they are leadership qualities. In democratic societies eloquence has always been valued as a concomitant and necessary ingredient of leadership, for it was assumed that the political or spiritual leader's discourse expressed the values, aspirations, and hopes of the flock in a more felicitous and memorable way than other individual members of the flock could attain. That was in the days, however, when the notion of an elite was tolerated by the masses as a positive part of life, because the elite accepted and met the obligation to lead by example and to teach in many other ways.

The success of great orators like Adolf Hitler in swaying large numbers of people reminds us that exceptional ability to articulate does not always lead a flock upward. The ability to speak cogently and persuasively implies neither morality nor good taste. The popular appeal of Howard Stern, Rush Limbaugh, and other radio polemicists suggests also that naysaying, denigrating oratory is easier to produce than eloquence of a more positive sort.

One may be articulate without being eloquent, and eloquent without being articulate. Those artificially elevated portions of roadways through parking lots that Americans call "speed bumps" are known to Indonesians as "sleeping policemen." In Ingmar Bergman's *The Seventh Seal*, when the squire Jöns is sent by his knight to ask a man apparently sleeping by a crossroads about the progress of the plague, Jöns finds the man dead of the plague, a corpse with empty eye sockets, and comes back to his master.

KNIGHT: What did he say?
JÖNS: Nothing.
KNIGHT: Was he a mute?
JÖNS: No, sir, I wouldn't say that. As a matter of fact, he was quite eloquent.[4]

The Indonesian example demonstrates good articulate behavior that any of us can reach but that is not eloquent, and Bergman's, eloquent behavior from the corpse that is clearly not articulate, yet at the same time exhibits the artist's eloquent turn of phrase in describing it.

In the United States today, the speech of too few people achieves eloquence, and that of the vast majority does not even reach a tolerable level of articulate behavior. The examples of inadequacy begin at the top, with the current President and his predecessor. When American politicians speak without a prepared text, they frequently babble and blunder, mangling the language in ways not only painful to endure but that frequently obscure the speaker's quite reasonable intent and meaning. President

George Bush was all too often a victim of his own verbal ineptness. In response to a 1991 news conference question about tax cuts, he replied:

> I think it's understandable, when you have a bad—economic numbers come in from time to time, mixed, I must happily say, with some reasonably good ones—other people get concerned. I'm concerned. But I don't want to do—take—I don't want to say to them, "Well, you shouldn't come forward with proposals."[5]

What Bush surely wanted to say was that people were overly concerned about bad economic numbers, but he would still entertain any proposal to address what was perceived as an economic slowdown.

On taking office in early 1993, President Bill Clinton was heralded as a more lucid speaker and thinker than the man he had replaced, but within a few months even some journals sympathetic to Clinton were wondering about his rhetoric. In the *New Republic*, Leon Wieseltier took Clinton to task for living "at too great a level of generality" and for his "gift for saying nothing, and passionately,"[6] while others tired of the vague nouns like *change* and *community* and *hope* that continually dotted his many speeches.

By the time of Clinton's 1994 State of the Union address, though specifics had replaced generalities, his blurry style was full-blown, as in this paragraph about the need for health-care reform:

> There are some people who literally do not understand the impact of this problem on people's lives. And all you have to do is go out and listen to them. Just go talk to them anywhere in any Congressional district in this country. They're Republicans and Democrats and independents; it doesn't have a lick to do with party. They think we don't get it, and it's time we show them that we do get it.[7]

The listening audience was so confused by the President's mixing of antecedents that very few could "get it."

It is a central contention of this book that inarticulate behavior is being modeled for us by our leaders, including those in politics, entertainment, and in other highly visible positions. From the example of our political leaders, seen on each evening's television news, people learn how not to say what they mean, and that it is acceptable not to mean what they say. Fuzziness and lack of eloquence in Washington mirrors inarticulate expression in the arena of big business. The following samples are culled from a single issue of a newspaper's business section. A lawyer representing Macy's bondholders, referring to the actions of the retailer's recently installed chairman, worries in a series of deliciously mixed metaphors: "He seems like he's got the thing thought through, seems like he's got the right answers, but to me the proof of the pudding is in the eating, and the jury is still out." Former baseball commissioner Peter Ueberroth, at work on the rebuilding of Los Angeles after the 1992 riots, uses slightly more concrete imagery: "Supermarkets are a cornerstone in bringing life back" to inner cities, he says, because one of "the worst ills of America is that poor city people spend more for lower quality food; supermarkets give people more disposable income to spend to support local businesses." The connection between more supermarkets and support to local businesses is not immediately apparent. A business analyst, commenting on a proposed alliance between British Telecom and the American computer services company EDS, splits so many hairs that we can hardly follow his locutionary paintbrush: "While I can see the advantage for European carriers in a tie-up with EDS, I don't see the advantage for EDS. EDS can manage and coordinate the services of multiple European carriers far better than they can coordinate among themselves. And while EDS is independent of any carrier, they are all potential clients."[8] If these men are trying for clarity in explaining their various concerns to the public, they are not achieving their objective. All have interesting points to make but are making them in a way that the points are barely understandable.

At least those models are attempting to be articulate. Many of our models, these days, have no such pretense and might not know eloquence if they stumbled into it. Today, those who have won the right to speak directly into television's microphones more often than any other group are the players of professional sports—despite what becomes obvious after listening to the vast majority of athletes: They may play fine games, but they certainly do not make illuminating or cogent remarks. At best, they reach the unintentionally funny level of Yogi Berra, in such lines as "Nobody goes there any more—it's too crowded." Verbal infelicity might be expected of athletes, because their agility is physical and not necessarily intellectual, but still, audiences suffer through locker room chats that expand the boundaries of banality.

Television talk shows have proliferated. During one ear- and eye-splitting twenty-four-hour period, a *Washington Post* reporter who watched and listened only to television talk shows was subjected to conversation from professional wrestlers, sexually active teenagers and their mothers, long-lost twins reunited on the air, "reformed racists," television news reporters who had bad things happen to them while chasing stories, country music stars, and women engaged to mass killers, along with discussions about breast-feeding in public, housing for the homeless, and gay men and women in the military.[9]

Guests on television talk shows tend to be either famous or emotionally impaired. It would be unfair to expect the latter sufferers to be articulate about their conditions, although some do manage to be quite emotional. On the other hand, actors and actresses who trot around the talk circuit to publicize their latest ventures can be expected to be articulate, because they are performers and are generally speaking about subjects on which they have had time to prepare their thoughts. But exposure to a morning, afternoon, or evening's worth of television talk programs will bring most viewers to the conclusion that the majority of actors and actresses have little to say and say it poorly.

Ten thousand of the country's stations now broadcast some "talk" programming. The world of talk radio has lately been touted as the ultimate town meeting and the home of free expression. It certainly serves as the home of free expression—so free that it sometimes raises eyebrows at the FCC because of profanity and other verbal excesses—but it constitutes neither a true forum of debate nor the playground of good articulate behavior. The arbitrariness with which incoming calls are screened and the abruptness with which most program hosts and hostesses treat the callers violate not only the rules for proper debate but the civility that must be a concomitant of such debate. Callers to talk radio tend to be passionate and ready to express their feelings, but they are mostly unable to couch their thoughts in articulate sentences.

A very large percentage of our population obtains its news from network television broadcasts, so it might be presumed that the responsibility for informing the public impels those programs and their producers to aspire to some reasonably high level of articulate expression. Nightly news broadcasts once did so, but the level has declined markedly over the years, a fact documented and analyzed in a later chapter of this book.

The ultimate farces of articulate behavior in our society are the trademark shouting matches of the public affairs programs *Crossfire* and *The McLaughlin Group*. Participants from the arena of politics and from the media are situated as though in debates, but no debate takes place, because each speaker has to fight for air time in which to expound a position. No participant ever tempers an opinion because of anything another participant says. The prize in the competition goes to the person who shouts the loudest and longest and is able to utter the nastiest quips about the others. Articulate behavior has been replaced by combativeness.

The above examples lay out some of the dimensions of the problem, but the issues are far larger than the immediate context. This book is part of three grand and continuing colloquies: that among cultural critics about the consequences of the increasing separation of elite from mass culture; that among political analysts about the effects of the rise of mass political movements; and that among educational analysts about the Socratic and Sophist modes of teaching and learning.

Following such writers as Orwell, Santayana, and Ortega y Gasset, I shall note the interlinkage of mass culture and mass politics and shall extend those writers' contentions to suggest that the decline in articulate behavior comes as a logical consequence of their conjoint rise. That contention is fundamental to the book's thesis that support for articulate behavior is being undermined by pressures to appeal to the masses in all endeavors. The argument will draw on foundations laid by Jürgen Habermas and Michel Foucault in their works about communication and its meanings. Habermas's demarcation of the boundaries of true and false debate and Foucault's distinction between discussants and polemicists are keys to identifying and separating helpful from harmful elements of rhetorical behavior. I will also build on the basic critique of mass culture and the commodification impulses behind mass culture that was originally framed by Adorno, Horkheimer, and others of the Frankfurt Institute of Social Research. Ortega's "mass man" has become so powerful a consumer that, as Adorno had predicted, his consumption and articulation habits have to be directed from the moment of his birth. The elucidation of these effects by such writers as Daniel Boorstin and Richard Sennet have informed my own interpretation of the effects of commodification.

Like Jacques Ellul, Marshall McLuhan, and Neil Postman, I shall delve into the effects of modern communications technologies in the cultural sphere. Ellul contends that technical civilization has transformed ends into means, and means (such as communication technology) into ends in themselves. He shows that first political doctrines are reduced to programs, then programs to slogans, then slogans to pictures so they can be impressed on people without benefit of words. I shall suggest other integral connections between the structure and intent of what is communicated and the decline in articulate behavior. "The medium is the massage,"[10] Marshall McLuhan proclaimed in the 1960s, and he prophesied that changes wrought by new communications technologies would reshape society to a degree not achieved since the introduction of the printing press and perhaps even as profoundly as the alphabet. Television and computers further distance people from one another, alter the structure of personal relationships, and in other ways erode a culture. McLuhan found clues to the nature of that erosion in an equivalent earlier time of transformation, when writing was first invented. Before that moment, McLuhan wrote, "man lived in acoustic space: boundless, directionless, horizonless, in the dark of the mind, in the world of emotion, by primordial intuition, by terror. Speech is a social chart of this bog. The goose quill put an end to talk." But today, having entered the new global village through the agency of the electronic media, we "are back in acoustic space. We have begun again to structure the primordial feeling, the tribal emotions from which a few centuries of literacy divorced us."[11]

McLuhan's contention is part hogwash, part prescient insight. Acoustic space is not boundless or directionless, and the goose quill certainly did not put an end to talk. The vision of a future society in which there will be a global village enlivened by tribal emotions rather than by literacy is insightful, but perhaps not in the way McLuhan meant it to be. He foresaw communications technology midwifing a feel-good utopia, but his vision can also be construed as the prescription for an inarticulate dystopia. Its dystopic potential will be made clear by reference to the work of McLuhan's former student, Father Walter Ong, S.J., who has pointed out the distinctions between the different ways of being of oral and literate societies. Ong differentiates between the oral societies that actually existed in acoustic, emotion-filled, boundless space before the invention of writing, the literate societies whose language and culture are based on the written word, and certain postliterate enclaves that Ong labels as "secondarily oral," because they derive their literacy not from the written word but from the language as communicated through such devices as the telephone, television, and popular music.[10] This book will contend that if the inarticulate society comes into being, it will be as a consequence of spreading secondary orality.

Since articulate behavior is the product of learning, we shall first make an excursion into the battle in learning theory that has been raging since Socrates and the Sophists attacked each other's methods. Following Mortimer Adler and other Platonists, I shall argue that Socratic teaching holds more potential for inculcating the skills necessary to articulate behavior. Following Erving Goffman, I shall maintain that context strongly affects performance in school and in extracurricular situations. Controversy over teaching advanced literacy, the concomitant of articulate behavior, still simmers among the successors of John Dewey, who revolutionized American education near the start of the twentieth century by championing "progressive education," which meant broadening the curriculum and function of the schools to include many subjects that were previously the concern of extracurricular educators—health, vocation, and family and community matters—as concomitants of the attempt to educate more and more children in the increasingly disparate country.[11] Today's battles are among those who feel that learning in students is best produced in an environment where social skills and creativity are stressed, those who argue for setting certain basic building blocks in place in order for literacy to be properly taught, and, finally, those who teach elements of thinking and problem-solving as the entry into higher literacy. I shall argue that a synthesis of all three approaches, plus a new emphasis on some pre-Dewey principles, is necessary to reverse the crisis in eloquence.

The giant panda, the snow leopard, and the black rhino are examples of what natural scientists call keystone species. Scientists study such species in a region, rather than every indigenous variety of flora and fauna, for two reasons: because the species' health is a good indicator of the vitality of its ecological surroundings, and because the keystone species has a totemic value in the public's mind. I study articulate speech for much the same reasons. This book will argue that the crisis in eloquence is culturally based, that fundamental weaknesses in our basic culture have produced the decline, and that addressing those faults, rather than the outward symptoms, is the only certain route toward reversal of the decline. In other words, the argument advances the idea that articulate speech is a fulcrum that today is being shifted in one direction, whereas it can and should be moved in the opposite direction.

Parents and schools blame each other for children's poor use of words, and both blame the media, which affect the children more than the home or the classroom does. The media say that creeping inarticulateness is not their fault, because they are merely a mirror of society. Our elected leaders chalk up their equivocations and lack of eloquence to what they perceive as the social necessity of scaling down their messages so they can reach all the people. All these institutions can and should share the blame. None currently accepts it. What we have now is equivalent to a circle of people who all point their fingers at each other instead of at themselves, and simultaneously hide their heads in the sand, hoping the lions will not eat them while they are thus concealed. Make no mistake, there are lions to fear: an inchoate, inexpressive populace and the demagogues it can empower, for instance. The most alarming aspect of the decline in articulateness, I shall argue, lies in its undermining of our democratic system.

The process of beginning to face the crisis in eloquence begins by identifying its sources, by reconstructing its history to determine which among our ways of living, acting, and learning are deepening the morass, and then by using the knowledge gained to devise programs and philosophies to reverse the downward slide. We should not despair, because renewal is possible. Our history and the innate richness of our language provide resources on which we can and must draw.

PART I

MASTERING THE PROCESS

$\mathcal{B}$iographical stories about the most eloquent men of all times, from Demosthenes to Jesus to Churchill, stress that they were not born with great oratorical gifts but rather developed them over time. Even though there is some evidence that the human species possesses certain innate abilities to comprehend language and especially that aspect of language known as syntax, it seems clear that advanced articulate behavior is learned, not inherited. As such it must be taught, and the teaching of it is not a one-time exercise in transfer of information but a lifelong process. Mastering the process requires dialogue partners for the individual learner. At first the partners are in the home and in the surrounding speech community; later they must be provided through the educational system.

Formal educators generally acknowledge that their function is to educate, and they set about consciously to do so. They are the subject of this first section of the book. The influence of extracurricular educators on the inculcation of articulate behavior is the subject of the remainder of this book.

One of the principal casualties of the seismic changes that have roiled American society during the past fifty to seventy-five years has been the environment in which children first learn and use the English language. That environment comprises first the family, then the speech community, and only then the informal schooling of play groups, day care, and kindergartens. "The family is the institution in which the children have their earliest education, their earliest experiences in the learning of language . . . and the assignment of meaning to the world," Lawrence Cremin, a historian of education, wrote. In a series of lectures given just before his death, he traced current language-usage difficulties to such root causes as the high proportion of American households with fewer than four members which had reached 82 percent, and the epidemic upsurges in the number of divorces, in single-parent households, and in the entry of mothers into the workforce—all of which contribute to having fewer accomplished language-speakers in the child's immediate environment. Educators have long known that the greatest effect on language abilities is produced prior to the time that the child enters formal school, for it is in the very earliest years that children develop what Cremin calls their "educative styles—their characteristic ways of engaging in, moving through, and combining educative experiences over their lifespan."[1]

Psychologists and learning specialists now generally concur that the manipulation of symbols, which is the key to higher learning, and the understanding of relationships and hierarchies, which is essential to taking one's place in a society, are intricately interwoven with language. Thus, mastery of the language is the most critical skill a child develops in the early years. William Fowler, director of the Center for Early Learning and Child Care in Cambridge, Massachusetts, who has studied childhood language acquisition and how it affects later school performance, holds that in terms of language "competence," what happens during the early months and years is crucial to the rest of a child's life:

> A poor foundation makes it difficult for children to master what is culturally expected in the next stage [of learning], while a strong foundation enables children to assimilate successive demands very easily and even go beyond the average range of these demands and learn on their own. . . . How clearly children speak, how fast they learn and, more important, how well they learn all the intricacies will depend on the quality of their language environment from day to day over the first few years of development.[2]

Once past the early years, the child's educatory process depends even more directly on mastery of the language, and in particular on articulate behavior. The central task of formal schooling, the development of higher-order thinking skills, is intertwined with articulate endeavor. What sort of classrooms, what sort of teachers, and what educational methods this development requires and mandates is of principal interest, for the quality and type of teaching has perhaps a more direct bearing on the mastery of articulate behavior than on any other subject in the curriculum.

Chapter 1

LEARNING TO SPEAK

*L*anguage is the symbolic universe through which we come to understand the world around us and by which we relate to that world and everyone and everything in it. A dog is called a dog not because that is the animal's innate quality, but because "dog" is the label by which we identify the creature.

The language a child speaks depends on the language environment in which he or she is raised. In turn, the quality of the language environment of the child's first few years depends in large measure on the workings of the child's "speech community." That technical term refers to a social group whose speech is relatively uniform and whose homogeneity is a direct result of the group's members having common experiences and common interpretations of that experience. What one adult in that community means by "home" or "pet" or "happiness" is substantially the same as what any other adult in it understands those words to mean. When people from similar backgrounds say that they understand one another, they mean that the words they use carry the same symbolic baggage: That is the essence of being members of a common speech community. Children begin to "acquire" the language of the speech community as soon as it is voiced to them, the psychologist Naomi S. Baron writes, and the process is "largely complete" by the age of five or six.[1]

In the days of the intact and extended family, typically consisting of many siblings, when the family's neighbors were likely to speak the same language in the same way as the family, there were fewer problems with proper language acquisition. However, Baron reminds us, "today's parents are the first post-immigrant generation to be raising families in isolation from relatives," the first to grow up entirely during the television era, in which child-minding is frequently ceded to the electronic babysitter, and the first in which the majority of mothers whose children are below the age of six work outside the home, a circumstance that also affects the amount and quality of time that the parents expend in teaching their children language usage.[2] In short, current childrearing practices are affecting the processes of language acquisition in ways we have not adequately recognized or addressed.

To understand why the makeup of the speech community and the methods it uses have such an impact on language acquisition by the child, we must look more closely at the process. It is a continuing dialogue between the child and those around the child that begins at birth and before verbalization. Psychologists believe that the infant and its primary caregiver mutually work to influence each other through vocal and physical behaviors. Eye contact, one of the most compelling cues a baby can give, strongly affects the caregiver's actions—positively when contact is held, negatively when it is broken off. Turn-taking, a principle of social interaction that is central to articulate exchange, is one of the earliest behaviors learned by the infant, at the breast or on the bottle. Thereafter, the joint enterprise of infant and caregiver proceeds in stages that are defined by developmental tasks that have a lot to do with pre-articulate expression. At two months, the principal task is the regulation of mutual attention and responsiveness; at five months, it is how to incorporate objects (pacifiers, mobiles, rattles) into their social interactions. During those early months the child discovers the meaning of some of his or her own actions from the ways in which parents (or other caregivers) respond to them. A big change occurs as the child begins to relate with intention, that is, to make an action specifically for the purpose of affecting the parent or caregiver. An additional developmental leap takes place in the eight-to-ten-month period, writes Daniel N. Stern, an infant development expert: The child discovers that his "subjective life—the contents of one's mind and the qualities of one's feelings—can be shared with another."[3] When more reciprocity becomes possible in the relationship, more give-and-take, the infant develops a sense of empathy; learns what strategies are better or worse for influencing the dialogue partner; accepts certain realities of life, such as the need to tolerate delay and to adapt to other people; and becomes able to recognize differences among situations. In other words, there is a continuing conversation or dialogue between infant and caregivers that not only defines how the child gets along in the world but also is crucial to becoming articulate.

A British linguist, M. A. K. Halliday, observed his son Nigel as he began to voice sounds and then words, the latter at about eleven or twelve months. Halliday was able to identify seven different functions in his son's attempts at speech—categories that show how much the child had already learned about the capacities and uses of speech in his first year or so. Nigel's communications were *instrumental*, a way of satisfying his wants; *regulatory* of those around him; *interactional*, a way of engaging those around him; *expressive* of himself as a person; *heuristic*, which Halliday defined as enabling the child to learn by asking questions; *imaginative*; and (the last function to appear) *representational*, a way of identifying objects in the environment.[4]

Research by psychologists has documented how and when a child's more complex mental abilities appear. Around the age of fifteen months, a child often plays mother to a doll or makes a block drink from a cup— evidence that he or she has developed an ability to use symbolic representation. It is from such abilities that complex speech in children sprouts. That process is what happens in a magic moment experienced in all families in one form or another: The caregiver points to an animal that is somewhat recognizable, the child responds by mentally matching it to the family pet or to a representation he or she has seen, and immediately afterward utters a word/concept the caregiver has been trying to teach the child for some time: "dog." The general principle is *Comprehension precedes articulation*. Once the internal support beams and floors of the house of language have been firmly set in place, the cladding of words is rapidly affixed.

That is the reason behind the "naming explosion" characteristic of the eighteen-month-old, who goes around attaching words to things with great gusto. At eighteen months, however, most children are not yet ready for words that reflect mastery of more subtle aspects of categorization, such as the notion that objects have permanence; only when that intellectual concept has been understood can a child know that a ball covered by a cup has not entirely passed out of existence and will reappear when the cup is removed.[5]

Command of such concepts allows a rapidly expanding vocabulary and permits most children aged 24–27 months to talk in three-to-five-word sentences. Catherine Garvey found in her studies of how children learn to speak that during the third year of life, children exhibit the "most dramatic changes" and make the "most impressive achievements" in language acquisition. In one experiment, she reports, at the age of twenty-two months three boys playing together made verbal utterances 27 percent of the time, but as the boys approached thirty months they made verbal utterances 64 percent of the time. Children usually learn and put to active use a five-hundred-word vocabulary by their third birthday, and by the age of four a child's vocabulary often expands to more than a thousand words.[6]

What do those thousand words do for the child, aside from permitting him or her to converse with caregivers and with peers? To put it briefly, they socialize the child into the speech community's culture. That culture depends on symbolic words even more than it does on the other component of vocabulary, narrowly descriptive words. In fact, the Canadian philosopher Willem Vanderburg argues, the artificiality and technological complexity of today's world have pushed our language toward becoming ever more symbolic and at the same time have made the language more difficult to apprehend. While most of the connotations and the mechanical workings of a concept like "sailing canoe" could be made understandable to a child through the use of very few words, a wider range of symbols is needed to convey all the workings and connotations of "supersonic jet transport." A second, more serious problem in regard to language acquisition by today's children arises from the fact that each culture has its own symbols. Vanderburg has been studying the parallel growth of minds and cultures and the ways they interact. He argues that maturation from infancy to adulthood is accomplished by the child's successively accepting and understanding more and more of his or her culture's symbol-filled way of viewing the world. Following philosophers from Rousseau onward, Vanderburg identifies language as the preeminent means by which children are transformed from natural beings not much different from animals into cultural beings. He points out that during the socialization process, the child's vocabulary changes in character. What happens is that the "world of immediate experience recedes" as children prepare to "enter the world of their culture," to which, Vanderburg reminds us, "language is the gateway." As the child grows, the newer words he or she acquires have less to do with concrete experience and more to do with concepts, so that "reality as children know it will increasingly resemble the symbolic universe of their culture."[7]

The mediator in this learning of symbols is the speech community, which in the past had always been made up of parents and the other relatives and neighbors who frequent the household and with whom the child interacts. The addition of outsiders to this important group—other caregivers, people on television, multiple peers—broadens and alters the group's character and thereby changes what it conveys to the child. It affects every function of human communication. In a textbook on the subject, F. E. X. Dance and C. E. Larson identify three essential functions: the linking of the individual with the world, the development of higher mental processes, and the regulation of human behavior.[8] The speech community's interactions with the child have to do with all three, but perhaps most with the last. Regulation of behavior is part of making the child aware of the social structure.

At the same time that they are learning language, children slowly become cognizant of what roles various people play in the society—policeman, mother, cook—and what is and is not acceptable and customary behavior. The normally almost invisible process by which a child's perception of the world and his or her ability to attach words to the perceptions proceed can be readily seen, Elaine Slosberg Andersen, a student of comparative language acquisition, writes, in how the child successively refines an understanding of the father of the family. Before entering grammar school, the child in a nuclear family describes the father in terms of his typical behaviors in the home; in the next stage of growth, the father is described by the child as having children and taking care of them; greater breadth is added to the child's description when the child is slightly older and can comprehend (and articulate) that it is possible for the father to have children, and that the father can change into a grandfather when he has grandchildren; still later, children come to understand and be able to talk about the idea that the father can have two roles at once, can be simultaneously both a father to his children and a grandfather to his grandchildren; even later, the child realizes that the father fulfills three roles, as father, grandfather, and son. Complete understanding by the child of the interaction of the father's spousal and parental roles, and of further complexity, often has to wait until the child reaches adolescence. "Children proceed from simple behavioral categories, to simple relations of categories, to complex systems of categories as they come to understand social roles, Andersen concludes."[9]

The most important social understanding may be mastery of the dialogue process itself, the give-and-take of life through words. This "rhetorical sensitivity" must be developed quite early, according to the psychologist and philosopher Harold Barrett. He defines a rhetorically sensitive person—the ideal—as one who "tries to accept roletaking as a part of life, tries to avoid counterproductive stylized language, is willing to adapt to existing conditions, seeks to distinguish between information that is useful and that which is not, and tries to understand that an idea may be rendered in a number of ways." Barrett emphasizes that articulateness includes the ability to listen properly and to interact genuinely with other speakers. The complex give-and-take perceptions of the rhetorically sensitive person, Barrett contends, must be well on the road toward full development before a child reaches the age of eligibility for play groups, and it is of great importance that they are properly instilled before that time.[10]

One would think that the process by which rhetorical sensitivity—indeed, all of language—is instilled in children through the speech community is something that could be discovered experimentally and not subject to debate, but it is actually the focus of intense disagreement. We can examine the controversy and the subject by looking at the interaction between mother and child. (It is important first to note parenthetically that linguists now agree that all languages are acquired with the same degree of ease by children in the heart of their own cultures—that Mandarin Chinese, for instance, is no more or less difficult to acquire for a child of a Mandarin Chinese family than Russian is for a Muscovite.) Andersen discusses a very common installation technique used in a variety of cultures around the world: babytalk, or "Motherese." She defines this as one among a number of "register variations," which are ways one group has of addressing another; two other register variations are "foreigner-talk" (how a native speaker talks to a tourist or to a recent immigrant), and the special, simplified, and ultra-controlled language in which doctors speak to their patients. The common features of babytalk in any language, Andersen found from an exhaustive review of the subject, are short sentences, incomplete forms of syntax, exaggerated intonations, duplicated syllables, and a slower than normal rate of speech. These adjustments on the part of the adult speaking to a child, Andersen writes, seem "especially well-designed to help children in deciphering the structure of the language being acquired." Babytalk assists acquisition in two ways. First, it attracts and holds the child's attention, for instance through high-pitched sounds that children hear better than they do low-pitched ones, allowing them to focus their attention. Second, it provides "consistent clues to the child about how to map ideas onto language and how to segment the flow of speech which he hears, in order to identify sentences, phrases, words and morphemes"; for instance, while adults speaking to other adults pause only half the time at "utterance boundaries," when speaking to small children adults pause at these boundaries 90 percent of the time, especially when demarcating the end of a sentence.[11]

On the other side of this controversy is an MIT linguist, Steven Pinker, a follower of Noam Chomsky. Chomsky and his associates have undertaken many experiments and observations that show very convincingly that children acquire certain highly important and complex language skills almost without being actively taught. Chomsky and Pinker attribute the phenomenon to certain universal similarities in grammatical structure, which children apprehend long before they are able to speak in complete sentences. Young children who have never been taught certain grammatical rules, for instance, are able to use those rules to answer questions. If children acquire language abilities in a sort of innate way, this argument goes, then such strategies as babytalk and Motherese cannot have much to do with acquisition. In his book *The Language Instinct*, Steven Pinker suggests that the efficacy of Motherese must be attributed more to folklore than to scientific fact:

In contemporary middle-class American culture, parenting is seen as an awesome responsibility, an unforgiving vigil to keep the helpless infant from falling behind in the great race of life. The belief that Motherese is essential to language development is part of the same mentality that sends yuppies to "learning centers" to buy little mittens with bull's eyes to help their babies find their hands sooner.[12]

This is a strong as well as a strongly worded argument, and Pinker is undoubtedly correct in contending that Motherese is not *essential* to acquiring basic aspects of language development, because many people learn languages like English without ever having been exposed to babytalk. Joseph Conrad and Vladimir Nabokov, two of the great stylists among writers of English, learned the English language only after they had reached adulthood. They are the exceptions, however, for many studies have shown that languages are best and most fully learned when the learner is young, and when the learner has a lot of help.

Andersen points out that the transmittal strategy of mothers making babytalk is not used by every society. The point is significant, because the societies that do use babytalk differ from those that do not in a critically important way. Andersen's review shows that such cultures as native Samoans, other Pacific Islanders, Athapaskan Indians, and American Southern working-class blacks do not use babytalk but instead employ quite different strategies in their transmission of language to the very young. What those other strategies are, and how they differ from those of the societies that use babytalk, was the subject of a field study by Bambi Schieffelin and Eleanor Ochs, anthropologists and linguists. They conducted studies among Asian peoples and compared their strategies to what is known about transmittal strategies in Western European cultures. They suggest that the axis along which societies differ in communicating language has to do with whether the culture is "child- centered," as in middle-class Western cultures, or "situation-centered," as in the Pacific cultures:

> In highly child centered communication, the caregiver takes the perspective of the child in talking to and understanding the child. Highly child centered communication is also characterized by child centered topics, a tendency to accommodate to the child's egocentric behavior, and by a desire to frequently engage the child as a conversational partner. In highly situation centered communication the child is expected to accommodate to activities and persons in the situation at hand. Highly situation centered communication is characterized by a range of situationally appropriate registers

addressed to the child as opposed to the heavy reliance on BT [babytalk] register characteristic of child centered communication.[13]

In other words, how language is communicated reflects cultural differences, especially in regard to how the child is to be taught to behave in various situations. In certain cultures, speaking frequently and in a highly articulate manner to the child is not as highly valued as is the transmission to the child of knowledge about where he or she fits into the culture and what roles he or she can or will play within it. But which cultures are those in which knowing where one fits in is more valued than articulate expression? They are precisely those cultures whose general characteristics were established in preliterate times, or those that appear to have entered a secondarily oral phase.

Children may acquire *basic* language skills through innate capabilities, as Chomsky and Pinker contend, but a higher level of language learning is necessary to make one's way in the modern world. William Fowler, director of the Cambridge Center for Early Learning, points out that what may have been appropriate for children entering an old-style oral culture is not the proper training for children in a society where literacy and articulateness are increasingly the keys to knowledge and economic advancement. "The era of informal communication and direct action skills so prominent in the past," Fowler writes, "has been replaced by an era that is built on manipulating language in highly abstract and varied forms. . . . Communication can no longer be confined to using familiar expressions with familiar people who share common local concerns." Essential now, Fowler argues, is to "adapt methods of child care and stimulation needed [by children] for the highly verbal, abstract symbol-oriented modes characteristic of contemporary institutions."[14]

Fowler has been working for more than twenty years to help children become adept in these "highly verbal" modes and has had considerable experimental success. His research provides, if not a direct refutation of Pinker's and Chomsky's argument that grammar-learning skills are innate, then at least a demonstration that the work of the language-inculcator— the mother, caregiver, or peer group—is vitally important in the process of acquisition.

By providing children with "an early start [and] an enriched environment," Fowler has been able to produce what he calls "significant positive influences on cognitive development." His methods raised the IQ scores of the tested children by fifteen to twenty points, while stimulating "excellent performance in school." He writes in a review of his work that with sustained support from parents, those early gains "continue through later periods of development." More than 90 percent of the children he tracked from tutored infancy through high school had "exceptional competencies," Fowler reports, concentrated in "language, reading and other verbally related skills" and carrying over into mastery of foreign languages and mathematics. They were also "very much self-directed in learning and achievement," able to take charge of their own further development. When Fowler's results were compared with other programs that stimulated preschool children through three different means—"social interaction" and "play," in addition to "language"—it was determined that the concentration on language "was the most effective of the three."[15]

To enhance early language training, Fowler has concluded, the key factor is what the adults do. From his research, Fowler makes a book's worth of recommendations. Here are a few. He starts with "vocalization play" from birth to three months, and then adds on "labeling play," along with introducing nouns that represent small, familiar objects (hand, cup), concrete action verbs (touch, kiss), and some prepositions, adjectives, and other small connective words that are high on frequency-of-use lists. At nine months, Fowler encourages story book reading by adults to children, and "sentence play," in which words are combined into phrases and adjectives or alternative phrase combinations are substituted one for another. By fourteen months, Fowler's training has parents and caregivers involving children in conversations and discussions, encouraging them to relate their experiences and happenings, and leading them from talk of "concrete, immediate and simple events" to talk of things and people and times that are "abstract and general," which deal with people, things, and situations that are not directly at hand and may have to do with the past or future as well as with the present. The parent or caregiver must carefully structure what they say and how they interact with the child. Instead of holding up a ball and asking, "What is this?" the questioner should ask, "Where is the ball?" so that the child can fetch it and then verbally identify it; such a "meaningful cognitive strategy" moves the child more and more into active learning. As a result of this early language training, children were able to talk in sentences at sixteen months (as contrasted to twenty-four months for the untutored, "average environment" children), to relate experiences at 21–24 months (versus 33–36 months for the untutored), and use basic rules of grammar in their speech at twenty-four months (versus forty-eight months for the untutored children).

Fowler found that it was possible to raise the language abilities of any reasonably normal child by orienting the child's environment toward good stimulation of those abilities. He conducted studies in which children from varied socio-economic and linguistic backgrounds—from families that spoke Italian, Chinese, and Afro-Caribbean languages at home, in addition to English, and from very poor as well as from middle-class households—had their language skills enhanced through the efforts of psychologists and sociologists who assisted mothers and other primary caregivers in that task. Exceptional progress was made both in families where the care was given by middle-class, well-educated mothers and in families where the mothers were not that well-educated but accepted the instruction and assistance methods of the experimenters. Children of the latter families, in fact, made as good progress as did children of the middle class. All the "stimulated" children reached defined benchmarks of acquisition-of-language growth earlier than did children in ordinary homes, and when they entered school, most of the "stimulated" continued to do well. Fowler came to the conclusion that even when the caregiver was not the parent but had been trained in giving clear examples and in correcting misuse of language, the children speedily learned proper use and were well prepared to enter school. Some of Fowler's experiments were carried out in day care settings, others in homes. Interestingly enough, the day care children did as well as those who were "home-reared," if—and that was a big if—the language stimulation was carefully carried out in the day care facility and was reinforced at home. However, if the stimulation was *not* reinforced at home, or if the families of the children in day care failed to continue their interest and participation in their children's language development when the child entered regular school, the tremendous boost that the children received from the stimulation gradually subsided and was lost.[16]

The implications of Fowler's careful research are clear: Anyone who is properly trained in the techniques of inculcating language will help children in learning their language. It is just as clear, however, that those who are not trained, or who are inadequately trained, or who do not bother with communicating well to their children, may actually hinder their language development. Research has determined that parents spend as little as eight to eleven minutes a day in real conversation with their children; most of the rest of the approximately thirty minutes per day during which parents interact with children is taken up with voicing commands or criticism. Even more "family time"—a quarter of the total—is spent jointly looking at the television set.[17] To communicate well takes time, knowledge and purposeful activity. Support for the idea of the positive effects of parental language training on children comes from a number of sources. In a study conducted by the British linguist Gordon Wells, children who were exposed to a greater proportion of conversation in which the adult partner provided clear examples of how language was used, and positive feedback in response to the child's correct use of language to communicate his or her intentions, learned their language more rapidly than others who weren't so exposed.[18] Similarly, in another study of interaction between mothers and children, researchers found that mothers who make more use of "metalinguistics," language that defines words, corrects grammar, or teases out extended verbal answers from the child, have children who develop better language abilities.[19] When language is presented to the child in a way that is literate and relatively error-free—as it is, researchers have found, by middle-class college-educated mothers in the United States—it is learned that way by the child. Many important basic points of grammar, syntax, and pronunciation, as well as a rich vocabulary, can be conveyed readily by those whose everyday speech approaches standard usage. The paradigm holds true even in the acquisition of American Sign Language. In one experiment reported in a book by Philip Lieberman, when ASL-using parents signed the correct morpheme (a unit of language that contains no smaller parts) less than half the time, the child learned to use the incorrect form, but when the parents used the correct morpheme 60 percent of the time, the child would use the correct one almost all of the time. Imitation is not only the sincerest form of flattery, it is, as Lieberman suggests, "probably the most important mechanism for the transmission of human culture."[20]

What is being transmitted to children first learning the language, and who are the transmitters, varies today from situation to situation, even in middle-class homes. Naomi Baron points out that several factors have an impact on the effectiveness of the training, for instance the parental age and education level, the amount of time the parents spent with the child, and parental awareness of modulating their speech in order to help the child learn. Fathers who work away from the home may not be as effective as language teachers of their children as the at-home mother who spends a lot of time with the child, she postulates. A study found that such fathers do not know how to imitate and feed back the child's words as the mother does in an effort to facilitate conversations with the child. Fathers tend to use more mature language and more sophisticated vocabulary and syntax than at-home mothers—in other words, fathers do not reflexively use metalinguistics.

What if the principal caregiver and transmitter fails not only to use metalinguistics but also to provide clear examples of good language use or positive feedback for correct choices, either because the caregiver's own language is full of errors or because the caregiver does not know how to manage the feedback? That is often what happens in many of the poorest households in the United States; when compared with children from middle-class households, those from the very poorest tend to be "linguistically disadvantaged," Baron points out, but she is quick to add, research suggests that their "problems principally derive from inadequate education and non-supportive parenting styles, not personal finances."[21]

What if it is precisely the "linguistically disadvantaged" who are used as primary caregivers to children from households that are otherwise linguistically advantaged? What if the principal caregivers at a day care facility are less skilled than parents in the inculcation of language skills? What if the structure of the child-minding facility is such that the sort of language teaching recommended by Fowler will not take place? The raging controversies as to whether or not mothers of young children ought to stay at home to raise them and over the efficacy of day care as opposed to care at home take on a new depth with the understanding of how critical the caregiver is to the all-important process of language acquisition by the child. The matter in question is not reducible to whether or not it is better for the child's language development to have a mother who stays at home rather than goes to work. In a recent study, two psychologists found "little difference in both quantity and quality of time" spent by comparable groups of working mothers and stay-at-home mothers in conversation with their children.[22] The issue is what sort of language instruction will be given to the young child in home or home-substitute situations.

Day care represents a golden opportunity for applying the techniques of Fowler and other experts in language teaching, because it can be a learning situation, and the presence of other small learners may stimulate the child to learn alongside them. Head Start is day care on a high level and in an enriched environment. I worked with the Head Start program in its early days, and have kept in touch with its progress. A good deal of research has shown that Head Start children do gain what the program's name aims for—a head start on learning of all kinds, with an emphasis on those verbal skills that underlie articulation and reading. The childminders in Head Start are teachers and nonteachers who have had some training in education, and their modest but on-target efforts are assisted by materials and methods provided by the government. Head Start's techniques for stimulating articulateness could be substantially and rather easily improved, but even in their present form they are a definite plus for children. As for regular day care, the sad reality is that its opportunities for learning are seldom if ever seized. At most day care centers, the hourly wage paid to workers is barely above the minimum wage—low enough to ensure that most caregivers will be only marginally skilled in educating children and unlikely to be competent in the inculcation of language skills. Nor do such workers have much time for such a task. The economics of day care means that the workers have to mind up to a half-dozen toddlers at once, an exhausting task in any circumstance. The substitution of other caregivers for the mother and/or the sending of the child to a day care facility—acts which many people have viewed as neutral in terms of their ultimate impact on childrearing—must now be viewed as changing the composition of the speech community, sometimes to the good of the child, but not invariably so. As Fowler determined, "The maintenance of quality care with enriched language need not be an elaborate enterprise." Nonetheless, some sort of fostering language environment does need to be in existence and functioning if children are to be properly set on the path toward becoming articulate. Families whose children receive their principal tutelage in language from caregivers of "linguistically disadvantaged" backgrounds or caregivers from cultures in which the principal function of teaching language to the very young is "situational" and designed to instill in the child a sense of his or her place in the hierarchy of the community, or in day care settings that do not recognize the importance of language development and do not actively and properly work on enhancing it, must recognize that such choices will adversely affect their children's language development. If the economic needs of the family require that a mother and father both work outside the home and must place the children in the care of people whose English language skills are less than their own, then at least those parents, during their hours at home, must work doubly hard to help their children properly learn the language.

The age of the mother, the sex of the child, the size of the family, and birth order all seem to make a difference in language acquisition. Precisely what sort of difference is a subject currently under study. Some of the pre-liminary findings have been reported in various issues of a single scholarly publication, *The Journal of Speech and Hearing*. Teenage mothers, who may not themselves have full command of the language and are likely not to have completed school, are much less aware of the need to talk to their children than are somewhat older and better-educated mothers. One study found that when American middle-class mothers talk with their daughters, they are more likely to use longer sentences and to ask ques-tions than when they talk with their sons. As for family size, it was long assumed that the first-born child and/or the single child of a nuclear family would be the beneficiary of the parents' undivided attention and would grow up having the greatest chance of becoming articulate; new research has contradicted that assumption. It has been shown that where more than two or three people inhabit the same living space, young children are not limited to interacting with a single caregiver, and the multiple dia-logues they conduct seem to assist in making them more articulate on the average, than children in smaller families. Birth order also seems to matter. Some children develop what is called a "referential" style of talk-ing as they begin to speak—their first fifty words refer to things by name. Other children develop more slowly and have an "expressive" style—they are more likely to speak late, and then to say action phrases like "please," "thank you," and "jump up." Referential children tend to be first-borns, while the expressive style usually characterizes younger sisters and broth-ers. However, the child most likely to be at ease with the language, when the acquisition process is finally complete, is not the first or the last, but the middle child, who has to adjust his or her speech both up and down to siblings, an undertaking that presumably gives the child a greater awareness of, and facility in, articulate expression.[23]

While there is plenty of evidence that Victorian era families contribu-
ted in many ways to the psychological difficulties that later afflicted their
children, in Victorian households there were plenty of minds available to
stimulate the child—several generations under the same roof, many siblings, an extensive and homogeneous speech community. In such homes
there were substantial amounts of reading aloud and other verbal-
interchange activities. There was conversation around the dinner table,
sometimes lasting for hours. There were parlor games in which the comments of the players were of as much interest to the child as the progress
of the game itself. Today's children, who live in smaller households, do not
reap the benefit of being spoken to by grandparents, aunts, uncles, and
phalanxes of siblings, all of whom might add measurably to the child's
storehouse of language knowledge and also might provide the child with
opportunities for verbal interaction.

Instead of trading words with such adults, today's children have for
home companionship the ubiquitous television set, which in many homes
becomes the electronic babysitter. Preschool children are positioned in
front of a television for several hours a day, and many parents rationalize
putting them there because they tune the sets to "educational programs"
like *Sesame Street, Mister Rogers Neighborhood*, or *Barney* the dinosaur.
Children love these programs and the principals in them, which is no
wonder, because these are their constant companions. Their quirks and
turns of phrase stay with the children even when the television set is
turned off, as any adult who tries to have a conversation with a three-year-
old will testify. What these electronic companions (and the toys that
replicate their images) cannot do is engage the children in dialogue. Even
though Kermit the Frog, Fred Rogers, and the purple dinosaur sometimes
encourage their little watchers to sing along, identify a letter or an object,
or answer a question about who loves them, the programs may actually be
repressing dialogue skills. The pace and humor of *Sesame Street* were initially judged by educational professionals in the United Kingdom and
other English-speaking countries as too fast and too adult to be suitable
for young children, and the program was not then broadcast in those
countries. Many children are threatened by *Sesame Street*'s noise, frantic
quick-cutting (reminiscent of commercials), and gaggle of nonhuman
speakers whose mouth mechanisms in no way resemble those of human
beings. Barney is lovable but so determinedly nonintelligent that he serves

as a powerful distraction from any activity that is more educational. Fred Rogers's program is the best of the three, because he speaks slowly and directly to children in the manner of a good Head Start or kindergarten teacher, and he reassures children about their innate abilities. These television programs are definitely tutorial, because children extract many lessons from them—mostly emotional "feel-good" lessons—but articulate behavior is not among the things being taught, because it cannot be taught in a nondialogue context. As Fowler and the Head Start programs show, what children need is not just instruction but feedback that helps them evaluate and improve their own performance.

Are television-saturated children different as learners from those who watch less at an early age? That is very difficult to measure. Gavriel Salomon has studied the problem and has concluded that children process information and other input from television in a "shallow" and more or less "automatic" way. He postulates the most devastating effect of television as being that "children acquire the expectation that pleasurable information can be obtained effortlessly, an expectation they then carry over to written material." Michael Morgan and Larry Gross, who also studied the problem, speculate that the shallow-processing style affects learning in a particular way. "Because watching television is 'easier' than reading, in that it does not require the same degree of sustained concentration for comprehension, heavy television viewing could reinforce impatience with reading; and reading skills hence would remain undeveloped." According to Morgan and Gross, the heavy television watchers among children read less well than do those children who watch fewer hours of television.[24]

Because of television and many other factors, students of today differ in many ways from those of yesterday, the psychologists Charles H. Wolfgang and Karla Lynn Kelsay write. They contend that "childhood is changed" as a consequence of the home environment having been altered from what it was in the past. Wolfgang and Kelsay are not just making a generalized rant against modernity but are identifying specific losses that have to do with how children understand certain key classifying concepts, for instance, the organization of time. Successful students are those who know how to organize their time and who produce work in a timely manner. Children who grow up in homes that view time differently—perhaps because parents are out of the home for longer stretches during the

day—do not understand what all the fuss is about when they are repri-
manded in school for turning in their work late. Similarly, many of today's
children do not know what behaviors are condoned or condemned in
what spaces—how behavior in the gym ought to differ from behavior
in the classroom—and do not have the same concept of property as those
in old-style homes, where the unauthorized borrowing of someone else's
jacket and not returning it is labeled as stealing. Problems arise in schools
when teachers view infractions in these areas as disobedience, and rectify
them, as Wolfgang and Kelsay charge, "with punishments and autocratic
classroom management." Because new-style children do not understand
the concepts, the only result of such teacher harshness is to prevent the
children from learning the appropriate values and how to work within
their structure. One school had to resort to dealing with the impasse between old understandings and new, the authors of the study report, by
declaring a six-week period to be "Mars Days," during which the entire
population of the school "pretended the students had just stepped off
rocketships from Mars and had no knowledge or understanding of the
new world culture of the school," so that teachers could help the students
"create a workable culture" that instilled "values and behaviors that have
traditionally meant success for children who possessed them."[25]

Parents who do not take the time or do not know how to inculcate
these values and behaviors are not only those from disadvantaged households. They are from every household that does not choose to do the work
of educating its offspring. In general, the psychologist Harold Barrett
charges, today's parents are "emotionally distant," and today's family atmosphere is "flat and sterile," conditions that lead to understimulated
children. Such stimulants as reading aloud to one another have all but
vanished from most households, as have the hours-long dinner with its
rounds of conversation (and tacit instruction in what is acceptable behavior and what is not) and the time for participating in parlor games with
their accompanying verbal byplay. Understimulation hurts children, Barrett writes, by cutting off or limiting the "spirit and process of discovery"
by which children investigate the phenomena of this world and learn
things in what educators consider the best way to learn—by discovering
truths themselves. Understimulation also curtails a child's creativity and
engenders a lack of appreciation for the past, both of which, Barrett
emphasizes, will impair the child's later performance in school and adjust-

ment to life. The proper family attitude can actually enhance creativity. One technique for making a child's later rhetorical success more likely, Barrett says, is "adequate mirroring" by the family, that is, responding to the child's actions and words in a way that helps the child know that those words and actions are proper and acceptable and exciting, and which give to children "a sense of their own being." The ideal sponsorship of emotional and rhetorical development, according to Barrett, entails the proper encouragement of play. Echoing Fowler's belief that an enriched language atmosphere need not mean an elaborate enterprise by the care-givers, Barrett writes that optimal conditions in a household are not difficult to achieve, but they must be there and they must not be too lax. Laissez-faire in childcare—allowing a child to do whatever he or she wants—does not help the child, Barrett argues; it is not bad for the child to be frustrated by the parent or caregiver, so long as this process pro-duces "useful adversity," that is, so long as it teaches the child the limits of omnipotence, which always has be to learned.[26]

There is new evidence that taking another person's perspective is the key attribute in learning to be what Barrett calls "rhetorically sensitive," that is, becoming the good listener who has the possibility of becoming a fully articulate person. In some interesting experiments, it has been shown that this process begins in the home when the child is young, and that the child's later "communicative style" remains tied for life to that immediate family situation. Tamar Liebes and Rivka Ribak report that in their own recent experiment, as well as in other experiments done on familial patterns of communication, the communicative style of the family tends to be reproduced in the child and to become more and more fixed as he or she approaches adulthood. Some families are "protective"—they teach the child to value harmony, not to show anger in a group situation, not to challenge their parents or argue with them, and in general not to speak about difficult subjects. "Protectives" do not often take the other person's perspective. On the other end of the discursive spectrum Liebes and Ribak place "pluralistic" families, which believe in the importance of fa-milial discussions and in the necessity of putting one's own point of view across even when others do not like it, but which also believe in listening to viewpoints with which the speaker may disagree. In between those two extremes are several mixed categories, but most families, Liebes and Ribak conclude, tend to be substantially like one or the other extreme. It is not the parents' *point of view* that the children eventually replicate, the researchers point out, but rather the parents' *patterns of interpersonal communication*. Parents with liberal views sometimes had children whose views were conservative, and vice versa, but families that did not encourage discussion seldom produced a child who liked to participate in discussions and who listened well to other people.[27]

It has long been an axiom that the children who do well in early formal schooling are on track for superior performance throughout the rest of their academic careers. What separates the adequate performers in early schooling from the less than adequate? Many investigators are coming around to the view that two elements are of the essence: command of language and the ability to take the perspective of the other person. The first is readily comprehended, but most people do not realize that these two skills—skills in the sense that both are learned abilities—are quite intertwined. Patrick De Gramont, examining language from the point of view of psychiatry, states flatly:

> Not only is language necessary if we are to share in another's perspective; we need language in order to consider and reflectively care about the needs of others, to become reflectively aware of who we are, and to share in the communal responsibilities that go beyond instinctual levels of conduct. Without language we would be severely limited in our ability to transcend the particular contexts of our experience, i.e., we would be trapped in our private worlds.[28]

Articulate behavior has as much to do with making sure that the listener comprehends what is being said as it does with expressing oneself well. That command of language and the ability to take the perspective of the other person are interdependent skills is a proposition supported by the experiments of Ionanna Dimitracopolou, a California linguistics professor. She studied language skills and "personal competence" at three nursery schools by means of a board game she had designed. To be a competent user of the language in nursery school, she found, meant more than possessing the ability to say words. What turned out to be critical to success was "the individual's attempt to act effectively in a structured social environment." "Successful speech" in this context she defined as that which aided the children in solving the exercise. On this small-child level, the ability to cooperate through communicating, rather than intelligence or pure verbal agility, was the key to completing the task. Cooperation through communication, in turn, depended on the children's "ability to take the visual perspective of another person, recognize the causal links in social events, and understand other people's inner feelings." The "socially successful" children, the ones who were able to cooperate with their teachers and peers in the board game and in other social tasks, were also the ones who were later evaluated as the most able learners in nursery school. Moreover, the children whom Dimitracopolou identified as having conversational problems—who were less successful in relating to others through language—were later discovered to be the ones experiencing difficulties in the more advanced task of learning to read.[29]

The interesting piece of evidence that language competence is intricately involved with taking the perspective of others brings us anew to the conclusion that articulateness in the growing child does not depend on the child's abilities alone, but is a jointly produced enterprise. It results from the work of at least two separate entities—the child speaker and the speech community. When there are unsolved and unbalanced problems with the adequacy or the constitution of that speech community or with its willingness and ability to help the child learn both the words of the language and the capacity to take the perspective of others, it is unlikely that the child—however brilliant in other respects—will be articulate.

Chapter 2

STANDARD ISSUE

$\mathcal{A}$ Puerto Rican–born woman in New York City neatly encapsulated a fundamental controversy in language use when she told a reporter, "Sometimes I intentionally try to lose the [Puerto Rican] accent totally, to assimilate" into the majority white culture of her adopted city, but at other times she chooses not to suppress her accent, in order to be more accepted in her own ethnic community.[1] In the previous chapter I argued that a language is learned in the context of a speech community and that articulateness in the maturing child requires a speech community composed mainly of those who themselves have a reasonably high facility in the language. However, there is conflict today between those who believe that using standard English is important, principally as a key to advancement in American society, and those who hold that standard English is a trap and insist on communicating in other languages or variants. The Puerto Rican–born woman is caught in the middle. Before examining in Chapter 3 the formal educational system and its methods of teaching (or not teaching) articulate behavior, we must first ask whether there is a standard English language to be taught and, if there is, whether all English-speakers must learn it.

The patron saint of Standard English in the United States is St. John de Crevecoeur, who emigrated to upper New York State from the Normandy region of France in the eighteenth century. In 1782 Crevecoeur wrote that the motto of all immigrants ought to be *ubi panis ibi patria*, "where there is bread, there is one's fatherland." He contended that in order to give the fatherland proper allegiance and become the best possible citizen, one must learn and use its language.[2] The perceived need to aspire to some standard of mastery of American English is very strong among many immigrants. New York City provides English as a Second Language (ESL) classes for 30,000 people; they are always filled to capacity, and the waiting lists are measured in years—recently, five hundred people applied for a class that has only fifty places. More than half of the 800,000 immigrants admitted legally to this country each year speak either no English or very poor English. According to scholars who have interviewed them, most of them want desperately to learn the official language of the United States. An accountant from Panama applied for an ESL class when she first arrived in New York, but two years later, when a slot finally opened up for her, she was working at two jobs, day and evening, and could not find the time for a class. "It's frustrating," Juliana Loma told a reporter in Spanish, "I'm stuck in menial work because I don't speak English, and I don't speak English because I can't afford to quit my menial jobs to take a class." Mary Cuadrado, a bilingual professor of sociology, in a similar vein, wrote that she knew many "brilliant Hispanic college students who perform well below their potential because they cannot clearly express their thoughts in English," which she thought a shame because "success . . . in most quarters of this country depends on one's ability to be fluent in English." Beyond job-related reasons, some immigrants want to speak English in order to deal more effectively with landlords, police, and other city officials, and to converse properly with younger family members who speak English and not the language of the old country.[3]

The desire to speak English is not confined to immigrants, nor is it exclusive to the United States. In a study of native Quebecois who learned English in addition to their first language, French, researchers discovered that those who improved their ability to speak English (as opposed to those who did not attempt to improve it) were able to raise their incomes 19 percent.[4]

Evidence that the step up into a higher socio-economic class may require the aspirant to employ the language in the same way and in the same tones as those already there is provided by the opposition, as it were, when it demands that this social requirement be changed. The objectors contend that American society must be more accepting of different languages and accents. To refuse advancement to anyone on the basis of a foreign or "lower-status" accent is discriminatory, they say, and so is forcing students to learn standard English when their home language is something different. Their view of standard English as discriminatory has sometimes been upheld by the courts, which, for instance, have mandated bilingual teaching in schools in order to counter the perceived discrimination.

The controversy poses the question: Other than to demarcate social boundaries, does a standard of English exist, and does it have important uses? To comprehend this complex matter properly, we must briefly examine the bases and purposes of human speech.

Some social actions that we consider to be quintessentially human—tool-making and tool use, for example—are possible without speech, but others are not. Neanderthals were able to build and live in wood-framed shelters and to produce art, Philip Lieberman writes in his investigation of the evolution of speech, but "they did not have human speech, because they did not have a human vocal tract." Lieberman suggests that Neanderthals may have died out because they lacked sufficient ability to communicate. Two anatomical mechanisms are considered essential for human speech production: a particular configuration of tongue, pharynx, and oral cavity that differs in important respects from that of other animals, and an advanced brain mechanism that permits voluntary control of vocal communication. Apes do not have those anatomical traits, and neither did most proto-humans. Fully human speech came into existence when the species developed a modern supralaryngeal vocal tract, "one with a curved tongue body that forms both the floor of the oral cavity and the anterior wall of the pharynx." Though there is no evidence of this vocal tract configuration in the bones of the earliest Homo erectus, it does show up in fossilized hominids of 100,000 years ago, the time of the emergence of Homo sapiens, and it has been specifically identified in the hominid remains recently uncovered at the Jebel Qafzeh and Skhul V sites in Israel.[5]

Further maturation of the human species probably had to wait for greater complexity to develop in the brain itself; that anatomical advance, Lieberman argues, strongly correlates with advances in human communication. Scientists have tried to figure out whether the ability to speak preceded or followed the more highly convoluted cortex; the developments were probably interrelated, Darwinian selection favoring those proto-humans better able than their brethren to encode and decode communications; the good talker (and listener?) stayed alive longer than the good hunter and had many more opportunities to reproduce.

The date of emergence of a fully developed brain capable of syntactical grammatical communications cannot be proved, because we cannot interrogate fossils to learn whether they knew how to diagram a sentence. But complex ability can be inferred from remains buried alongside the skeletons. About the 100,000-years-ago mark, the first ritual burials in tombs and cairns began, which included material goods as well as the bodily remains. Ritual burials have been interpreted as evidence that their practitioners believed in some sort of afterlife, rebirth, or reincarnation. To think about such concepts, to develop them among the members of a tribal group, requires communication beyond the mere transmission of warnings or of claims to territorial ownership; it requires a language that is syntactical and reciprocal. A moral sense—for that is what ritual burials demonstrate—and complex human vocal communication developed simultaneously; many lessons might be drawn from that conjunction, but one is inescapable: An early function of human speech was to articulate common beliefs, those primary means through which human beings were knitted together in community. *To communicate* has as its essential meaning, *to share*.

Speech as a means of bringing people together and not as a way to exacerbate what separates them continued to be a valued foundation for human affairs during the golden age of Greece. Aristotle's teachings emphasize that the central task for the speaker is to find or make common ground with the audience. This was done, in part, through full use of memory. Aristotle characterized memory as a system for organizing the storehouse of a person's knowledge in a way that permitted it to be drawn upon easily in the course of giving a long speech, for the purpose of providing "common ground" examples and ordering the successive stages of one's argument. One imagines a great building and then mentally situates in its niches, patterns, and details the items and sequences one will later need to recall and to which the audience will most readily respond. Full command of the language was not considered to be reflexive or instantaneously reactive—it was not the ability to retort, to come up with a one-liner; rather, one's full powers were in use when the speech was made by means of reference to memory and to what had been carefully prepared and arranged in it. One constructed eloquent phrases and salted them in memory, whence they could be produced at the proper time and occasion.[6]

Writing changed the equilibrium of this array of the mental powers. In a famous passage, Plato explains how. In part to demonstrate how rhetoric was then being distorted to serve other ends than persuading men to the knowledge of the truth, Socrates tells a story about King Thamus of Egypt entertaining the god Theuth, who brags that he has just invented writing. This invention, Theuth contends, will improve "both the wisdom and the memory of the Egyptians." Thamus says that the opposite is true, that those who acquire writing "will cease to exercise their memory and become forgetful," because they will rely on the words on the papyrus to call up matters by external signs instead of using their internal resources; eventually, this will result in people who are "thought very knowledgeable when they are for the most part quite ignorant."[7]

The Greeks were still too close to the changes wrought by writing to notice an even more radical alteration that it made to the thinking process. By what Father Walter Ong, SJ, labels "the commitment of the word to space," writing so fundamentally transformed the structure of language that the mind-set of the user was also greatly altered. Languages are inherently different after they become written from what they were before. Once writing has become deeply enmeshed in a culture, Ong insists, its users no longer think in the ways that orally based peoples do; rather, they think principally by reference to the written word. Writing becomes "interiorized" to such a degree that is impossible to separate the thought processes from writing. Languages formed by long and deep association with writing, Ong contends, have a power different from and far greater than that of purely oral languages. Ong reminds us that standard literal-based English

. . . has accessible for use a recorded vocabulary of at least a million and a half words, of which not only the present meanings but also hundreds of thousands of past meanings are known. A simply oral dialect will commonly have resources of only a few thousand words, and its users will have virtually no knowledge of the real semantic history of any of these words.[8]

A nonliterate, nonwriting, "primarily oral" culture is at a severe disadvantage in a writing-dominated world, Ong contends. Members of a primarily oral culture can learn by apprenticeship practices, but "abstractly sequential, classificatory, explanatory examination of phenomena or of stated truths is impossible without writing and reading." That is to say, according to Ong, oral cultures cannot study; they cannot learn a great deal from the past or from the work or lives of individuals who are not then present in the community. "Without writing, human consciousness cannot achieve its fuller potentials," Ong concludes, because literacy is "absolutely necessary" for the development of the disciplines that we honor as the crowns of human civilization: science, history, philosophy, literature, and many of the other arts.[9]

The thought processes of oral and literate-based peoples are remarkably different, a fact made clear by a series of observations in 1931–32 in the steppes of Russia. A team headed by A. R. Luriia chronicled and examined the enormous changes that were occurring as a group of peasants in remote Uzbekistan and Kirghizia were being brought from a preliterate into a literate-based culture.[10] For Luriia, one of the leading linguistic scholars of the Soviet Union, this presented a once-in-a-lifetime opportunity to investigate and document a process that must have occurred many times in the history of the world but had never been closely recorded for posterity. Luriia and his collaborators first talked extensively with their subjects in the informal setting of a teahouse, then, having gained their trust, asked questions, some of which were riddles. There were five major findings from the study, all of which help illuminate the difference in thinking between the oral-based and literate-based subjects.

1. The oral-based subjects identified objects by their names, rather than in abstract terms—a circle was called a plate, a rectangle was a door or an apricot-drying board. Students in a local literate-based school, shown the same objects, identified them by their categoric geometric-shape names.

2. The oral-based subjects were asked to do a task that has more recently become familiar to a generation that grew up watching *Sesame Street:* to tell which one of a set of objects is not just like the others. Preliterate people responded to "hammer, saw, log, hatchet" in practical terms, as though the objects were all related. A twenty-five-year-old man said, "They're all alike. The saw will saw the log and the hatchet will chop

it into small pieces. If one of these has to go, I'd throw away the hatchet. It doesn't do as good a job as the saw." When told that the hammer, saw, and hatchet are tools, and that a log is not, and that is the clue, the same man protested, "Yes, but even if we have tools, we still need wood—otherwise we can't build anything." By contrast, a fully literate man got the categories right and defended them under attack, while a marginally literate older man came down on both sides of the question, confusing categories and practical thinking.

3. "In the Far North, where there is snow, all bears are white. Novaya Zemlya is in the Far North. What color are the bears?" This question drew a response from one preliterate man that the only bears he had ever seen were black, and from another that you could only find out the color of a bear by looking at it. Luriia's preliterate subjects were unable to use formal logic—a discipline that came to the Greeks, not incidentally, only after alphabetic writing had been introduced into the culture. Literate responders said that by the questioner's logic, the bears were probably white. In literate riddles, the answer has to do with decoding the words, but to solve a riddle in an oral culture requires a different skill—canniness, which may have little to do with the words themselves.

4. The oral-based subjects could not define concrete objects. Asked for a definition of a tree, the peasants refused to give one, saying that everyone knew what a tree was, so it was not necessary to explain. Asked for a definition of a car, another person told the interviewer that the best way to understand it was to go for a ride in one. But a literate-based factory worker told the interviewer that the car was a machine made in a factory, that it could cover distances more rapidly than a horse, and that the engine was steam-based, requiring both fire and water in order to work.

5. The preliterate and oral-based peasants all had great difficulty in articulate self-analysis, preferring to imagine themselves in a situation rather than as individuals removed from the situation and capable of independent thought.

Luriia's work has been largely replicated with other societies (in Africa and Asia) that are on the cusp of changing from oral-based cultures to those that have strong elements of literacy.[11] The results have confirmed that the words used and, more important, the thought processes themselves are significantly different in oral-based cultures from those in literate-based cultures. Walter Ong cites Luriia's work as emphasizing the important distinction between oral and literate cultures. This distinction has many ramifications for a consideration of standards. To condense them: Without writing, there are no standards.

An oral language is continuously in flux, because it is passed from person to person and varies with each passing, especially when transmitted from an older generation to a younger one. The pace of change is very rapid: Oral languages, and in particular their dialects, can vary from one year to the next. Written languages also are in constant flux, but the pace of change is slower, because writing permits a society to freeze a language in one form. The written word becomes a record of past standards and acts as a partial brake on the language's continuing evolution. Colin Cherry, a communications theorist, likens language to "the shifting surface of the sea" and its words to "the sparkle of the waves like flashes of light on points of history."[12] John Earl Joseph, an analyst of standards in English, agrees that all language is "inherently unstable," because "the reality in which we live—and which language is our primary means of expressing, dealing with, and mitigating—is not static, but always changing. . . . With reality perpetually in flux, we could scarcely expect that language remain static."[13]

As we try to determine if there is a standard, we have to recognize that English is altering at a phenomenal rate of speed. Comparing successive editions of dictionaries, we find about 10,000 words per decade are added or dropped from the usual college dictionaries, those which contain the working vocabularies of most users of our language, somewhere around 100,000 words out of the entire corpus of more than a million. That is to say, what one generation accepts as its standard is, at least in terms of vocabulary, perhaps 10 to 15 percent altered from what its parents accepted as standard. Grammar also changes rapidly. President Woodrow Wilson so often used the phrase "may I not" in his letters and speeches that White House insiders joked that the presidential yacht could move at a speed of five may-I-nots an hour. Wilson's old-style grammatical construction is certainly still extant and understandable in English, but it is almost never used.

The question then becomes: Who is interested in having standards, and why? The Stoics were the first recorded language curmudgeons, the first to take an interest in grammar and in the standardization of linguistic form and meaning. Since then, purists the world over have been attempting to keep their own languages unchanged by erecting and maintaining some sort of standard. The urge to hold back language change may be universal. All speech communities are "sensitive to language quality in one form or another," Joseph writes. Across many different cultures the complaints about loss of quality display the same elements. The older generations of the speakers of various Native American languages, for example, dismiss the younger generations' use of their ancient tongues as too full of slang and as a decline from the golden age of pure speech; they also hope that this distressing change is an aberrant phase destined soon to pass. It will not pass, Joseph contends, and moreover, the elders' idea of a golden age is a myth, one that seems to be present in every society, and around this myth the desire for a standard rallies. The myth of a golden age is particularly insidious, because the linguistic harmony that the older generation yearns for is combined with many other elements in a grandiose misconception of "the good old days" when not only cultural harmony supposedly existed, but also spiritual and racial harmony. Whether this idea crops up in Navajo country or in the halls of Oxford, Cambridge, or Harvard, such myth-making is simplistic and flies in the face of the reality of continual change. Linguistic purity and acceptance of an unchanging standard may be appropriate for a culture that is monolithic like, say, the culture of a remote island that has no communications with other lands, but it is unrealistic and unattainable in a multifaceted, continually evolving culture.[14]

Charles Carpenter Fries, a historian of the changes in American English, wrote that there was always a separation between the mostly spoken "language of the people," which serves many functions, and the language of "great literature," which serves only one of those functions—beauty. Fries likened literature to the especially lovely hothouse plants and flowers developed by specialists, flowers that are not reproducible in everyday natural, outdoor circumstances. The moment when the gap between spoken and written language began to crystallize, Fries speculates, was in a 1765 book by William Ward entitled *Grammar of the English Language*. Ward attempted to standardize the ways in which many words were used—for example, "shall" and "will"—and did so, Fries shows, in an arbitrary way. It was arbitrary because Ward's book did not describe how "shall" and "will" were used in 1765, or even earlier; Fries writes that

Ward "definitely repudiated usage, even that of 'our most approved authors,' as the basis of correctness in language," and sought to correct instances "'where Custom is erroneous'" in order to make the language seem more rational. That is to say, the grammatical "rules" for the use of "shall" and "will," which have vexed a dozen and more generations of English users after Ward, have no real historic basis. As far as Fries was concerned, the only rational basis for judging correctness in language was usage or practice. Writing in the 1940s, he cited as an example the phrase "to get on one's nerves," saying that it was considered colloquial, not used in serious writing but frequently overheard in conversation. Fries contended that such colloquial usage was neither correct nor incorrect; it simply denoted that the term had not yet entered the lexicon of most writers.[15] Today, of course, it has, and the phrase is regularly used.

Ward's 1765 book reflected a mid-eighteenth-century urge to rationalize, catalogue, and preserve many things—not just words but also books, paintings, and sculptures—and to consolidate collections of them into coherent structures called libraries and museums. When the museum of English came to be regarded as the only socially acceptable repository of our language—indeed, as its sacred teaching institution—the idea of a standard was really hatched.

Old countries make museums; new ones have neither the time nor the inclination. In the American Revolutionary era, the museum of English was predominantly a British concern, not an American one. It echoed the codified class distinctions of a country separated into those who could enter the House of Lords and those who could aspire only to Commons. The idea of a museum of English was also an egregious British instance of pronunciation envy—a modified version of the concern for linguistic purity espoused by the French, who had established an Academy for the express purpose of immutably fixing their own language. The British thought such an academy was a capital idea, though there was never enough enthusiasm to generate one in London, and in the early days of the American republic, John Adams sought to set up an American Academy "for refining, correcting, improving, and ascertaining the English language." Thomas Jefferson, asked to preside over such an enterprise, adamantly rejected the post and the idea. He ridiculed what the French were doing, contending that, because new notions were always entering any language, it would be silly to restrict change, and he lambasted the idea of trying to fix English in amber at that particular time, because to tie the United States to the then current standard would mean tying it to the very aspects of England that we had shed so much blood to leave behind.[16]

Joseph, Fries, and Jefferson permit us to understand that the idea of a language standard had become fused with a way of making class distinctions. This aspect of standards was articulated best by Thorstein Veblen. A passage at the end of *The Theory of the Leisure Class*, published in 1899, has had a great impact on the way several generations of investigators have viewed standards. Veblen wrote that one of the chief differentials employed by the leisure class to express their distance from the classes below them was "elegant English . . . great purity of speech" of the sort that could only have been acquired during a life spent "in other than vulgarly useful occupations. . . . Elegant diction, whether in writing or speaking, is an effective means of reputability," that is, it conveyed membership in an elite club; the more archaic the language usage of the member, the greater the warrant of respectability. Refined speech had been lauded as the concomitant of principled behavior; moreover, Veblen, wrote "it is contended . . . that a punctilious use of ancient and accredited locutions will serve to convey thought more adequately and more precisely than would the straight-forward use of the latest form of spoken English; whereas it is notorious that the ideas of to-day are effectively expressed in the slang of to-day." He charged that the use of refined language was no more than an attempt to signify that the user was socially superior to the slang user, no more than a tool by means of which the moneyed ruling classes defended their privileges and kept down the impoverished classes.[17]

Veblen's blast is at the core of why the use of standard English has ever since been castigated for being a social distinction rather than a sign of advanced learning. In the remainder of this chapter, I want to demonstrate why this Veblen diatribe is misguided and unhelpful. In order to do so, we must first trace the various ways in which Veblen's idea was employed and railed against.

In the early decades of the twentieth century, a series of linguists, accepting Veblen's basic social-classes critique of Western society, formulated a notion that the power of the museum of language was a potent force inside a person's head that affected every aspect of thought. In 1929

Edward Sapir crystallized this notion in an essay: "Language is a guide to social reality [which] powerfully conditions all our thinking" to the degree that people are "at the mercy of the particular language which has become the medium of expression for their society." Benjamin Lee Whorf adopted and amplified Sapir's thesis. From studying a Hopi dictionary, Whorf concluded that the Hopi language did not include tenses that divide time into past, present, and future, which, he thought, went a long way toward explaining why the Hopi had a hard time handling those white-man's concepts. In a 1940 article he extended Sapir's notion into what has become known as the Sapir–Whorf hypothesis: "Every language . . . incorporates certain points of view and certain patterned resistances to widely divergent points of view," so much so that a person's language becomes "not merely a reproducing instrument for voicing ideas but rather . . . the shaper of ideas, the program and guide for the individual's mental activity."[18]

The Sapir–Whorf hypothesis—that we are the language through which we think—has been shown by later scientists to be inadequate as an explanation for the generation of thought. Chomsky and Pinker have demonstrated that all languages contain a number of basic structures that are strikingly similar, that all languages have the capacity to express human beings' most complicated thoughts, and that the differences between languages are mainly in the order in which words are used in sentences and in the labels that we variously attach to objects and concepts.[19]

As Walter Ong's work shows, the differences are in language *usage*. Pinker's book does not mention Ong, but a Chomskyan insistence on a Universal Grammar does not compromise the idea that thought processes of oral and literate societies differ in level and quality of discourse. Both Chomsky and Ong refute Sapir–Whorf.

Before leaving the Sapir–Whorf hypothesis in the dust, where it belongs, we have to understand why it was so influential. When Sapir–Whorf was posited, it seemed eminently logical, especially when one language was superficially compared to another. Arabic has six thousand words that pertain to camels, while English has only a few; a tribe in the Philippines can distinguish among ninety-two kinds of rice, the staple of its diet. The Chinese have no single words for yes or no; in order to say something in the negative, the speaker must negate a verb. Many other languages similarly stress process over things. In the parlance of the Nootka of Vancouver

Island, the speaker cannot refer to an object that we would call a house, but instead says "a house occurs," or "it houses." In English the adjective usually precedes the noun, while in French the adjective follows it; this, some people contend, is a fundamental difference. "The red wine" is a phrase that shows the "inductive" thought patterns of English: it begins with a particular (red) and builds to a more general notion (wine). "Le vin rouge," as the same phrase would be worded in French, reflects the more "deductive" French thought pattern, which starts with the general (vin) and from that deduces the specific adjective (rouge). "Deductive-versus-inductive" so distinguishes French from English thought that it has been used to describe the basic dichotomy between the French and English legal systems.[20]

Did that mean French was superior to English, or vice versa? Or that either language was or was not superior to Hopi? Or that standard English was better than nonstandard? This latter question became the focus when a devastating sociological inference was drawn from Sapir–Whorf: that people who do not use the standard language for their thought processes have a quality of thought inferior to that of those who do use it. Trying to figure out why some native English-speaking children did well in school in Great Britain while others of presumed equal intelligence did not, the social scientist Basil Bernstein studied several groups and determined that the real difference lay in the ways that various economic classes used the English language. The middle-class groups used what Bernstein called an "elaborated code" for speech, while the lower class used a "restricted" code. Both codes were inculcated by the respective sets of parents when the children were infants. Poverty-level parents, his observations showed him, produce the restricted code by ordering their children about and giving the children no explanations or analyses; at most, they offer reasons for their behavior by making reference to metaphors that are common only within the immediate community. Poor parents' language, Bernstein decided, was "particularistic," specific, dramatic, and colorful, but meaningful only within their own limited group and not useful in many other situations. That was why the children who used it had such a hard time in school, Bernstein guessed. The middle-class parents he observed often formally explained to their children why they should behave in a certain manner and did a lot of analyzing. Middle-class language was less colorful, but the explanations and analyses were "universalistic" and had more utility in situations outside the home and community—in the most important instance, in school. The middle class was able to shift from one code to the other as the situation demanded, Bernstein concluded, but poor people, locked into the restricted code, had trouble "generalizing . . . at the higher ranges" and suffered from "a low level of conceptualization," which, he believed, caused them not to do well in school.[21]

Bernstein's first volume in his trilogy on the sociology of language was published in 1971, and he soon came under attack because the conclusions were used to justify "tracking" of lower-class children—at the extreme, they were used as a basis for dismissing such children altogether from the possibilities of academic education by shunting them into vocational schools. The reasoning used: Since lower-class children used substandard English and thought differently, they could never climb to higher rungs in society, and so would be better served by being removed from strictly academic venues. Controversy over the use of Bernstein's conclusions obscured what has since became apparent: that Bernstein's basic research identifying and elucidating differences between the groups' language usages was solid. Working-class and white-collar parents *do* talk to their children differently. Bernstein's sociological conclusions based on that research were flawed, however, because in effect they blamed the victims for their incapacity. In a most succinct refutation of Bernstein's conclusions, John Earl Joseph writes: "To assume that a person's use of the [language] is a measure of his or her intellectual development is to commit a basic deductive flaw. It is to judge a book by its cover."[22] Joseph is only partly correct in this analogy, because intelligence is often (and perhaps most easily) measured in terms of command of language; as we will explore in a later chapter, the ability to correctly identify and use certain "rare" words is the key to high rankings on standard intelligence tests. However, having low articulate ability does not necessarily mean that a person is of low intelligence, because intelligence may have other correlates—it can consist of mathematical, athletic or musical adeptness, for instance, in addition to or in place of verbal ability, as Howard Gardner pointed out in a recent book. As important, William Fowler has shown, and I have reported in an earlier chapter, that IQ test scores can be enhanced if children are exposed to good articulateness training.

A strong, research-based refutation of Bernstein emerged as African-Americans and other minority populations in the United States began to assert their rights as citizens and to celebrate their own cultures, which placed considerable emphasis on the distinctiveness of their language usage and its capacity for full expression. It came in the work of William Labov and his associates at the University of Pennsylvania on Black English Vernacular (BEV). Labov first distinguished himself in an ingenious and elegant 1966 study of the dialects used by New Yorkers, a study that elucidated some principles that underlay his later work. Labov gathered data on such matters as when his subjects did or did not drop the letter "r" from pronounced words—a missing "r" being characteristic of extreme regional lower-status dialect, so that New Yorker becomes Noo Yawkuh, while enunciating the "r" is believed to sound upper-class. Employees from three department stores were asked questions to which the answer had to be "fourth floor." Labov discovered that the "r" was pronounced by upper-middle-class members about 20 percent of the time in causal speech, 25 percent of the time in careful speech or in ordinary reading aloud situations, but 55 percent of the time when the employees were given lists to be read aloud. In contrast, lower-middle-class subjects said the "r" less frequently in the first three categories, but when it came to pronouncing lists, they enunciated the "r" an astounding 80 percent of the time. Labov concluded that people regularly and voluntarily shift their styles of speaking, depending on their relationship with their hearers, the context in which the language is being used, and the topic.[23]

Those three factors—dialogue partners, context, and subject—are the key to understanding differential language usage. Labov's next studies were on the use of "Black English Vernacular." After studying its usage in many different situations, Labov concluded that BEV was not a substandard version of English but rather a separate and distinct vernacular that followed its own grammatical rules, had its own vocabulary, and had been successfully transmitted from generation to generation. He also found that users of BEV relied on more than words to communicate; in addition to BEV's vocabulary and grammar, BEV communication included certain types of rhyming, joking, and intonations, as well as body movements that conveyed meaning. Whereas Bernstein considered the lower classes of the inner city to be linguistically damaged, Labov, based on the evidence he had amassed, pointedly disagreed:

Black children in the urban ghettos receive a great deal of verbal stimulation, hear more well-formed sentences than middle-class children, and participate fully in a highly verbal culture. They have the same basic vocabulary, possess the same capacity for conceptual learning, and use the same logic as anyone else who learns to speak and understand English.[24]

Dialogue partners, context, subject: The use of BEV was very understandable in those terms, because it was employed principally in the home or among friends, and in casual conversation. It was the language, in other words, of a particular localized speech community. Widely used in that community, it was the principal determinant of a child's speech before he or she entered formal schooling. Labov argued that for children who first learn to communicate in BEV, having afterward to learn standard English was equivalent to studying a foreign language, with all the difficulty usually attendant on mastering a new subject. In the early 1970s Labov reached the conclusion that BEV speakers were able to learn standard English fully only when they reached the teen years, which was why he suggested that learning standard forms of English could be delayed until then.

Problems arose when, as Bernstein's conclusions had been used to justify "tracking," Labov's conclusions were now used as the intellectual foundation from which others argued that BEV-speakers in lower grades should be taught in that language, rather than in standard English. In some urban districts, the complete changeover was made; in most areas of the country BEV was not instituted formally as the language of instruction but was accepted informally. The Labov conclusions were also used as part of a package of arguments that resulted in the institution of bilingual education in many states. The law of New York State, for example, now stipulates that when there are twenty or more native speakers of a foreign language—Spanish, Mandarin Chinese, Farsi, or whatever— in a school, instruction in a few subjects must be given in that language, even while the majority of subjects are taught in English.

It was once thought that learning to speak in BEV was an insuperable barrier to learning standard English. Later research, however, has shown that children as young as first-graders are able to switch back and forth from BEV to standard and use the standard forms of English in 50 percent of their responses; by the third grade or the fifth grade, in some other studies, these children are employing standard forms regularly 70 percent of the time and with even greater frequency in academic classroom discussions, while continuing to use BEV in social situations.[25] In other words, knowing BEV does not prevent a child from learning and using standard English; children who have come from a culture in which BEV is used at home and in the community can and generally do switch over into standard English in situations where that standard, rather than BEV, is understood to be more appropriate.

That is to say, when the speaker has also been able to learn standard English, the use of BEV—or of Spanish, Mandarin Chinese, or Farsi—is a situational choice, rather than something made inevitable by a child's background.

Today some African-Americans vociferously reject the use of standard American English and employ BEV in their speech, writing, and other art forms, in part to accentuate their differences from the mainstream culture. While the need to distance themselves from what has been an oppressive culture is understandable, the insistence on the use of nonstandard English produces problems in the classrooms, where some children who try to use standard English are castigated by their peers and pressured to employ *only* the language of the speech community.

Aligned against this peer pressure to use BEV are those in the African-American community and from the mainstream culture who believe that insistence on the use of nonstandard English will severely limit children's future possibilities of employment and advancement. The impasse between the two groups is highlighted in the following dialogue from a comic book about an African-American superhero named Icon. Addressing an angry African-American woman, Icon asks, "Finally, what does it mean to 'talk black?'" "You know," says the woman, "With it. Down in it . . . street!" "I see," Icon responds. "To speak as though I didn't get an education, improperly conjugate a few verbs, mangle some syntax. I shall never understand why ignorance should become fashionable." To which the woman replies, "You can't understand because you're not *really* black! You're an alien! You can fly!"[26]

As Icon and his antagonist make clear, the argument is between her form of speaking, which seeks to stay within the in-group, and his, which uses the more formal language of the larger society. This conflict should not be mistaken for a black-versus-white issue, because the same relational paradigm emerges when the choice involves the use of other languages. BEV in many respects is quite close to mainstream American English, and the ability of children to learn and use the more or less standard forms as well benefits from that closeness. Other "birth languages" used in various communities in the United States do not have as much overlap with English. Nonetheless, in the United School District of Los Angeles, some immigrant children as they enter grade school are now being taught exclusively in their birth language—Korean, Chinese, and Spanish—until they complete the third grade. Only after that will they be taught English.[27] The Los Angeles school system is betting that the children will be able to learn enough English to get along in the larger society if they study it later rather than earlier. This could prove disastrous to the children, because if they do not learn English well enough to work in the larger society, they will have been restricted by their education to making their way solely within their immigrant community.

Cajun-speakers in Louisiana have been agitating to have their language taught to kindergarten and grammar school children. The difficulty here is even more acute, because Cajun is almost entirely an oral language, a variant of French with strong Native American and African-American elements. Adult Cajun-speakers wanted their tongue used for the same reason that Spanish-speakers in Los Angeles and BEV-speakers in Michigan wanted their own languages used: so that their children would not be penalized or stigmatized upon entering the school system. The State of Louisiana offered a compromise: the teaching of standard French in place of or in addition to standard English. The Cajun-speakers rejected it; they wanted their children taught only in the language the children had already learned at home, even though such instruction could severely limit the children's prospects in the wider world they might later inhabit.[28]

The issue is not black versus white, nor is it immigrant versus native-born. Studies in European countries show that whatever the majority language, it is the groups of people lower down on the economic scale who either reject or have difficulty accepting the dominant standard form in their speech and writing. In Swedish as well as in some other European tongues, Elaine Slosberg Andersen notes a "consistent finding of the adult studies is that the lower a person's position and status in the social class hierarchy, the less likely he is to use standard forms. In the case of grammatical variables, the contrast between middle class and working class usage is particularly marked."[29] Such research observations are remarkably similar to those Basil Bernstein, made a quarter-century ago in regard to English.

Once again, Walter Ong's work helps to illuminate the basis on which one group employs the forms thought of as standard while the other does not. Ong pinpoints some dramatic differences between the communicative strategies, on the one hand, of a culture that is almost wholly literate, and on the other, of a "secondarily oral" culture that contains many elements of preliterate, "primary oral" cultures and that derives what literacy it has secondhand from electronic media, such as television. Secondarily oral cultures have reembraced primary oral communicative strategies, even though the society around them is basically literate. Many pockets within English-speaking society, Ong argues, now learn their language from the telephone, the television set, the radio, and CD or audio cassette players—from technological instruments that principally transmit the language in an oral style, even though their actual language is literate-based. In a "culture of secondary orality," people tend to have less direct touch with the literate-based language, even though the dominant culture around them remains literate. Despite being surrounded by words whose meanings and usage have basic reference to the written standard language, people in these pockets communicate in ways that may bypass or reject literacy. Instead, people in such pockets embrace the oral style and its characteristic communicative modes.

In primary oral societies, according to Ong, one's "thought must come into being in heavily rhythmic, balanced patterns, in repetitions or antitheses, in alliterations and assonances, in epithetic or other formulary expressions . . . in proverbs which are constantly heard by everyone so that they come to mind readily and which themselves are patterned for retention and ready recall, or in other mnemonic forms."[30] Ong's description, though it is of a primary oral culture, reads like a prescription for a rapper's next opus. Rap, in fact, may be the first full flowering of a secondarily oral culture.

Rap is far from illiterate; in fact, one of its prime glories is words. By definition, rap exists without benefit of melodic music, and each rhythmic and repetitive lyric contains many more words and ideas than occur in most popular songs. It features nonstandard spellings—"trix" for tricks, "ruffneck" for roughneck—and alternative meanings—"strapped" to denote carrying a gun, and "law" translated as ruling power. The misspellings are deliberate, not accidental, and the alternative meanings, too, have been chosen for the express purpose of distinguishing the culture of those who adopt them from the mainstream culture. A tee-shirt with alternative spellings on it, for instance, is understood by wearers and savvy viewers to signal that the wearer is a rap practitioner or fan.

Rap, which began among young, poor inner-city African-Americans, has many positive, community-building purposes. For instance, the director of a Washington, D.C., program "connects" to boys in juvenile detention by means of rap, which he says helps them "to let go of the stress and strain they experience as subjects of a judicial system not necessarily concerned with the scars they carry."[31] Rap music has also been embraced and its CDs and cassettes purchased by many young white suburbanites, so its appeal cannot be said to be confined to inner-city minorities alone. Richard Wesley, an African-American playwright, has observed that the popularity of rap stems from the same impulses that in previous decades had attracted young people to rock-and-roll: "It is anti-establishment, anti-authoritarian, and it is rebellious, which are all things to guarantee that it relates to youth." In rap's efforts to include the young and to exclude all listeners who are not young and rebellious, it goes beyond the boundaries of usual language. Some lyrics are deliberately obscene, sexually explicit, and violent. Also common to many lyrics is anger at whites, sometimes coupled with a dismissal of what are considered black middle-class attitudes and aspirations. Those latter aspects have convinced some African-Americans that rap's language, while it may well help to create a coherent audience of young listeners, also produces problems. One such difficulty was in evidence during a session on rap at a meeting of the National Association of Black Journalists. When Bushwick Bill, of the Geto Boys, explained his choice of lyrics to the audience by saying, "I call women bitches and hos [whores] because all the women I've met since I've been out here are bitches and hos," most of the women in the audience walked out.[32] The harshest criticism of rap comes from the African-American cultural critic Stanley Crouch, a champion of jazz as an African-American art form. Crouch dismisses rap entirely, contending that it is "either an infantile self-celebration or anarchic glamorization of criminal behavior."[33] The Reverend Calvin O. Butts III, pastor of the Abyssinian Baptist Church in Harlem, while insisting that some rap is uplifting and that he does not condemn all of it, nevertheless believes that the "vulgar and negative" aspects of rap have been "eroding the moral fabric of our community and society at large." As a countermeasure, Butts undertook a public campaign to crush rap recordings and videos that promulgated "social irresponsibility and immorality." The Rapper Preacher Earl responded to Reverend Butts's charges by claiming that his particular art is a mirror of the world and must be understood in its proper business context. Rap, the rapper said, is "about what happens every day," and—perhaps more to the point—"it's entertainment."[34]

Rap is only one example of speech to an in-group that is meant to exclude others. Similar exclusionary uses of speech are all around us. In-group conversation is of the kind linguists label as "phatic," used for establishing a channel of communication and for cementing social and psychological bonds, not for conveying information. Phatic speech is unplanned and repetitive, and it makes more use of simpler sentence formulations than do other sorts of discourse. Incomplete exposition is another hallmark, which is to say that phatic speech uses code words or shorthand to convey meaning quickly. Code words are also used for such secondary purposes as demonstrating the implicit understanding that exists between the speakers, shoring up the group, and engendering suspicion of anyone who does not use the same shorthand. The frequent repetition of idiomatic phrases, for instance, is thought to validate the in-group's already established beliefs.[35]

To speak effectively to the in-group—and this is the group to which any of us speaks most of the time—we ordinarily use the oral-based strategies, contexts, and shortcuts that facilitate such communication. It is conversation appropriate to the first or second levels of the four tiers that I postulated in the introductory chapter. To put it another way, it is conversation that, as Labov pointed out, depends on context, subject, and dialogue partners. We must not make the mistake of believing that the in-group way of speaking is confined to gangs hanging out on big-city street corners; it is found among any delineated group that speaks a common dialect. W. Ross Winterowd, a college English professor, recalls in this connection the "Sanpete" dialect of his youth in a Mormon area of central Utah. Sanpete is an English variant that according to Winterowd differs from standard English in pronunciation, vocabulary, and structure, for instance using the word "man" to mean "husband," "drink" to mean "water," and the phrase "and them" to denote the other people in a family or group.

Sanpete users, Winterowd writes, are "unaware that they speak a minority dialect," because their language is not a problem within their own community; it causes difficulties for them only when they interface with outsiders.[36]

The specialized language of any distinct small group, even if it is not a dialect, exhibits similar social characteristics. Larry Rivers chronicled the atmosphere of the Artists Club in Greenwich Village in the early 1950s, when every member was a commercially unsuccessful abstract artist. Certain things were never discussed. "There were no doubts about the necessity of being modern. It was inarguable. It was so inarguable that it wasn't even mentioned. . . . If you weren't interested in the avant-garde, in being avant-garde yourself, no one was interested in you." The real purpose of the discussions in the club, Rivers later concluded, was to make him feel good about himself and his art, and to solidify his feeling that he was part of an important group. Rivers likens the experience to being a member of a church, where all the congregants believed in the same things; in this instance, a major tenet was the irrelevance of commercial success: "Not receiving any rewards for making art somehow made the concerns even stronger." This in-group cohesiveness dissolved at a precise time and in a precise way: "After people started selling their work the club didn't last long," Rivers writes. He attributes the sudden decline to the fact that the penniless style and common concerns that had earlier bound its members together had irretrievably changed. In the last phases of the club, discussions of figurative versus abstract art gave way to gossip about people having shows in galleries and being featured in magazine articles.[37]

Rivers and his artist peers, and Winterowd and others from his Sanpete community graduated or moved out of their in-group environment and joined the mainstream in which standard English is more regularly used. The question remains as to whether those immersed in other in-groups that use phatic communications will or will not choose to also join.

There *is* a standard English, and it is a literate-based language. Communications that are more secondarily oral are not only not standard but also tend to be drawn from a substantially narrower base, and therefore to have many fewer possibilities for complete expression. They are articulate, but not fully so.

I must also emphasize that the standard of English that various groups have tried to uphold and maintain is increasingly unrealistic and exclusionary. Perfect command of English, which a true standard might require, is virtually unattainable—a Nirvana to which humans may aspire but only the gods will ever reach.

The time has come to stop thinking of standard English as a locked and isolated museum and to begin to understand it as a fabulous realm that exists all around us, rich in possibilities for articulate expression, and with an open-door policy for immigrant words, expressions, and turns of phrase.

English, like all languages, continues to evolve and will never be a fixed entity. Nonetheless, there can be a version of it that can be considered a standard and held up for emulation and possible measurement. Any up-to-the-minute college dictionary—Merriam Webster's Tenth Edition has just been published—can provide a fair, though hardly complete, benchmark for vocabulary and word usage. Combine that dictionary with a brief teaching grammar such as the most recent edition of Strunk and White, and we have a standard that is like a topographical map of our realm, something realistic and measurable, though not completely descriptive, a map that covers more words and grammatical possibilities than most people will ever be able to explore, more language possibilities than most of us will ever have occasion or need to employ in spoken or written communications, say a hundred thousand out of the more than a million extant words. (Shakespeare used more of them than anyone else, and he employed a mere 29,066).

Given such a huge and subtle map, we shall be able to know what we know, and—perhaps more important—can get a sense of how much there is left to learn. And the very size of the map ensures that there will always be a great deal to be learned, no matter what academic degree has or has not been awarded for our studies. Another consequence of the size: Because the map is so large, if for no other reason, we can insist that this standard ought not to be construed as a restrictive canon, yet still insist that becoming competent and comfortable in the use of literate-based English must be everyone's goal—something to value and toward which to strive, not something to rebel against. The new standard must be considered a grail, perhaps forever beyond one's complete grasp but always worthy of the effort put into its pursuit.

The compilation of words that we now call a standard dictionary should be more properly referred to as a book of ideals. Similarly, the compilation of rules that we now call a standard grammar—with all the negative connotations that having rules implies—we should henceforth refer to as a book of possibilities. Even if no one any longer uses "may-I-not" or "if-I-were-you" or "leapt," it is senseless to throw away those constructions. They should be included in our ideal books and possibilities books so that we can continue to be dimly aware of them as potential communicative choices on the map, even if individually we decide that we never want to use or visit them.

Conceiving and celebrating the standard in this way, we acknowledge that English is a literate-based language and will hereafter remain so, even if secondarily oral culture and its products make substantial inroads upon it. Moreover, we acknowledge that the oral variant learned at a parent's knee, even if it is a coherent, complex, and socially useful dialect, is not the language of the larger territory; it can only serve as an introduction and foothill to the mountain of literate-based English. No oral variant can usefully replace literate-based English.

Just as important, our goal also demands affirmation that literate-based English need not exclude any variant of the language; rather, in the realm of English, we ought to know and to celebrate our many mansions. American English is and always has been as inclusion-minded as the country itself; in recent dictionaries, homage is paid to the enriching influences on English of words from the languages of Native Americans, dozens of European tongues, regional dialects, African and Asian languages, and the social dialects of sports, law, medicine, and other subcultures. Our realm will continue to be larger and more inclusive than any single dialect or vernacular. And our realm provides a service that no smaller unit within it can offer: the ability to communicate to numerous and diverse audiences. Use of literate-based English is like broadcasting, which reaches toward an audience of almost the entire population, while use of a variant of defined ethnic, racial, age or regional boundaries more resembles—in that new word—"narrowcasting." More particularized versions of English are often better for communicating messages to localized and specialized audiences, but not to the broader audience. Those who choose not to communicate in the broader standard language must understand that in this distinctive exercise of their right to free expression, their choice may limit the audience available to them, and if in consequence the audience does remain limited, they have no basis for complaint.

We must also urge everyone to employ, and make it possible for all children properly to learn, standard English, because knowing it will afford them wider life choices for the future. Command of literate-based English permits its users to be more precise and incisive communicators, and—no less important—to be audience members who fully understand what is being communicated to them. The articulate behavior I want everyone to master is an ability to put one's tongue on the most appropriate, effective, and beautiful way of saying what one means to a very broad audience. It is an articulateness that strives for grammatical perfection because the grammatical is the most effective way to speak, and not because that is what some outmoded canon of use once dictated. It is a schooled articulateness, because it is through formal analysis in an educational setting that the largest numbers of possibilities for communication are learned. And it is a supple articulateness that aims high, out of pride in its linguistic heritage and out of a desire to use all of that heritage to reach for eloquence.

Chapter 3

THE
UNHELPFUL SCHOOLHOUSE

*E*ducation for articulateness begins in the home and in the speech community, but well before children's thinking processes are mature they are delivered into the schools. There a child must learn standard English, which will be a foundation if not always a requirement for articulateness. Other components of articulateness must also be instilled there—an ability to use logic, an ability to listen properly, and a supple vocabulary are just a few. Were the schools performing well the task of education for articulateness, there would be little reason to inquire into the efficacy of the teaching. But they are not.

One way of measuring what children have learned is the Scholastic Aptitude Tests (SAT), taken by high school seniors. General scores have been in decline since 1963, and the decline is greatest in the verbal ability sections. The downturn has been explained by pointing to the addition to the test-taking pool of inner-city minority students after that date. That is not the reason for the decline, because since 1976, the first year minority student scores were separately tallied, minority scores have been steadily improving, while the overall scores continue to sag. In a heartening recent trend, the results of the 1992 and 1993 SAT tests showed a slight improvement over those of 1991—on the verbal section, a rise of three points in two years. However, the figures are still nearly thirty points below the average scores of the 1960s. Moreover, since a test-taker gets 200 points for signing his or her name, and a perfect score is 800, today's average verbal score of 424 is significantly below the midway number and hypothetical average score, which would be 500. Scores on the A.C.T. exams, rival tests that are preferred by some state university systems, parallel the decades-long downward trend of the S.A.T scores and also show the same slight gain in recent scores. The sag in the scores of the average test-taker may be due to the radical expansion of the entire pool, since many more people now take college entrance exams than did so in the 1960s, but that does not explain the decline in the scores of those on the upper end of the scale. In 1972, 11.4 percent of S.A.T.-takers scored above 600 on the verbal section, but in 1992 only 7.3 percent managed to reach that level.[1]

The intimate connection between the decline in verbal facility scores and articulate behavior is pinpointed by Daniel J. Singal, a college writing supervisor at Hobart and William Smith colleges: "We see so many kids coming in here with such weak command of language that even if we put in a tremendous amount of time it's not going to make a difference. Sometimes they are very motivated, but they are hindered by what happened in their previous twelve years of school." Sandra Prior, director of composition at Columbia University, echoed Singal in telling a reporter that her students also have difficulty writing coherent essays and dealing with the verbal give-and-take of the classroom. She contends that they are unable to construct or to conduct proper arguments. Moreover, "When students do challenge you, they speak from the gut or from anger and hostility. If you say, 'What about this, or this?' they think you are not hearing them."[2]

The result is that many students pass on to graduate work without having repaired a weak command of the language. Since 1964, Graduate Record Examination (GRE) scores of college seniors seeking admission to graduate schools have been declining in eleven of fifteen subject areas, precisely those areas that depend most heavily on verbal and word-based skills. A more specific postadmission test of those skills was recently given to entering graduate management students at the Wake Forest University business school. The graduates of some sixty different colleges in twenty-one states did very poorly: of 250 business words and phrases, the students were able to identify on average only 43. "Amortization" was recognized by 30 percent of the students, "capital gains" by 38 percent, "lien" by 21 percent, and, in the nonbusiness categories, "adenoids" by 8 percent and "suffrage" by 35 percent.[3]

Colleges are convinced that problems with verbal facility start in the high schools, while high schools testify that the damage has been done before the teenagers reached puberty. Trying to measure the end product of high school classrooms, in 1986 the National Assessment of Educational Progress (NAEP) gave a test on history and literature to 7,812 seventeen-year-old students. The group had been carefully chosen to reflect the demographic makeup of the country's population. According to the educational researchers Diane Ravitch and Chester Finn, the "questions were not difficult." They were multiple-choice queries about such literary characters as Robin Hood, Job, and Gulliver. Nevertheless, the average student's score was in the 50-percent-correct range. Even that level was suspect, Ravitch and Finn contend, because many of the subjects of the test questions, such as the tortoise and the hare or Tom Sawyer, were most likely to have become known to the students through the medium of cartoons rather than through reading. A second reason for alarm: The average score of the top quarter of the students was in the 70–79 percent correct range, meaning that the scores for three-quarters of the students were actually far lower. Since there was no box to be checked off for "don't know," Ravitch and Finn considered it likely that students' guesses raised their scores by five to ten points. The nine-year-olds have also been doing badly, the NAEP found out in a study—but Jane Healey, an educational psychologist, reports that when NAEP officials planned to publish research showing a drastic decline in students' reading, writing, and speaking abilities between 1971 and 1990, "these plans were canceled because no one wanted to believe the results." One NAEP report that did make it to publication traced students' problems in dealing with the written and spoken materials to their inability to understand verbal reasoning.[4]

Edwin De Lattre attributes the most common failings of students in regard to language to three refrains he has heard over and over again in university classrooms. "That's just semantics," students complain when meanings of words are being discussed, when accurate definitions are sought and they can't come up with them. Their dismissive phrase, De Lattre writes, conveys a judgment that "examination of the meanings . . . is not really necessary and is somehow trivial. . . . They do not grasp that how we use words is directly connected to what we believe, what conclusions we reach, and that what we believe is directly connected to what we do and how we behave." The second common phrase identified by De Lattre is, "Well, you mean what you mean, and I mean what I mean." The third—and capstone—student phrase is, "I know what I mean, but I can't say it." Students who believe it possible to think clearly without using words are condemned to the sort of thinking, De Lattre writes, that "is often limited to vague, largely ineffable sentiments or preferences rather than to ideas. Their sense of language, unless it matures into a more thoughtful one, will keep them outside forever."[5]

Command of the language, the ability to have and to express complex thoughts, articulate behavior and literacy, are all intertwined. To separate out the elements key to the inculcation of articulateness, we need to have reference to a time when writing was relatively new and not much used in the educatory process, but when articulate behavior was prized: in Athens of the fifth century B.C. The Sophists, then the most successful educators, claimed to be able to teach anyone. They decried philosophic notions such as the search for truth and attempts to discern the essence of man; instead, by means of the public lecture—for which their audiences paid—they offered instruction in the art of success in politics, which they insisted would be guaranteed by learning how always to make one's own point of view prevail. Many principles of persuasive speech were developed and perfected by The Sophists. Opposed to them was Socrates, to whom their utilitarian doctrine was anathema and who maintained that only the search for truth would truly educate someone. He wandered the streets and the gymnasia of Athens, not lecturing but engaging friends and young men in conversation with the aim of bringing all the participants closer to wisdom. He recognized the value of rhetoric but never embraced it for the sole purpose of persuasion. Socrates claimed that he was only a midwife to his pupils' thought; just as a midwife is usually old and barren, he said, a teacher does not furnish ideas and is not the fount of wisdom, but rather is a stimulus and critic who helps the student bring forth his own ideas. Socrates held that truth in particular cannot be taught, but can be learned by the student as a product of joint inquiries with the teacher.

One of Socrates' typical educatory dialogues takes place during his trial for being a corrupter of the young. He draws a main accuser, Meletus, into dialogue in order to make the real issue clear to those who are judging him:

S: Come hither, Meletus, and let me ask a question of you. You think a great deal about the improvement of youth?

M: Yes, I do.

S: Tell the judges, then, who is their improver?. . . .

M: The laws.

S: But that, good sir, is not my meaning. I want to know who the person is, who, in the first place, knows the laws?

M: The judges, Socrates, who are present in court.

S: What, do you mean to say, Meletus, that they are able to instruct and improve youth? . . . What, all of them, or some only and not others?

M: All of them.

S: By the goddess Hera, that is good news! There are plenty of improvers, then. And what do you say of the audience—do they improve them?

M: Yes, they do.

S: And the senators?

M: Yes, the senators improve them.

S: But perhaps the members of the assembly corrupt them?—or do they improve them?

M: They improve them.

S: Then every Athenian improves and elevates them; all with the exception of myself; and I alone am their corrupter? Is that what you affirm?

M: That is what I stoutly affirm.

S: I am very unfortunate if you are right. . . . Happy indeed would be the condition of youth if they had one corrupter only, and all the rest of the world were their improver.[6]

Both education and the art of conversation can be said to begin, and—not incidentally—in a way that emphasizes their interpenetration, with the teaching method of Socrates. For Plato's teacher, philosophy was a search for meaning and the making of distinctions, which could be finely drawn only during relaxed and lengthy conversations among friends. Socrates was concerned with the practical use of reason, and the dialogues Plato has reconstructed drew examples from the work of shoemakers and carpenters to help students reach their own conclusions about universal truths.

Alfred North Whitehead has said that Western philosophy is a series of footnotes to Plato. Before discussing the Socratic method and its relationship to articulate behavior, I want to pick up on one of those footnotes, from the twentieth-century philosopher Kenneth Burke. Speaking of the sources and action of democratic process, Burke constructs a magnificent parable of an "unending conversation," held in a parlor, that was going on long before any of the present participants were born and in which no one can reliably trace all the steps previously taken. During a person's lifetime, each of us takes part in this heated discussion: "You listen for a while, until you decide that you have caught the tenor of the argument; then you put in your oar. Someone answers; you answer him; another comes to your defense; another aligns himself against you, to either the embarrassment or gratification of your opponent." The process goes on and on, the hour grows late, and the discussant departs "with the discussion still vigorously in progress." The democratic political process is that unending conversation, Burke maintains.[7] We shall explore this idea more thoroughly in later chapters that deal with political expression, but for the moment I simply want to draw attention to the notion, well expressed by Burke's parable, that both education and democratic governance can be thought of as having strong similarities, each to the other and both to the process of articulate, Socratic conversation.

Conversation was long considered an art unto itself, part of an articulately expressive environment that valued the continued exchange of dialogue in social situations more highly than individual eloquent expression. That environment was well captured in the Virginia Woolf novel *Orlando*, a purported biography. In a seventeenth-century literary salon scene, Alexander Pope displays such "true wit, true wisdom, true profundity" that conversation ceases after the hostess calls sarcastic attention to his feat. Twenty minutes of embarrassed silence follow, after which the other conversants—among them Dryden and Addison—leave the room, and it is feared that they will never again take part in the salon.[8] Conversational flow, not profundity, was the point of clubs regularly attended by Addison, Steele, Congreve, Samuel Johnson, Edmund Burke, Oliver Goldsmith, and other writers in the late seventeenth century.

Little is known about conversation in the middle ages, but after Gutenberg manuals on the art of conversation appeared regularly from the seventeenth to the nineteenth century in England, France, and other European countries. According to the language historian Peter Burke, those constituted a subgroup of treatises that addressed problems of civility and what the novelist Henry Fielding called the "reciprocal exchange of ideas." Burke calls attention to the nonspontaneous character of the best conversation in that period; a balance between spontaneity and study was needed, in order for a participant to be at his or her best. Among the most frequently repeated tenets was an admonition not to speak of oneself all the time.[9]

From the era of Pope to that of Churchill, in Great Britain as well as in the United States, schools for the elite, especially the relatively small and cloistered universities, had both the time and the talented faculty to use principally Socratic methods. In the democratic countries they were ideally suited to do so, because only in a democratic society can the hierarchical rules of conversation that prevail in monarchies or other court-dependent societies be breached and all participants provided with somewhat equal chances to say something. "Liberal arts" education's premise of nonspecificity in training, along with its emphasis on old models, was an adaptation of the elite curriculum. As an educational focus it combined the Socratic search for truth and methods of inquiry with the emphasis on rhetoric of the Sophists and, more particularly, of the Aristotelians, who turned the art of rhetoric to the purposes of argument rather than to the lesser pursuit of oratorical success.

The basic divide in education between Socratic discussion methods and Sophist lecture methods continued to exist after the time of the Greeks, with Sophist methods usually chosen in two important circumstances: when the student group was large and when the objective of the teaching was the transfer of information rather than training toward wisdom. Neither of those circumstances obtained in small colleges, which made them an almost ideal setting for Socratic discourse. Indeed, rhetoric was a central focus of the elite curriculum from the Renaissance until about a hundred years ago. In the mid-nineteenth century rhetoric was a set of courses in college that lasted for two or three years. Since the meaning of rhetoric has now changed, it is important to recognize that rhetoric was then a discipline that encompassed and intermingled the arts of speaking and writing and the formation of good character. For rhetoric, literature and language were inseparable, and literature encompassed both imaginative works such as novels and poetry, and such nonfiction works as essays and histories. Included in the latter group were speeches made by famously articulate men from the ancient Greeks onward. Those were studied, often copied out in longhand, memorized, performed aloud, and used as models on which the student based his or her own speeches. Memorization—today much deprecated as a learning tool—was considered essential, because it was indispensable for making use of that large fraction of one's vocabulary that did not come readily to the tongue, for storing images for use in speeches, and for mentally organizing material. Recitation—also much decried today—was prized because it not only acclimated the student to speaking in public but also emphasized the careful preparation necessary for addressing an audience. Writing and speaking were considered very much the same thing, for formal speech was generally written out first, or at least was based on written notes.[10]

James A. Berlin, who studied instruction in rhetoric in nineteenth-century American colleges, wrote about the process of "composing" for writing or speaking as it was then construed. In the composing, the composer was supposed to bring "all his faculties" to the task, not simply his identity as a Christian or a scientist or an artist, and must always keep the audience in mind:

> The audience is an important part of composing, since the individuals comprising it must be appealed to on all levels of their being. For this reason . . . rhetoric commonly considers oratory superior to written communication, primarily because it uses all features of consciousness, sensory—the voice, the body—as well as the intellectual. It is also possible for the orator to respond to the audience as the presentation is made, creating a dialectic of speaker and listener that corresponds to the dialectic of subject and object.[11]

While articulate speech was synonymous with literature, colloquial speech, used in everyday conversation, was not, and was not considered appropriate when one had something of importance to say, either in person or in writing. That was an implicit recognition of the difference between the usual spoken vocabulary—shown by later researchers to consist, on average, of a thousand or two thousand words—and the literate vocabulary of ten times as many words, which the average literate person can command during the process of writing.[12]

In the late nineteenth century in the United States, three trends converged and together had a tremendous negative impact on the teaching of articulate behavior. The first was toward the use of colloquial language in more and more situations, generated in part to counter the overblown speechifying of the era. Kenneth Cmiel, who studied that era's popular speech writes: "Less and less did the educated worry about presenting themselves as refined gentlemen, articulate in the old rhetorical sense. Colloquial informality became more acceptable."[13] The second trend was a serious attempt to find better ways to transmit the language to immigrants whose native language was other than English, and who needed to learn English rapidly. The third was the dividing up of the universities into departments, each a fiefdom with its own territory.

Together, these trends succeeded in separating and segregating the study of literature from the study of language, and then in moving both studies toward colloquial expression. The study of rhetoric was taken from its central place in the curriculum and parceled out to the new departments— literature here, language there, public speaking yonder, composition elsewhere. Language became an elective course. So did literature. Soon businessmen like Andrew Carnegie were complaining that college graduates could no longer read, write, and speak well enough to be of use to employers. The response by the universities was to institute a course in Freshman Composition. New textbooks were written for those courses, but in them, composition no longer had anything to do with literature, ancient models, the making of public speeches, or the building of character. With the publication of an influential composition text in 1891, Cmiel points out, the break with the past was complete: "Writing had become an introductory, utilitarian subject for freshmen. The old tradition was gone. Composition, unlike rhetoric, taught basic skills; it was not part of a larger formation of character."[14] Now, college students were expected to learn to write as they learned to swim—by doing it. One result was to make the students more subject to colloquial and contemporary influences. A second was to relegate rhetoric to the realm of the theoretical, while composition and public speaking became practical—that is to say, they were pushed into the Sophist realm, and away from the Socratic realm, where theory and practice are commingled.

In 1898 the aptly named Alphonso G. Newcomer published a text called *Elements of Rhetoric*, subtitled *A Course in Plain Prose Composition*, in which he asserted that the "bulk of matter in our rhetorics is traditional, and, except for higher critical purposes, useless."[15] Reformers considered literature beautiful, but by segregating it, Cmiel contends, they divorced it from the close connection with practical writing and speech that it once enjoyed.

By the progressive era of the early twentieth century, the purpose of language studies had changed radically. They were now used to "socialize" children, that is, to make the children of foreign cultures accommodate themselves to the mainstream culture and foster their assimilation. The term "socialize" was used expressly to contrast it with the old intention of such study, "character building." In the seminal textbook of the era, two professors at Columbia and one at Michigan wrote: "The living language is the spoken language. The written language is merely a conventional form of the spoken language." It followed that the "most important aim of education in the mother tongue must, therefore, always be the development of power over the spoken language rather than over the written language."[16]

Here is the budding point of the growing divide between popular and literate language that eventually exacerbated, if not actually engendered, the split that Ong refers to between the literate-based language and the language that is not solidly based in writing. After World War I, literature continued to decline as a subject connected to speech and everyday writing, while students were introduced to good writing more in the form of contemporary articles in popular magazines and newspapers, and even radio speeches. Literature was restricted to imaginative prose only, and it was argued that the thoughts of most importance to modern people came not from literature but from the disciplines of history, economics, and social science.

As if in a final gasp, it was at this time that the last groups of great conversational salons for English came into existence in London, with Woolf and her circle, and in New York City, in the salons of Mabel Dodge and others in Greenwich Village. Their participants had been educated for the most part in the old style at elite colleges, where rhetoric had not yet yielded entirely to Freshman Composition.

After World War II the effort to extend secondary and tertiary education to all Americans mandated so great a widening that the system itself changed in character and focus, as Lawrence Cremin has documented. In 1950, just 34 percent of Americans twenty-five or older had completed at least four years of high school, and only 6 percent had completed at least four years of college. By 1985, 74 percent of Americans twenty-five or older had completed at least four years of high school, while

19 percent had completed at least four years of college. An even larger fraction had completed at least two years of college, because one-third of all colleges were now junior colleges. Cremin writes, "As had been the case historically, these increases in enrollment were accompanied by fundamental changes in standards. . . . It proved infinitely easier to juggle the substance of the curriculum than to develop pedagogies for conveying the more intellectually demanding materials to most or all of the students." The new high school graduates, many of them not well prepared academically, went on to junior colleges in record numbers, and they also proved attractive to regular colleges, whose standards, Cremin says, then also dropped. The unintended result: "Except for a few highly select institutions—some 50 to 100, perhaps, out of the 2,000-odd four year institutions—admission and graduation requirements had diversified to the point of near meaninglessness." The widening, in other words, produced a dilution of quality in the preponderance of the college-level institutions. Cremin's findings are seconded by a recent Department of Education Adult Literacy Survey, which contends that large numbers of college graduates may be technically literate but lack true reading, writing, and comprehension skills. Nearly half of the nation's 100 million adults, the survey concluded, were not proficient enough in English to be able to write a letter about a billing error. The National Alliance for Business, sounding a similar note of alarm, estimated that only one-quarter of the nation's adults are "highly literate." A group of foundations active in educational philanthropy recently conceded that proficiency is higher among college graduates than among those who have less schooling, but charged that undergraduate education in the United States consists of "little more than secondary school material—warmed over and reoffered at much higher expense," and that our universities "certify for graduation too many students who cannot read and write too well, too many whose intellectual depth and breadth are unimpressive, and too many whose skills are inadequate in the face of the demands of contemporary life."[17]

The exigencies of educating the masses rather than the elite became the driving force in American education. The consequences are still being felt today. The most important may be that because the classes for the masses have to be so large and are so diversely constituted, the methods used to teach them are, now more than ever, being forced in the direction of the Sophist/lecture/training-for-success mode and away from the Socratic/

discussion/ideals style. This fits in well with modern universities' predilection to pursue research and alumni dollars rather than excellence in the teaching of undergraduates.

In one of the most ambitious and far-reaching recent considerations of elementary and secondary education in the United States, a year-long study for the Education Commission for the States, Dr. Rexford G. Brown and his team of evaluators observed hundreds of teachers and classrooms and recorded hundreds of hours of interviews with teachers, educators, and administrators.[18] Brown was looking for how, if at all, the schools were inculcating in the pupils what he calls a "literacy of thoughtfulness," which he defined as literacy "that goes beyond basic skills and includes enhanced abilities to think critically and creatively; to reason carefully; to analyze, synthesize, and evaluate information and arguments; and to communicate effectively to a variety of audiences in a variety of forms." Those skills very much overlap what I consider prime elements in articulate behavior. For Brown, they constituted the ingredients of "higher-order-thinking-skills," or HOTS. To many professional educators, HOTS constitutes a red flag, because for a decade our schools have been under a mandate to go back to basics, a mandate encapsulated in the comment of one educator to Brown that "in order to acquire higher-order-thinking-skills, it is first necessary to acquire the basic skills." Brown's research prompted him to express pointed disagreement. He found "that children can practice various kinds of thinking and problem-solving at any age, regardless of whether they have mastered the basics." The educator David Perkins echoes Brown's conclusions: "The conventional pattern [of schooling] says that first, students acquire knowledge. Only then do they think with and about the knowledge they have absorbed. But it's just the opposite: Far from thinking coming after knowledge, knowledge comes on the coattails of thinking. As we think about and with the content that we are learning, we truly learn it. . . . *Learning is a consequence of thinking.*"[19]

HOTS may be better understood if we refer to its elements rather than to its label. It is those reasoning, argument, and problem-solving skills that must be learned in order for children to use the knowledge they are stockpiling. If a child knows Newton's laws by heart but cannot apply them to new examples, then the child does not truly understand those laws. Brown did not find a "literacy of thoughtfulness" very often in his travels, and he concluded that its absence could be traced to the "recitative" classroom, where teachers and pupils take turns speaking in a sing-song, expected dialogue. In such classrooms, the "teacher exercises total control over the right to speak, tends to ask questions to which students already know the answers, tends to move fast, and tends not to show any tentativeness or doubt." Such a classroom appears to use Socratic methods but does not, because the dialogue is solely about the transfer of information. This has also been labeled the "banking" system, for the students' minds serve as repositories into which information is first loaded so that it can be then spewed out again by the students, often in smaller quantities or in slightly changed denominations.

Students taught in these classrooms, Brown found, were severely hampered in activities that require more than the ability to answer by rote. When given the opportunity to ask thoughtful questions or to offer their own opinions, they cannot do so. They "prefer recitation to open-ended, think-for-yourself kinds of activities. They are tuned in to looking for the right answer, filling in the blank. They get confused by other types of questions." So well entrenched is this recitative classroom configuration "that it seems natural, and its limitations are invisible to the people caught up in it. They try to get a discussion going, without realizing that a discussion would violate all the unspoken rules of discourse to which they are habituated. They get frustrated, decide discussions cannot take place, and remain stuck in recitations."[20]

At one time or another we have all been mired in such settings; putative discussions in boardrooms, no less than in classrooms, founder on just such a divide, and become recitations. This is the setting where the leader asks a question and there is only one correct answer, where one- and two-word responses from students always suffice, and where all texts are assigned and only one interpretation of each is accepted. When students in these classrooms were evaluated by the NAEP, the judgment was harsh: "Students seem satisfied with their initial interpretations of what they have read and seem genuinely puzzled at requests to explain or defend their points of view. As a result, responses . . . requiring explanations of criteria, analysis of text or defense of a judgment or point of view were in general disappointing."[21]

To explain criteria, to analyze a text or defend a judgment or a point of view requires thinking that understands the notion of causation. Frank J.

DeAngelo identified three types of people who are unable to understand causation properly. Adults who are marginally literate, people who have substantial "features of electronic orality in their thinking," and children who are just learning the language. All three types think in visual and concrete terms, and in narrative progression rather than in causal terms. DeAngelo concludes that the only way for such people to reach "analytic competence," the level of thinking at which they can properly express and understand causation and other complex ideas, is through increased literacy of the sort Rexford Brown calls a literacy of thoughtfulness.[22] Without it, children are severely hampered but may never know they lack it.

Now and then, during Brown's research, he and his associates would come upon classrooms where recitative had been eclipsed and the elements of the literacy of thoughtfulness were being transmitted. The difference between those and the recitative classrooms was like night and day. Questions were intelligently asked and answered at length. There was not a single right answer put forth, but many. Students seemed excited by the materials being studied and willing and able to argue about their meaning. Brown noted that those "thoughtful" classrooms were invariably ones in which "real discussions" took place. He was tickled to discover the tipoff to the presence of such a class: The discussions would not end when the bell rang but would spill out into the hall, students pursuing the teacher to continue the thread, or pairs or small groups of students walking down the corridors, their conversation still reflecting their involvement with the subject.

Brown attended a session at the Schenley Teacher Center in Pittsburgh, where a group of old-style teachers were asked to read a purposely ambiguous text from Plutarch and to use it as the basis for a discussion among themselves. As the teacher-participants struggled with the meaning of a couple of paragraphs about Pericles, Brown was "struck by the difference between this discussion and so much of what I have observed in classrooms around the country. Here, meaning is hard to fix; lots of interpretations seem reasonable. People talk for an hour about a short passage and still have disagreements and loose ends to pursue." In a debriefing session, the master teacher also pointed out just those aspects to the participants and asked: "If that's true for you and for this passage, why isn't it true for your students and the stuff they're reading?" "Because," one of the English teachers answered, "in the material they read, there *really* is only one main idea."

Such a conclusion indicates either that the materials chosen to be read by the students are without depth, or—more likely—that the teachers regularly fail to fathom the depths of the selections. "Transfer of what these teachers learned [in the conference] to their classrooms," Brown glumly observed, "has some way to go."[23]

If, as this example makes clear, and as Brown and dozens of other evaluators of teacher education have charged, the teachers are unable to teach articulateness, it is largely because our teachers in general are unprepared for their teaching tasks.

"He who can, does. He who cannot, teaches," George Bernard Shaw wrote in *Man and Superman*. Shaw meant it as provocative hyperbole, but it became a calumny accepted as the way our society thinks about teachers—people unable to do anything truly productive who have fallen back on teaching. One cogent argument places the blame for poor teaching on the unattractive salary structure of the profession. Teachers below the level of college have historically been underpaid, after all. However, over the last ten years, teacher salaries have risen at a rate greater than inflation, to a point where new teachers can look forward to salary ranges that in the more generous states begin around $25,000 annually and can eventually reach $60,000–$70,000, though in other states the range remains as low as $18,000–$30,000.[24] Despite pay hikes, the old charge that teachers' colleges attract mediocre students and turn out teachers who are poorly prepared to do their jobs is still mostly true, as a former teacher, Rita Kramer, discovered during a yearlong tour of training institutions. State university systems turn out more than half of today's teachers—California's system alone produces 10 percent of the nation's total—and the requirements for would-be teachers, Kramer found, are not high; future teachers are permitted to overload on pedagogical instruction while giving short shrift to academic subjects. This is true all over the country, a 1989 survey discovered: More than three-quarters of all education-college graduates had no academic major other than education, and almost that many had no academic minor.[25]

In another study, the Southern Regional Education Board (SREB) showed that three-quarters of the teacher candidates graduated seventeen state universities without having taken *any* courses in foreign languages, philosophy, economics, or physics, and that half graduated without taking any political science. But those same graduates took 50 percent of their credits in education and physical education, receiving college credit for such courses as "Standard First Aid and Personal Safety," "Coaching Track and Field," "Lettering, Posters, and Displays in the School Program," and "The Culturally Diverse Classroom," in the last of which, according to the education reporter Thomas Toch, the main point was to instruct teachers how to seat white students near black students to foster racial harmony. Academic requirements for prospective teachers were lower than for arts and sciences students, the SREB study found. Prospective teachers took mostly introductory-level academic courses, and many took remedial courses, which nonetheless were accepted as satisfying academic requirements. Education graduates of the Arizona State University, another study reported, obtained 95 percent of their math, English, and science credits from freshman-year courses; moreover, 90 percent of teacher candidates had taken some academic courses at community colleges and then transferred the credits to the university, thus avoiding even the college's introductory courses.

The SREB also found that one-third of all grade school and high school instructors are teaching courses for which they have had *no* academic preparation and that the majority are instructors for courses in which they have had only minimal academic training. Of the elementary school teachers, only 6 percent had taken their college work in math, and 9 percent in English, even though those were the main subjects they taught to children.[26]

The National Council for Accreditation of Teacher Education established new guidelines in the mid-1980s. They required teacher education programs to demonstrate compliance with tougher new standards. When forty-six such institutions were monitored during the 1988–89 academic year, fourteen failed to meet the new standards. Moreover, when veteran teachers were forced to take new certification exams, some who had taught for years were exposed as nearly illiterate. In Arkansas, Georgia, and Texas, about 10 percent of the teachers who took the first such exams in the mid-1980s failed to pass them, even though the exams were considered so simple that a ninth-grader would do well on them. Similarly unqualified people were still trying to get into teaching, a fact that came to light when many states instituted stiffer tests for new teachers: The failure rates were even higher, in such states as New York, Florida, and California reaching an average of 20 percent.[27]

* * *

Teachers are not the sole culprits for the decline in articulate behavior, and it is a trap to consider them as such. The larger culprit is the divide between the literate-based and oral languages, a chasm into which many children fall because our system of teaching them the language does not adequately bridge it.

Despite problems in the home with the inculcation of language, most native-speakers enter grade school able to understand 4,000 words when they are spoken to them. Children of that age, if they can read at all, can recognize only about 600 of those words. The 4,000 words approximate about one thousand "lemmas"—a single lemma, for instance, incorporates the word forms *go, going, gone*. Research on frequency of word used has shown that those 1,000 lemmas are the most commonly used words in the language. For instance, they constitute the first level of words in *The American Heritage Word Frequency Book*, which was compiled as a source for a dictionary serving fourth- to eighth-graders. That book considers that the first thousand lemmas account for 74 percent of all the 5 million words in the written materials from various sources on which the list was based. The first 5,000 lemmas account for almost 90 percent; beyond those 5,000 are "rare" words—those that occur in the reading materials only once or twice per million written words. The compilers point out that many relatively rare or "hard" words—such as *allegation*, which turned up only twice in the AH sample—are important for students to know. One compiler, John B. Carroll, wrote that even if the most esoteric words from the list are dropped from consideration, "there still remain many rare words whose meanings must be learned if the student is to attain full comprehension of the verbal materials to which he is exposed."[28] Note that Carroll is not discussing adult comprehension here, but the comprehension expected of children, perhaps not children at eight or nine, the lower end of the range, but certainly expected of those at age thirteen or fourteen.

It is just these full-comprehension words that are used in the standard Stanford-Binet test to determine adult intelligence. In an important study, the sociologist Donald P. Hayes figured out that of the 45 test words in the vocabulary section, 25 are listed as "rare" in the AH corpus, and 13 others are so rare that they do not even occur once in the five-million-word sample of children's literature. Those comparatively rare words,

Hayes writes, are precisely the ones that "provide the language with its breadth, depth, and subtlety of reference and meaning. Knowledge of such rare words distinguishes those at the highest levels of 'verbal intelligence' (the mastery level) from the novice, the competent, and the proficient word users."[29] That is to say, someone who does not know these "rare" words is not truly literate.

Hayes recently developed his own index, called LEX, to find out how words are used. To focus on the distinction between the patterns of word choice exhibited in speaking and writing, Hayes recorded conversations between parents and children in homes, and between other conversants in such locations as schools, hospitals, courtrooms, dormitories, a bar, and a fire station. He also took samples of written words from newspapers, comic books, school readers, television shows, and scientific treatises. He assigned every word a value based on its rarity in the frequency lists, then made a computerized scale in which the average difficulty of reading prose in sixty-one different newspapers was taken as zero. Based on the LEX scale, the most difficult text was a technical article in *Nature* magazine—58.6 LEX units—as against a sample of *Time* magazine at 6.8 and samples of *The National Enquirer* and *Sports Illustrated* at minus 10.3. He found that the average difficulty of most popular television sitcoms was "approximately the same as that for school readers designed for third and fourth grade pupils." Absolutely terrible on the scale was the number for dialogue on *Sesame Street*, at minus 45.1, nearly as bad as the number Hayes assigned to the speech of farmers addressing their dairy cows with such lines as "Let's go, girls. Come on, honey," which he calculated at minus 55.7. In casual conversation—and that is what these latter uses are, or mimic—the natural tendency is for speakers to use only the most common, most easily remembered words. Speculating how the minds works in these situations, Hayes believes that it is as if "the less common the term, the longer the latency for its recognition and retrieval from memory." This is an important point. When people are writing, they usually have more time in which to think about the most appropriate word, and usually their search leads them eventually to the most suitable word, which often is *not* one of the first to come to mind. Hayes found "greater reliance in writing upon words belonging to the much larger, but less frequently used, lexicon beyond the first 5,000 types." The fact that too many people today rely on the more common types of words, Hayes concludes, can be traced to the introduction of oversimplified early-grade textbooks after World War II, because "if you simplify texts, you deprive children of concepts associated with uncommon words."[30]

A fascinating comparison of "the use of words in context" from the periods 1943–45 and 1979–81 suggests that American vocabularies have indeed diminished since World War II, and in interesting ways. Four language researchers, John W. Black, Cleavonne S. Stratton, Alan C. Nichols, and Marian Ausherman Chavez, used the records of a large study of American college students done from 1943 through 1945, in which several hundred students' short speeches in public speaking classes were analyzed, as a basis of comparison for speeches made by an equal number of college students in public speaking classes during 1979–81.[31]

The various speakers used between ten thousand and twelve thousand different words, a fairly good sample of the vocabulary of literate-based, spoken English; most of us in our daily conversations choose from a considerably smaller base. The 10–12,000 number is evidence that the speeches were first written out and then presented. Of the words employed, 2,170 were what the researchers called "unique" to 1943 and 3,595 unique to 1979, while 4,430 appeared in the speeches of both groups. The authors attributed the significant change in the vocabulary over the course of one and a half generations to a "dialect of time." By that lovely phrase they mean that many words appropriate to 1943 had retreated (if not disappeared) from vocabularies by 1979—in particular words that had to do with World War II—and many words frequently used in 1979 had either never existed or were not on the tips of student tongues in the pretelevision, precomputer era of 1943.

Of greater significance than the dialect of time is an overall loss in the range of words. The 1943 students were able to use 8,786 different "word types," while for the 1979 group the number of word types had declined by 13 percent to 8,121. (In a 1932 study the word types had been even more numerous than they were in 1943.) The 1979 group also tended to repeat certain words more frequently than the earlier group: In 1943, only seventy words were used at least twenty times by various speakers; in 1979, 282 words were used at least twenty times. It appears that the earlier speakers displayed more originality in their choice of words, each speaker taking care not to use the same words as the other speakers in his group. We know that the 1979 speakers have been more assaulted by the products of mass culture and can be presumed to be more subject to the siren calls that lead to secondary orality. Is that why they used so many of the same words over and over? The answer is not clear from the statistics.

The authors of the study worried that critics might contend that the 1979 college students were from a larger and more heterogeneous population and were therefore a less select group and less likely to have a vocabulary level equal to the earlier group. Partly to address this notion, the investigators looked at groups of students from both predominantly white and predominantly black colleges, and found that while there were differences in terms of vocabularies—each group used a great many words that the other group did not—there were "no consistent qualitative differences between the two lists of words" culled from the speeches of the two groups. So the addition of minority students, who were perhaps not as well trained in the standard language, was not to blame for the disparity between 1943 and 1979 groups. What other hypothesis could explain it?

Vocabularies are often studied to detect the patterns behind them, the implicit evaluations and cues for social behavior that they sometimes reveal. The drop in vocabulary documented by the researchers of the 1943 and 1979 groups, instead of reflecting that the universe of words has simply diminished for the 1979 generation of students, may show that it is also the way these students view the world and their own actions in it that has altered.[32] Consider, as examples, the first ten unique "A" words of 1943, *abdominal, abide, aboard, abound, absent, accent, acclaim, accommodate, accustom,* and *acoustic,* and the first ten unique "A" words of 1979, *abbey, abbreviated, ABC, abdomen, Abe, abnormal, abolition, aborted, Abraham,* and *abrasion.* Consider also some large declines from 1943 to 1979 in the frequency of use of such words as *absolute* (from 25 instances down to 7), *administer* (12 to 6) and *along* (157 to 93). Together with these are some large increases in the frequency of use of such words as *abuse* (9 to 27), *achieve* (16 to 46) and *adjust* (9 to 24). Judging simply from these vocabulary lists, modern college students have narrower fields of interests than the college students of World War II, bandy about fewer ideas, use fewer conceptual and abstract words—which are usually taken as evidence of agile verbal development—but are inordinately concerned with processes and personal strivings. I find in this vocabulary decline additional evidence of the long-term trend identified by Cremin, the bias toward mass rather than class that is a seemingly inevitable consequence of the widening of popular education.

Most of a student's vocabulary is learned between the first and sixth grades. If children are progressing properly in language learning, a tenfold increase in the use of the words on the frequency lists considered "rare" can be achieved in those years. Donald Hayes cites this statistic but cautions that progress is not automatic: "To advance beyond the limitations of conversation and popular television . . . the child must both become literate and practice that literacy. As with chess or dance, the most rapid development occurs with hours of daily practice, carried on over many years with language sources rich in topic breadth."[33]

Now we are again at the heart of the matter: The written word as the center and mainstay of the language. Other research conducted with schoolchildren bears out the importance of the written word to development of a child's English competence beyond a very elementary level. For years, educators have been troubled by the existence of a "third-grade slump," which often erases the initial boosts given to children by Head Start programs, tutelage at home, and educational television shows. Educators have also been frustrated by the persistence of an even more troubling separation in the postprimary grades between the achievements of lower socio-economic status children and of middle-class children; with each passing year in school, the gap seems to widen. In an effort to get at the root of these slumps, the educational theorist Jeanne S. Chall conducted research that led her to conclude that the slumps could be traced to the manner in which children's reading development proceeds. In the early stages, what is necessary for reading is *recognition* of the alphabet and of individual words. That recognition is what *Sesame Street* and Head Start teach. In later stages, however, increased *comprehension* of meaning is required—and obtaining that comprehension means mastering a larger and more abstract vocabulary, as well as less familiar syntax and grammar. By the time children get to the third grade, they are usually able to recognize 9,000 words and can read and understand a full 3,000 of them. Beyond that point, achieving literacy becomes a different ballgame, Chall and her associates documented.[34] The task of a child changes from "learning to read," which has gotten the child to the third grade, to "reading to learn," which will take the child further into literacy. Chall's team showed quite convincingly that the third-grade slump occurs precisely when "direct instruction in advanced decoding skills," or recognition, must give way to comprehension, or "reading and study of texts . . . that contain new ideas and values, unfamiliar vocabulary and syntax." Children from the middle class recovered from the slump, Chall found, but those from poor homes did not do so as readily, and thereafter did not increase their vocabularies or mastery of grammar as quickly or as thoroughly; by seventh grade, the poor children had fallen two or more grades behind the norm and "did not know the less common, academic, and abstract words needed for reading their texts in science and social studies, as well as their library books." Other sociological research has shown that it is in the seventh or eighth grades that children begin to drop out of school. It is now clear that part of the reason for dropping out is being two or more grades behind in comprehension. Chall and her associates showed that the more the children read and wrote, the greater their comprehension of the language and their ability to use it. The obverse was also true: the less the children read and wrote, the lower their comprehension and use of the language.[35]

It is important to note that Chall's and Hayes's conclusions strongly echo those of Walter Ong about the divide between those who have continual reference to the literate-based language and those who are or who become secondarily oral. The third-grade slump and all that unfortunately follows from it, for those unable to get over that slump, show us precisely when and where many children fail to make the leap from oral to literate language accomplishment.

Part of the difference between the literacy levels of middle-class and poor children, Chall says, can be traced to the quantity, level, and use of reading materials in the home environments. The middle-class homes had more reading matter in them, and more educated parents who encouraged the reading of those materials, than did the poor homes. Chall points out that the basic underlying mental abilities of children from poor homes were confirmed by her group's research. What is now needed, she writes, is for schools to compensate for the lack of reading materials and encouragement in poor homes by adding more of those elements within the schools.[36]

The stamping out of children's early fascination with language occurs beyond the third grade, too, and cannot be blamed solely on a dearth of reading materials. It has to do with the curriculum. Mary S. Temperley, a college English professor, notes that most children love and delight in language games and wordplay, but by the time they reach high school their fascination vanishes, with unfortunate consequences for speaking, writing, and reading. One likely villain, according to Temperley, is what is taught in the name of grammar, namely, pedantic emphasis on a huge superstructure of rules such as deciding when to use *shall* or *will*; the attention paid to those matters, she writes, "has vitiated or invalidated much English language instruction" and made children think of it as boring, irrelevant, and unduly difficult.[37]

Sitting in on English classes throughout the country during his travels, Rexford Brown was "reminded of how much I hated teaching grammar: it was so clearly uninteresting to my students, and I didn't know what to do about that." Successful businessmen, lawyers, and doctors who met Brown at cocktail parties would tell him how much they had hated the study of grammar and would admit that they did not consider themselves good at it. Yet, Brown mused, there was no subject to which these people had been more relentlessly exposed, year after year. Unfortunately, that exposure "seems to have had the opposite effect from the one intended. It appears to have created a nation of people insecure and unknowledgeable about their native language."[38]

There may be no way to make grammar interesting. Nonetheless, it is one of those things that must be learned in order to function well in society. However, most educators, instead of reacting to student boredom and burnout in regard to grammar with innovative attempts to make its study more exciting, have chosen to decrease instruction in grammar and to substitute less demanding work. This accommodation is part of an overall trend in which educators have capitulated to the demand that all schoolwork be interesting or be gone. As a result, pupils are promoted from grade to grade without learning how to construct complex sentences, use previously unfamiliar vocabulary words, or employ better syntax. When children are not able to incorporate into their thinking the language structure information that grammar contains, they are deprived of their best path to mastering the upper levels of English.

Those successful people who braced Rex Brown at cocktail parties, though they felt "insecure and unknowledgeable" about using their language, were nonetheless among the more articulate people in our society.

Study after study has shown a strong correlation between articulation and achievement, and, supporting the contention from the negative side, a correlation between *not* being articulate and nonachievement, often to the point where inarticulateness becomes a principal reason for students to drop out of the educational system. It is well known that financial success is correlated with educational level, but recent studies conclude that it is not lack of schooling or poor schooling that condemns people to the lower part of the heap, but poor communication skills, especially poor oral communication skills.[39]

Given the number of children that do graduate from high schools in this country, presumably able to read and write at levels considerably beyond that of the third grade, why is it that they are not successfully articulate? According to some theorists, it is because they lack the ability to deal with abstract concepts and are stuck in literalness—the same literalness that is conveyed to them every day through the television set and other purveyors of popular culture. Stanley Aronowitz pinpointed the problem in his college-level social science and literature courses. During his many years of teaching, he wrote,

> I have never met a class that did not complain with either bitterness or bewilderment that the "reading was too hard," that the ideas associated with critical thinking were beyond their preparation. Students are overwhelmed by the factuality of the observed world and have enormous difficulty making the jump to concepts which may controvert appearances. I refer not only to concepts that have obvious ideological content such as socialism and capitalism, imperialism and national independence, but also to ones like metaphor and metonymy, or even the logical principle of syllogism, that demand some leap beyond experience.[40]

At stake here, Aronowitz concludes, is the tradition of critical, analytical thought itself, the center of the liberal arts curriculum.

Critical thinking of the sort Aronowitz and most other educated people value—and that, as I shall argue in a later chapter, is central to the functioning of a democracy—may well depend not on literacy alone but also on direct training in articulate behavior. As we have seen, training in rhetoric began to disappear in American classrooms about a hundred years ago. Although its vanishing has been lamented throughout the intervening years, what has actually been lost with it has not been well understood. It is the notion that being able to articulate thoughts and to say them aloud is as essential to the development of intellectual analytical ability as is the recognition of those rare words from the *American Heritage* word-frequency list that appear on the Stanford-Binet intelligence test.

The main theoretical underpinning for the view of articulate behavior as a concomitant of intellectual development comes from the work of the twentieth-century Russian language theorist Lev Vygotskii, who contended that in order to be truly educated, people must develop oral competency, because it contributes to the development of intellectual ability.[41] This notion is partially embodied in the old saw that if you can explain something to another person, then you successfully understand it. Socrates and his students arrived jointly at such understandings, and the thinking-on-your-feet process that Plato chronicles in their dialogues is strong anecdotal evidence that oral competency and intellectual ability are conjoined.

Vygotskii's theories underlie a renaissance of interest in oral competency that is just beginning to take hold in a handful of colleges and universities across the United States. Michael Cronin and Phillip Glenn, professors of communication, echo Vygotskii's dictum when they write: "Oral communication activities represent a fundamental mode of learning." Cronin and Glenn argue for the inclusion of such activities in all courses, because they permit students to "take a more active role in mastering and communicating course content." Their view is considered close to radical by the vast preponderance of the two thousand colleges in the country, which either reject the argument or are too hide-bound and lazy to change their instructional ways. However, some among the fifty or so institutions that do accept this view use "oral competency" as a way of testing whether students are really learning the material being taught to them. According to a recent national assessment, most college students lack sufficient oral skills. Inculcating such skills is not simply a matter of having students learn to overcome their fear of public speaking, because a study showed that students who took only a public speaking course were not much more competent in oral skills than those who had not. The heart of oral competency, according to Sherwyn Morreale and her colleagues at the University of Colorado Center for Excellence in Oral Communications, is not learning how to give a speech but rather "the development of organized and logical thinking and the communication of organized thought to others."[42]

What if the student is seriously lacking in oral competency? Other researchers have found that those who are less able to communicate have a particular set of problems: In their conversations and speech they demonstrate "high global uncertainty," a term that means they are wary of everything and everybody. They avoid people they do not already know, and when forced to deal with someone new—a new teacher or an unfamiliar fellow student—they exhibit a particular and quite negative interaction pattern. They do not ask many questions, though they do flaunt a "high level of personal disclosure," that is, they try to tell the new person who they are, while in the process they avoid trying to learn much about who the other person is or what the other person might have to say.[43]

Refusing to ask questions while simultaneously tooting their own horns and not responding to what the other person has to offer—a pattern usually thought of as characteristic only of high school dropouts—has become the style of many mainstream college students today. Catherine Zizik, a Seton Hall communications professor and debate coach, observed that in class these students are loud and aggressive rather than articulate and are also unable to tolerate anyone else's speaking. "They can't shut up, they can't listen, and they can't analyze," Zizik concludes.[44] Asking questions, listening to others, and analyzing what they say constitute essential factors in articulate behavior. The absence of those abilities in a student, Zizik suggests, may well be no more than bravado that masks substantial inadequacy in articulateness.

Oral communications and competency, if not articulate behavior *per se*, can be taught, and this is being done in the work of groups led by Cronin, Glenn, and Morreale at a few universities across the country. It is of note that these institutions are not in the tier of small, elite colleges of the sort identified by Cremin, which are likely to be more Socratic than Sophist in their orientation; rather, they are the large state universities and relatively small colleges (Hamline, Radford, DePauw) not generally lionized for academic excellence, where most instruction is given in lecture courses. Even so, these leaders in the field of teaching oral communications have insisted that their courses be more than college versions of Dale Carnegie courses. Morreale's team at the Center for Oral Excellence teaches its students that in addition to *cognitive, behavioral*, and *affective* dimensions of oral communications, they must also actively demonstrate in their speeches an understanding of the *ethical* dimension. To be orally competent, Morreale writes, one must "take moral responsibility for the outcome of the communication event and its impact on the receivers."[45]

Articulate behavior, in short, can and must be modeled and sponsored, but how can teachers know when students are successfully on the road to mastering the tasks of articulateness and when they are not? Learning theorists are beginning to find clues in the distinction drawn between novices and experts in other fields. The distinction is not in the level of knowledge each group has—knowledge, as we are beginning to understand in a society flooded with information, is readily accessible and does not have to be stored inside the mind when there are libraries and computers available. The difference between novice and expert lies in the level of critical skills of analysis—the ability to solve problems. If you are able to analyze and solve problems, you are an expert; if not, you remain a novice.

In the field of articulate behavior, analysis and problem-solving have well-known components, and they are precisely the ones so pithily identified by Catherine Zizik earlier in this chapter. They also echo the essence of the difference between the Sophist and Socratic methods that constitute the chapter's underlying theme.

Listening is more than being quiet while another person speaks. According to Michael Purdy, an oral communications expert, the skill of listening is one that must be learned and practiced. He identifies seven elements in this critical analytical skill. They include being aware of all the facets of what is being said, remembering all of them, intently focusing one's attention on the speech and speaker, and "volition," wanting to listen—an aspect that requires the listener's courage, because in taking account of what one hears, one may be obligated to change. Socrates would surely agree that change may result from intelligent listening. Purdy also identifies seven ways that people often block the possibilities of effective listening, for instance, by saying something instead of remaining silent, by asking leading questions, by expressing instant approval or disapproval, and by responding in clichés rather than in specifics that show the listener has actually heard what the speaker is saying.[46] *Questioning* is one of a constellation of strategies that have been identified as helping students to attain and to demonstrate higher learning. Asking questions requires that students move from passivity to active involvement. According to the debate coach Catherine Zizik, questioning, like listening, is becoming a lost skill. People fall silent either because they are unable to concoct good questions or because they believe the ones they do have may be judged stupid if voiced. There are no stupid questions, only unasked ones, Zizik suggests. Moreover, the quality of questions can improve when additional work goes into formulating them. She has seen an increase in quality occur among the debaters she has coached to championships. Questioning is possible not only in Socratic classrooms. In information-transfer settings such as a history classroom, asking questions permits students to figure out whether or not what is being taught makes sense and to go beyond the information presented to seek out matters that are implied or collateral; the best student questions are often those that cannot completely be answered by the materials provided in class. Other strategies linked to this process are *summarizing* what has been taught, *clarifying* one's own difficulties in understanding the material, and *predicting* what other lines of argument can be next expected.

Analyzing what is said or presented—which is what summary, clarification, and prediction of rival argument really amount to—is even more crucial. Some college teachers who assumed that their students were able to analyze discovered to their chagrin that the students had never learned certain basic skills that underlie analysis. The students needed to find out how to deconstruct the reasoning behind an argument or a set of allegations that were intended as facts, how to recognize where rational explanations were being sidestepped and logical fallacies or specious examples had been substituted. Here we are back again at something referred to earlier in the chapter, Frank DeAngelo's analysis of the inability to understand causation, which he traces in part to secondary-oral residues interfering with thinking processes. One cannot be an expert articulator without being an expert analyst. In fact, no advanced degree of mastery of *any* subject can be attained without the ability to analyze the work of others, and one's own work. The more specific, detailed, objective, and rational the analysis, the higher the degree of mastery.

Listening, questioning, the elements of analysis—these "strategies" or techniques can trace their lineage back to Socrates. And in the classroom experiments that are in the forefront of educational reform today, though used in a minuscule fraction of schools in this country, they are triumphantly present. A "reciprocal teaching" method based on those strategies, in which students took turns with the instructor in being the teacher of the class—that is, the person who asked the questions—was found to have raised students' comprehension of a subject from 15 percent to 85 percent accuracy in one study, and in another study from 30 percent to 80 percent accuracy. The reciprocal teaching studies discovered that all students need practice and prompting in how to ask questions, until they develop the confidence to formulate their own. They also found out that students listen better when they know that very soon they will be the ones doing the teaching and asking the questions.[47]

The listening, questioning, and analyzing activities are central to having good discussions, as another group of experiments in learning has showed. In the best discussions—that is, the most freewheeling and productive ones—what happens bears many similarities to what goes on in experimental classrooms when students take turns being the teacher. In the discussion, the goal is usually expressed as a jointly agreed-upon decision; in the classroom, it is a jointly understood body of knowledge. In both situations, people take turns. They present alternatives. They listen to what each person has to say and then analyze the alternatives, a process that itself encourages better articulation among all the participants. (Shades of Kenneth Burke's depiction of the "unending conversation" that is the basis of democracy.) In several experiments, it was found that both the alternative teach-and-be-a-student mode and the discussion mode enabled students to gain a better sense of their own progress in the problem-solving activities of analysis and articulation and to achieve better control over their own progress. The reciprocal teaching and discussion methods go by the name of "cognitive apprenticeships." One additional common factor has been noted in several widely variant styles of such apprenticeships, and that is the kind of teaching that goes on in them. After an initial burst of instructing the students, the good cognitive apprenticeship teacher then fades into the background and remains present as occasional coach rather than as continual instructor.[48] In other words, the teacher becomes the midwife that Socrates insisted he was, the facilitator rather than the keeper of knowledge, the person who assists the students in engaging in the higher-order-thinking sort of learning in which people teach themselves to be articulate through their own senses of curiosity and inquiry.

PART II

EXTRACURRICULAR EDUCATORS

*F*ifty to seventy-five years ago, if dividing the educational influences between formal and extracurricular educators, one would have been apt to include the church and other formidable social institutions such as the Boy Scouts in the category of formal educators, and to make a fairly small set of extracurricular influences, principally teenage peer pressure and the "school of hard knocks." One would also have had to conclude that the formal training in articulate behavior obtained in the home, at school, and through religious education far outweighed the effects of all other influences. In Part I we saw how formal education's influence in this regard has diminished and that it has deemphasized training for articulate behavior. In this section we shall see what has taken its educative place. The decline of religious institutions and clubs like the Boy Scouts, and the concurrent rise in importance of mass culture—of television and other entertainment purveyors—has shifted the balance: now extracurricular educators are more influential than the formal educators. Consequently, they are the focus of this larger section of the book.

Mass culture and mass politics arose together, and in this section I shall argue that their sources, aims, and effects are still conjoined, and that as our prime extracurricular educators, they are principally responsible for fostering and accelerating the decline in articulateness. From politics and entertainment come our society's most puissant models of behavior, whether of articulate behavior or of its obverse, models that are much admired and imitated.

Before the nationalistic upheavals of the mid-nineteenth century, most politics and entertainment were essentially local, small-scale matters. Groups were led a few thousand at a time, even on a military field, and audiences were entertained in even smaller aggregations. The theory in politics and in entertainment was that a statesman or a composer aimed for and influenced the elite few, whether in a parliament or in the audience gathered around the music chamber in a sovereign's presence, and that this elite would then spread the statesman's or composer's messages to ever wider audiences. Printed transcriptions of speeches, no less than the printed scores of musical compositions and texts of plays, might then further extend the reach of the great thinker. The masses might occasionally be moved to storm barricades or to sing a national anthem, but they were not sought out as natural constituencies.

Empowering individuals regardless of class began with the revolution of Martin Luther and the enlightenment, and found political expression in the populism of President Andrew Jackson and the 1848 nationalistic upheavals in Europe. In the latter half of the nineteenth century, from Karl Marx's theoretical bifurcation of the population into the exploiters and the exploited arose attempts to form the exploited masses of a particular country or region into coherent groups that could agitate for change in their political and economic status. Where the residue of feudalism held sway, nationalism also began to provide a rationale for the old feudal constituencies to cohere for the purposes of organizing themselves in nonfeudal aggregates. Leaders whose abilities lay in mobilizing these masses came to the fore and pushed out those old-style leaders who had previously made their way up political ladders to positions of ascendancy and who saw their task only as influencing the elites.

Mass man as a political creature is very much mass man as a cultural creature, as Ortega y Gasset pointed out. We are all members of a very large crowd. With the increasing crowding of the planet, it becomes more difficult to exist as an individual, and easier to become subject to the tyranny of the commonplace. The real world recedes, artificiality pushes into every arena of life, and the mass man's days are filled with escapist thoughts and dalliances. Those who can provide escapist, unreal ideas and entertainments become society's leaders.[1]

Jürgen Habermas insists that the center of argument about the modern world has now shifted from Marxian contentions about how industrial production is organized to an examination of how communication in societies is organized and effected.[2] That contention is well founded. While a discussion about the bases of entertainment can be held without reference to the political sphere, it is no longer possible to discuss the modern political sphere without reference to communications techniques and communications technology. As far back as World War I, even such committed mass populists as Antonio Gramsci in Italy discussed politics in terms of the organizing the masses to send and receive communications, and of the purpose of culture as communicating political tenets to the masses.[3]

In the late nineteenth century, while the political arena was becoming more and more the realm of mass politics, the cultural sphere was also undergoing substantial structural change. Previously, most artists had made their living from the largesse of rich patrons, not from the sale of books or ticket receipts or some other direct or nearly direct monetary payment from the audience. As patrons of the arts disappeared, the need of artists and entertainers to reach audiences directly increased. From the beginning of recorded time right up until the end of the nineteenth century, entertainers (as well as politicians) had been able to reach only those people who could see or hear them in person.[4] Quantum leaps in reaching large and distant audiences first were realized with the introduction of the microphone in the late nineteenth century, then by means of the motion picture camera and the radio, inventions that were consolidated and considerably improved upon in the first two decades of the twentieth century.

Electronification can be said to have been the principal growth stimulant for both mass politics and mass entertainment. Before the advent of radio, Governor Al Smith of New York recalled, in a month of giving speeches every night he could reach perhaps 30,000 people, 1 percent of the eligible voters in his state; by 1928, when Smith was running for the presidency, he could get his message to millions in a single radio speech. Smith lost his campaign for the presidency, but in Europe and in Asia political leaders with more radical agendas based on appeals to class distinctions and nationalism, such as Hitler, Mussolini, Stalin, and the Japanese militarists, extended their appeals by means of the new communicative technologies and thereby achieved power over the masses. Similarly and simultaneously, such filmmakers as D. W. Griffith, Charlie Chaplin, and Sergei Eisenstein, as well as the early radio broadcasters, were transmitting their visual and verbal images to ever larger audiences, achieving in this way their own considerable power and influence. The filmmakers' and broadcasters' reach into the minds of their mass audiences became greater as well as wider than the influence such composers as Mozart, Beethoven, and Haydn had on the minds of their smaller, more elite audiences a hundred years earlier.

In consequence of its enlarged reach and power, entertainment for the first time achieved the status of an industry, most readily visible in the studios of Hollywood. Entertainment was no longer something created by individuals or by loose aggregations of artists as a way to make a living. It was products turned out by entrepreneurial entities that were in business for the purpose of making a profit for their shareholders. As the purposes changed, so did the objectives. More ticket buyers and radio listeners translated directly into larger profits, and so the larger the audience, the better. The presence of elite members among that audience was no longer of consequence, for each ticket buyer was of equal moment to any other. The only thing that counted was more and more of them.

The end result of this trend toward mass entertainment, especially since television replaced radio as the dominant form of dissemination, has been to transform the contemporary United States of America into the most thoroughly and continuously entertained society ever to have existed in the long recorded history of the planet.

Chapter 4

THE ENTERTAINED CULTURE

$\mathcal{A}$ published novelist moved to Hollywood to join her fiancé and looked for employment in the area's main industry. After she had cut her scriptwriting teeth on occasional television series episodes, she was asked to join the writing staff of a new situation comedy commissioned by a major network. She arrived at the first script meeting brimming over with innovative and quirky ideas for plots, character traits, lines of dialogue. The senior creators heard her out for a few minutes, then enjoined her to remember: "This is television—aim lower."

She was perturbed and a bit shocked by that directive, but she should not have been surprised, because aiming lower is what the creators have come to believe is usually required in order to reach the inordinately large audience necessary to keep a prime-time network television show on the air. And part of aiming lower has been to restrict substantially the vocabulary, sentence structure, word usage, and cultural referents in television scripts.

Similar directives directly or indirectly absorbed by the creators have affected the production of the most popular program on the channel that is the most watched by teenagers and people in their twenties—those who constitute a desirable audience because they spend a large fraction of their incomes and allowances on consumable goods—MTV's *Beavis and Butt-head*. Its defining characteristics are dumbness and meanness, expressed in the title duo's lack of eloquence and copiously displayed ignorance. The eponymous teenagers are continual watchers of television, particularly of rock videos. School dropouts, they work at a burger joint, and divide the world into "things that suck" and "things that are cool." Defenders of the series say it is a satire, and the audience is being encouraged to laugh at the title characters' asininity, not to emulate them. But a fourteen-year-old who dropped his karate class in order to watch the show regularly told a reporter, "We go around mimicking . . . not what they say, but how they say it." *Beavis and Butt-head* is written by recent Ivy League college graduates who seem to have passed through their schooling untouched by the literary basis of higher education. Matt Groening, creator of *The Simpsons*, a more witty forebear of the MTV show, said that the scripts of the new show "are based on what comes out of the collective memory of the writers, which is mostly memories of sitting in front of a TV set growing up."[1] The characters talk only about what they have seen and heard on television; their friendship—indeed, their entire relationship—is built around shared mass culture experiences. They have nothing else to talk about, no other frame of reference. The early *Saturday Night Live* programs also took the events and situations of television as their base for satire, but *SNL* subjected them to a broader, more literate-based series of humorous critiques.

Beavis and Butt-head is an example—not the worst one, but a typical one—of mass culture gone very wrong. It is the latest in a long line of products whose stock in trade is the deriding of merit, though in the guise of laughing at pretension; what seems new is its cruelty, admiration for destructiveness, and focus on obscene and deliberately inarticulate discourse.

We have become a country of mass audiences. The average American spends half of his or her daily waking hours watching, reading, or listening to some product of the mass media. Most Americans watch thirty hours of television a week, or 1,550 hours a year (during which, according to one estimate, they encounter 37,822 commercials), listen to the radio 1,160 hours a year, spend 180 hours a year reading some part of a newspaper and 110 hours a year reading magazines. We each buy fifteen books a year, and although this appears to be a substantial number, most of the books purchased are considered to be in the category of trashy novels. Surveys conclude that the "most read" portion of any newspaper is Ann Landers's advice column and that the most frequently read magazine is *TV Guide*. As reported in an earlier chapter, the vocabulary and sentence-difficulty level of such readings is quite low, not much above grade-school level. In 1992 Americans spent $12 billion to buy or rent videos, a figure that translates into 49.5 rentals per family a year, about one video each week. Add in a few hours for going to the movies or listening to audio cassettes and CDs, and the total number of hours that the average American spends attending to mass media products comes to more than fifty per week, more time than the average American spends on the job or at school, more hours than he or she devotes to any single activity other than sleeping.[2]

A trend toward convergence of the entertainment and news/information industries has made certain that the language practices of one sector largely reproduce the practices of the other, and both aim lower, with dire consequences for articulateness. This chapter will be concerned principally with fictional products of mass culture as they affect our articulate behavior. The next will focus on the nonfictional products.

In the past half-century, as our work week has shortened, we have increasingly given over our time to materials produced to entertain us. Some are of undeniably high quality; it is a happy consequence of the prodigious size and high economic standard of living in the U.S. that we can sustain the production of some quality books, films, dramas, and television programs, and the performances of dance troupes, orchestras, and popular musicians. However, these quality products are few in number and power, a half-dozen rowboats struggling to stay afloat in a harbor crowded with the yachts, international freighters, and cruise ships of the mass entertainment industry.

Because television has tremendous power to influence its viewers, it is legitimate to be concerned with the nature and the accuracy of the medium's representations of reality. Meticulous studies of program content and viewing habits conducted over the course of several decades by George Gerbner and his associates at the Annenberg School have reached the unsurprising conclusion that both fictional and nonfictional broadcasts give viewers inaccurate and misleading representations of reality. Among their findings: Crime is ten times more prevalent on television than it is in the FBI's annual statistics on criminal activity. More than half of television's fictional characters are involved in a violent confrontation each week. Habitual television watchers—defined as those who turn their sets on for more than four hours a day—come to believe the skewed version of reality that is broadcast and to disbelieve reality itself. Not only do such "heavy viewers" perceive crime unrealistically, with a serial killer lurking behind every tree, but they also develop other misperceptions about our society: Their sense of reality comes to reflect television's inaccurate portrayal of who we are and what we do. On prime-time television, nine out of every ten characters are middle-class, less than 1 percent are lower-class, and only one-quarter have blue-collar jobs. On television, only one out of every ten characters is married; women age quickly—there are many youthful female characters and some recognizably older ones, but few are in their middle years. Conversely, the facts show that two out of every three jobs in this country are classified as blue collar, and most women in the country are married and middle-aged. While 80 percent of the convicted criminals in the United States are young, male and largely from a minority background, the villains seen on television are even more disproportionately young, male, lower-class, minority or foreign-born or mentally ill. "Losers" on television programs are mostly likely to be female, old, unmarried, and/or poor. Similarly, heavy viewers overestimate the number of people in this country employed as doctors, lawyers, and managers, and hold such mistaken beliefs as that the older population of the country is sick, ineffectual, and makes up less of the whole than do the young people whose counterparts fill the bulk of the roles on popular television shows. In a report published in 1993, Gerbner concludes that in terms of reflecting reality, television hasn't changed much in the last thirty years; it remains "frozen in a time-warp of obsolete and damaging representations."[3]

What do these misrepresentations have to do with the decline in articulate speech? The answer lies in a further investigation into the nature of the misrepresentations, for they are not accidental. Rather, they are a result of marketing analysis, which consistently advises the creators of television programs to aim lower in order to reach broader audiences. That has precipitated the industry into a self-perpetuating cycle of infinite regression, a cycle in which the most effective product is always the one aimed lower than the previous one. The prime target audience is relatively young and monied, between 18 and 34 years old. Betsy Frank, director of television information and new media at the advertising giant Saatchi &

Saatchi, recently told a reporter: "The most important thing for our clients is the demographics—*who* is watching." The cost of a thirty-second commercial on the highly rated *Murder, She Wrote* series is $116,000, but a commercial on a lower-rated program scheduled opposite it, *Lois and Clark*, which is known to appeal to younger viewers, is $132,000. A media time buyer suggested that the latter program was put on the air principally as counter-programming, to corral advertisers for products who did not want to reach the older viewers of the Angela Lansbury show.[4]

That reasoning is a variation on the industry commonplace that more viewers tune in to an episode of a commercial television program than have ever attended a live performance of a Shakespeare play in the nearly four hundred years since the plays were written. The dark side of this commonplace is that industry executives come to believe that the requisite huge audience will not tune in any broadcast that is too complex, witty, or highbrow. Even though public television, whose offerings are acknowledged as more artistically elevated, consistently reaches an audience numbered in the millions, that audience is considered by network producers and executives to constitute an unacceptably small minority—3 percent—of potential viewers. Similarly, the critical acclaim reaped by foreign-made films is deemed by the creators of Hollywood mainstream motion pictures to be of no importance, because foreign films consistently place far behind Hollywood's products in total boxoffice receipts. To achieve mass appeal, in other words, the industry belief is that one must aim low. That belief permits network and studio executives to assign blame for aim-lower entertainment to the audience and to contend that they are able to give us only what we say that we want, judging by Nielsen ratings and box office receipts. Michael Fuchs of Home Box Office told a group at an academic conference, "Everybody says they want to watch documentaries, but nobody watches. All of you act like you're going to watch 'The Mayan Civilization' and then you tune in to Geraldo Rivera. I've got the numbers [to prove it]."[5]

Must the need to ensure a large audience automatically mean that the makers of mass media entertainments should trim their creative sails? Clearly, the industry itself has concluded that an entertainment product cannot be both widely popular and of high quality, but there is no intrinsic reason why quality and sales appeal cannot be combined. One of the more popular programs in the early days of commercial television was

Omnibus, a program of decidedly elite culture but aimed at a mass audience presumed to want to be led upward rather than downward. Other, occasional broadcasts also aimed higher. In a 1950s program designed for young audiences, Leonard Bernstein electrified a generation of viewers and listeners with his demonstration of why an orchestra needs a conductor. Bernstein and the producers of the program assumed that most children—indeed, most people in the viewing audience—had never been to a live concert, but that did not deter the program's creators from making an intelligent point. The composer began at the podium, started the orchestra on a familiar classical theme, and then walked away, leaving the orchestra to its own devices; within a minute, the music turned dissonant and sour, as each instrument player followed his or her own beat. When Bernstein returned to explain what precisely a conductor does, very few in the home mass audience dared turn to another channel.

It had been the function of entertainment producers for many centuries to adhere to elite standards and to assume that part of their task was to bring wider and wider audiences up to those standards. That task was most overtly pursued in the age of Addison, Steele, and Henry Fielding, who wrote popular plays and novels. Many of their works were transparently about the spoken word. They offered readers choice phrases to repeat as well as models of good and bad speech. Television now provides models of words to say and how to say them; however, the models are too often based on the worst uses of language. Rather than use their reserves of ingenuity to entertain, today's producers totally abandon any adherence to high standards or to educating as well as titillating audiences and fall back on the most basic elements at their disposal—an attitude that fosters appeals to base instincts, the too ready exclusion of references to anything other than pop culture, and the endless recycling of familiar material. Why allude to Mozart if the audience is presumed to know only the music of Michael Jackson? *Amadeus* was a fine motion picture that not only won Academy Awards but was immensely profitable—and spawned an equally profitable revival in sales of Mozart's music—a fact dismissed as an anomaly. Circuitous marketing logic becomes self-fulfilling prophecy, and it is heresy to suggest that the intellectually more complicated products of the foreign film industry or the highbrow programs seen on public television might fare better in commercial terms if they had the same financial and promotional backing and the same wide distribution as the products of the mainstream. "Nobody ever went broke underestimating the taste of the American public" goes the phrase attributed to H. L. Mencken. He meant it as an indictment; today's pop culture purveyors treat it as a directive.

This directive implies a high degree of contempt for the audience. It expresses a belief that the audience is infinitely malleable and easily led, that it has no intelligence at all, or not enough to see through marketing tricks. It tries to turn audiences into mere consumers who have no more choice in how they react to a stimulus than do hungry animals confronted with food. As Theodor Adorno and the other members of the Frankfurt School pointed out fifty years ago, one of the main purposes of mass culture is to keep the consumer's responses at an infantile level, and thereby to manipulate the consumer with false promises of libidinal gratification.[6] In the ensuing half-century, the purveyors have only become more skilled at their task. The corollary of the directive about taste is that a product will make a great deal of money if it is aimed low. That belief—for it is only a guess— has become the engine of Hollywood, affecting every part of motion picture and television production, from casting to script development to the props on the set. The fact is that Hollywood producers cannot predict with any degree of certainty what will or will not make money. Out of fear of not making money, they resort to the elements that seem most likely to ensure that the product makes money. Certain stars are labeled as "bankable" because such a star's agreement to play a major role in a movie enables the producer to obtain funding for it. A star's bankability, in turn, derives from the presumed (and unproved) relationship between the degree of success of the star's most recent picture and his or her performance. Marketing considerations, then, are what causes actors and actresses to be frequently cast in roles for which they are unsuited. As in the recent box office failure *Robin Hood*, starring Kevin Costner, the results are all too often artistically as well as financially disastrous. Memoirs like Robert Evans's *The Kid Stays in the Picture* are filled with tales of how the marketing mentality overwhelms virtually every other aspect of filmmaking.[7]

The marketing mentality also skews the writing process. To make a point about just this, one of the most successful American scriptwriters, William Goldman, cites in his memoir a pithy line from Joseph Mankiewicz's *The Barefoot Contessa*, which starred Humphrey Bogart and Ava Gardner: "What she's got, you couldn't spell, and what you've got, you *used* to have."

In 1954, Goldman argues, that line could be put in the mouth of a minor character, Bogart's wife, but today it would have to be said by one of the stars, or it would be cut from the script: "Giving that line to the wife, in today's movie world, is not just incorrect screenwriting, it is lethal. Today, you must give the star everything."[8] Giving the star everything contributes to the downward spiral by centering movies more and more on the star's bankable presence. In similar moves based on marketing and appealing to base instincts, beautiful women and handsome men are always cast in the leading roles on the assumption that no one will want to gaze at a less than pretty face. When Farrah Fawcett was asked if it was the acting abilities of herself and the two other top models in starring roles that ensured the success of the television series *Charlie's Angels*, she reportedly replied that it was more likely to have been the fact that none of the women wore brassieres.

The marketing mentality has spilled over into areas previously immune from it, such as set decoration. For the first seventy-five years of moviemaking, set decorators thought in terms of what would best convey the atmosphere sought by the director of the film, with perhaps some consideration given to how to achieve that effect within budgetary constraints. Often care was taken so that the label on a bottle of liquor, or the brand name on an article of clothing, was turned away from the camera. Today, when a character in a movie drinks a beverage or bends down to tie a shoelace, the can of Coke or the Nike sneaker is prominently featured, its label easily read by the camera. The audience sees the labels because the manufacturers of those commodities have paid fees to have their products displayed on screen. Producers defend this shoddy practice by saying that the fees help to defray film budgets that are inordinately high.

Fees for displaying products may seem a trifling matter, but the practice is symptomatic of the commodification that is now at the center of producing mass entertainments, which threatens to overwhelm any lingering traces of attempts at artistry by film and television artists. Theodor Adorno saw the great divide in artistic products existing not between those aimed at a mass audience and those aimed at an elite audience but between "autonomous" art products and "commodity art." Autonomous products made no compromise with the marketplace, while commodity art products had no other purpose but to conform themselves to marketplace exigencies.[9] Commodification is a reduction in the purposes and aims of a product. It is a way of thinking that presumes everything has a price, all things can be bought and sold, and therefore all things *should* be bought and sold. This thinking is based on flawed and incredibly arrogant assumptions—that people will not consume what is good for them, and that only the marketers know what is best for consumers and should therefore dictate what can be consumed. When a product becomes a commodity, only marketing considerations have any meaning, and those that maximize the potential profit have the most meaning. No other objective—not art, not morality, not personal integrity, and certainly not the modeling of good articulate behavior—can be of any importance. Articulate behavior is not perceived as able to sell anything but itself, and as such it is useless to the commodifiers. Inarticulate behavior, on the other hand, has been construed as something that appeals to the masses, and thus a useful commodity.

Classic behavioral psychology experiments have repeatedly demonstrated that when image and sound are presented concurrently, a subject is better able to recall the image than the sound and retains that image in memory for a longer time. Producers seize on this, too, as rationale to get rid of words and to rely only on the visual nature of moving pictures. Where filmmakers err is in assuming that audiences always prefer the visual to the verbal or that film is only visual. There has always been tension between literacy and the visual image in films, but in the talking films of the 1930s and 1940s, dialogue was considered supremely important. The verbal byplay of Nick and Nora Charles in the *Thin Man* series of mystery films was one of its glories; by comparison, the character of the supposedly literate mystery novelist played by Angela Lansbury in *Murder, She Wrote* on television is entirely witless. The notion that a picture is worth a thousand words has wreaked insidious and far-reaching havoc in Hollywood, for now the film and television industries have embraced visual storytelling without pausing to determine which words a picture can or should replace. As most film and videotape editors will readily admit, the ultra-rapid cutting between images best exemplified by MTV videos, which has already taken over commercials and is creeping into all Hollywood feature and television production, is incapable of telling complex or subtle stories; it is most appropriately used in conveying emotional impact. The end result of choosing only pictures to tell stories is products in which rapidly changing images convey information in ways that are often deliberately illogical, disorienting, and surreal. A video game commercial that features forty-eight images in thirty seconds stops only once to have someone speak: the football star Joe Montana, who lip-syncs the phrase, "I forgot what I was going to say."

In martial arts films and tapes the stars do not have to forget lines, because they have virtually none to utter. As for more mainstream motion pictures, a poll taken in Hollywood in the spring of 1993 underlined the predilection for the visual. A group of thirty-five marketing executives, heads of advertising agencies, and motion picture producers were asked to rate forthcoming summer movie trailers for excitement and promotional impact. Most of the trailers emphasized physical action over dialogue, but none more so than the one for *Cliffhanger*, starring Sylvester Stallone. This two-minute, 84-clip montage, set to the music of Wagner's "Ride of the Valkyries," won the laurel from those who were polled and was singled out by the film critic of *Los Angeles Weekly* as "the best example of American moviemaking so far this year." It was the only trailer in which there was absolutely no dialogue.[10]

Many observers contend that heavy television viewing may be an addiction. Addictive behavior follows certain patterns, whether the addicting substance is liquor, drugs, or images. The addicted person comes to believe that the addicted situation is somehow normal, even though it is not. The addicted person also does not notice a gradual lowering of normal bodily and mental functioning and of articulation levels. The Italian philosopher Franco Ferraroti points out some other severe consequences of television addiction:

> The semihypnotic condition in which most people follow TV broadcasts often leads, apart from a considerable difficulty with and distaste for expressing one's own ideas coherently, to a series of real dyslexic disturbances, especially the inability to distinguish between written words, written fully, and those abbreviated. . . . The atrophy of the imagination thus leads progressively to reducing the habit of reading and at the same time to the satisfaction induced by the contemplation of images, even better if the words no longer appear. . . . We are faced with a new form of illiteracy which prefers acquiring knowledge through images.[11]

It is perhaps impossible to prove whether or not television is addictive, but there is evidence that the vocabulary of images learned through television has in many ways replaced earlier literate-based understandings of the world. As a teacher of scriptwriting, I tried to encourage students to utilize the pictorial dimension of film properly. But I discovered that I first had to disabuse them of preconceived visual-based ideas about what constitutes dramatic action. For far too many students, action meant the exciting scenes they had seen in countless television shows: a car chase, a bullet being fired, a woman running from a stalker. This is action construed as something in physical motion. Aristotle defined dramatic action as what happens when characters act upon one another. Thus an extended car chase may be visually stirring, and it certainly has movement, but it is often not essentially dramatic, because it does not reveal much about the emotional forces that move the story forward.

However, in *Stroszek*, a film by Werner Herzog, there is a moment of real action. The title character is about to lose his mobile home because he has not kept up the payments. He stands with back to camera, in the foreground of the frame, and looks at the side of his home, which otherwise entirely fills the screen. Off camera, a truck is hooked up to the trailer and then pulls the mobile home laterally out of frame, revealing an empty field at which the hero and audience must stare. This striking and dramatic image helps the audience to appreciate the impact of losing his home and helps us to imagine what effect the loss may have.

Herzog contends that films are "the dreams of illiterates," though his own films have for the most part reached only an elite audience outside of his native Germany, and in the English-speaking world they have not become part of mass culture. His critique repeats the criticism of early silent movies, one that faded only with the introduction of talking pictures in 1929. For decades after that change, Hollywood's need for scriptwriters who could provide good dialogue lured playwrights and novelists to write for the silver screen and to help turn out movies that were both entertaining and reasonably literate. *My Little Chickadee*, starring Mae West and W. C. Fields, sparkles with the clash of words of those two outrageous characters, both of whom had written material for themselves and other performers.

Today, the need for writing good dialogue has been obviated by the producers' belief that audiences prefer physical action to words. Filmmakers are urged to give the audience more and more physical action, fewer and fewer words, and characters who are even less inclined to speech than the audience itself. Sylvester Stallone—more precisely, the roles in which he has achieved his greatest commercial success—is a prime example of the current generation of inarticulate screen heroes who make John Wayne's strong-and-silent cowboys and soldiers seem loquacious by comparison. Stallone's Rocky Balboa and John Rambo, and the appallingly similar characters played by Arnold Schwarzenegger, by Clint Eastwood as Dirty Harry, by Mel Gibson in the *Lethal Weapon* series, by Bruce Willis in the *Die Hard* films, and even by John Travolta in *Saturday Night Fever* or *Pulp Fiction* speak in fragments or incomplete sentences when they voice words at all, and employ a severely stunted, reflexively profane vocabulary. Equally important, they and virtually all the other characters in these films are ignorant of history and make no references to literature, art, or anything else except other recent products of popular culture, such as commercial advertisements. When they have a choice between physical and verbal solutions to a given problem, they unhesitatingly go for the blow. If they have any breath to spare, they accompany it with a wisecrack.

To have characters speak lines that are brief, pithy, and memorable is one of the goals of all Hollywood films and the source of the scriptwriter's imperative to "write short." Never say in ten words what you can get across in five. Linda Seger, a script doctor, gives this advice in *Making a Good Script Great*: After a writer prunes the script so that it focuses mainly on the images and actions of the story, the writer should reexamine what has been removed. "If these sections were long speeches, see if you can reduce the pertinent information to a sentence or two. . . . If some of [the scenes] reveal character through talk, try to find an image or an action you can substitute for the dialogue."[12] The imperative has corollaries, such as never have a character who overexplains, and never continue a scene past a trenchant "button line." William Goldman, the screenwriter of *Butch Cassidy and the Sundance Kid*, a movie well regarded for its quips, quotes in his memoir the scene in which Butch walks up to a modern-looking, heavily-barred bank and asks a guard, "What was the matter with the old bank this town used to have? It was beautiful." The guard says that people kept robbing it, and Butch walks off, saying, "That's a small price to pay for beauty." Seventeen years after the movie, Goldman reprints the dialogue in his memoir, and comments:

> I happen not to believe Butch's final retort—I don't think he'd say it and I think it's smart-ass. There's a lot about the screenplay I don't like, the smart-

assness just being one of them. I also find that there are too many reversals and that the entire enterprise suffers, on more than one occasion, from a case of the cutes.[13]

The idealization of writing short and cute in movies is the logical result of competition with television and its cult of the one-liner, the quotable joke that enlivens situation comedies. Each sitcom character must respond to any comment with a single, snappy, mirth-provoking line; just in case we miss the joke, it is highlighted by a laugh track that reminds us to join in the fun. Let us cheerfully admit that the writing in sitcoms is frequently funny—I myself cannot watch a good sitcom without being often moved to laughter, and neither can you. The problem is that the producer's compulsive need to make the audience chortle at every second or third line is, for the writer, a smotherer of invention. Plot and character development, or the interplay of themes and ideas, must be forgone in the all-consuming quest for the perfect retort.

It is an odd feature of American films that inarticulate screen heroes are frequently matched against villains who are decidedly better spoken and better educated—smart guys apparently gone wrong. The well-spoken English actor Alan Rickman has made a career of playing literate villains, opposite Kevin Costner in *Robin Hood* and Bruce Willis in *Die Hard*. James Bond's opponents have, to a man, always employed good diction and vocabulary. The tradition dates back as far as Milton's *Paradise Lost*, in which Lucifer is more articulate than the angels, but in the modern era the interesting dissatisfaction with the world that Milton's devil expresses has entirely vanished. A textbook on advertising written forty years ago traces the American fascination with this plot device back to what became an ingrained bias against the con man, the barker, the pitchman, the seller of snake oil—to a distrust of anyone, Pierre Martineau writes, who is too facile with logic and "too glib with words."[14] Articulate villains are a further attempt to pander to the prejudices of the audience, which is presumed by producers to be inarticulate and willing to vent anger at those who can and do bandy words.

Apologists for Hollywood like lobbyist Jack Valenti, Chairman of the Motion Picture Association of America, contend that there are no adverse social consequences for motion pictures that promote dislike of articulate villains and exalt inarticulate heroes. That is nonsense. While the physical exploits of modern movie heroes may be beyond the capacity of most audience members, their inarticulate condition is ripe for imitation and widely emulated. "Hasta la vista, baby," growls Arnold Schwarzenegger before terminating someone—and 10 million ticket buyers incorporate this witticism into their daily discourse. The inarticulate heroes' influence over us might perhaps be counterbalanced by the utterances of articulate public figures, but our modern political pantheon no longer includes a Winston Churchill and has had to settle for a speechwriter-dependent John F. Kennedy. President Ronald Reagan's most remembered remark was not from his highly praised D-Day memorial speeches, nor even his telling phrase about "the evil empire," but his re-iteration of a warning line originally snarled by Clint Eastwood in a Dirty Harry movie: "Go ahead—make my day."

The celebration of Dirty Harry's proclivity for violence in a series of films is indicative of a deep shift in the focus of mass entertainment. The shift is more evident in television than in movies, perhaps because in television the relationship between the dollars paid by commercial advertisers and the marketing mentality of the producers is more overt. In the era before cable television, the prevailing theory of programming was based on the view that Americans wanted to watch something, few choices were available, and the least objectionable program, or LOP, would be the most widely watched. Now that the menu of viewing choices has been expanded, the LOP has been replaced by the LCD—the lowest common denominator. This principle operates, for example, in the decision to schedule the most sensational made-for-television and feature movies during May and November. In those "sweeps" periods, viewership is measured and ratings are established, and they become the basis for the advertising rates on which the networks' and syndicators' revenues depend. Among the principal ingredients in the offerings made especially for sweeps period are larger than usual doses of violence. Violence is hip right now, and highly commercial. For instance, violence is an accepted sales tool for the breakfast cereals and toys advertised on children's cartoon programs. A recent study by Gerbner and associates tallied 7.8 violent acts per children's program, or 32 per hour—more such acts per hour than in any other form of programming. The National Coalition on Television Violence says that the leader in showcasing violence is the cable network MTV, with 29 instances of "violent or hostile imagery" per hour, and with one-third of its videos containing some violent elements.[15]

A controversy rages over whether depicted violence in entertainment has any direct relationship to the raising of the level of violence in individuals or in society as a whole. What is more relevant to this discussion is the dire effect that the producers' craving for violence has on writers and other creators of entertainment. The creative difficulty lies in the fact that violence is often so visually and emotionally compelling that it tends to overshadow any other dramatic element. When Shakespeare wrote his *Henry V*, he made sure that the battle of Agincourt took place offstage, and he invoked a "muse of fire" to help his audience properly imagine it. In Laurence Olivier's film adaptation of the play, made almost fifty years ago, the battle appears on screen but in a relatively tasteful and limited way; in Kenneth Branagh's much lauded 1992 film version, the battle takes up many minutes, during which Branagh fills the screen with slow-motion shots of swords and spears impaling bodies amid mud and flying gobs of blood and bone—so much detail that the battle sequence nearly overwhelms the original text.

Violence takes focus. Violence is more quickly depicted than verbal action, and in films and television, every second counts. Violence obscures plots that make no sense and characters that have no depth. Violence does not require good actors and actresses, or even performers who have good speaking voices. Two other LCD elements are on the rise in commercial broadcasting, overt sex and profanity, and the same charges can be leveled against them: They take focus, serve to obscure silly plots and weak characters, are more easily portrayed, and do not require deft performers.

The 1993 fall television season, according to the critic Tom Shales, reflected an "obsession" with sex that "seems to have been cranked up to a new high." Shales reprinted examples of smutty jokes and profanity from pilots he had watched, including bits from such new programs as *Family Album, It Had To Be You*, and *The Trouble With Larry* (CBS); *Daddy Dearest* and *Living Single* (Fox); *The John Larroquette Show* (NBC); and *Grace Under Fire* (ABC).[16] By common consent, the worst offender of the fall 1993 season was not a sitcom but an hour-long drama, *N.Y.P.D. Blue* (ABC), which featured nudity and language previously considered too obscene for prime-time network television. The admired producer Steven Bochco, whose company created the series, told reporters that he had deliberately incorporated those elements because he is in a struggle for viewers with cable television, which runs full-length motion pictures with "adult" content. "I don't think we can at ten o'clock with our hour dramas effectively compete any longer unless we can paint with some of the same colors that you can paint with when you make a movie," he stated.[17] The shock value of the nudity and profanity attracted some viewers and repelled others, but those "colors" were toned down after the first few episodes. Later reviews, which were quite enthusiastic, stressed the series' good stories and believable characters. Indeed, *N.Y.P.D. Blue* has gone on to become a critical and commercial success, and many critics and viewers have wondered why the creators considered it important in the first place to pander to base instincts. It appears that nudity and profanity were deemed essential at the outset because the creators and the ABC network executives were somehow afraid not to include LCD elements, lest their enterprise fail commercially for lack of them. They were also enamored of the publicity generated by the controversy over the nudity and profanity. Heightening viewer interest through controversy is a well-known tool in the marketer's belt. With these craven (and possibly unnecessary) actions on the part of the creators and the network, the downward regressive cycle took another turn for the worse.

Chapter 5

TRANSFORMING THE NEWS

$\mathcal{E}$xcess commodification, the engine of mass entertainment production, has pushed entertainment into aiming at ever lower sensibilities and in the process has fostered a decline in articulate speech. The search for new areas to commodify has caused entertainment to spill over its former boundaries into areas once considered to be neither entertainment nor subject to the same marketing analysis as entertainment. Athletics and religion have been compromised by just this process, but in terms of having the worst effects on articulate behavior, the principal victim is news and informative television.

Survey after survey documents that 60 to 70 percent of Americans obtain their news from the ABC, CBS, and NBC television and radio networks, not from newspapers or magazines. But television supplies us with more than just information, it also supplies us with ideas and attitudes. It has been proved that television news plays a major role in setting our national, local, and even personal agendas. For a week, under controlled conditions at the University of Chicago, two groups watched television news. One viewed actual broadcasts, while the second watched broadcasts that had been altered to highlight certain social problems and downplay others. At the end of the week, watchers of the doctored broadcasts had realigned their views and now believed that the problems stressed by the experimenters were more much important than they had previously imagined.[1]

115

The steady encroachment of the marketing mentality has caused television news to become ever more shallow. Both the volume and the character of broadcast news is in steep decline. In 1976, in one five-day span, ABC, CBS, and NBC evening news broadcasts covered 265 stories, fifteen of which were features; in 1986, a similar study revealed that the number of stories had dropped 20 percent, to 212, while the number of features had nearly doubled to twenty-nine. Was there less news to cover? Not according to any index of newspapers. But television showed fewer hard news stories and more human interest pieces. Coverage of federal domestic policy dropped 37 percent during that decade, while soft stories about people involved in situations "linked to public policy" increased by more than 50 percent.[2] Accordingly, television audiences may be learning more about the poignant effects of government policies than about the policies themselves, with the result that viewers become less able to judge the pertinence or efficacy of those policies.

Television news has certain structural biases that it shares with televised fictional programs. The first is the visual emphasis of the medium. Psychophysiological research has shown that the information we perceive when we see images and hear sounds is not integrated and remembered in the same ways as what we extract from reading. For instance, studies have demonstrated that knowledge derived from newspapers tends to remain more detailed, to stay with us longer, and to be more broadly based than what we obtain from television. In one experiment tied specifically to election material, watchers of television news were able to recognize an image of a newsmaker but were less able than newspaper readers to recall very much about that person and that newsmaker's stances on issues.[3] Television news forms pictures in our head, Anthony R. Pratkanis and Eliot Aronson contend, pictures that "serve as fictions to guide our thoughts and actions; the images serve as primitive social theories—providing us with the 'facts' of the matter, determining which issues are the most pressing, and decreeing the terms in which we think about our social world."[4] For a while, during the ascent of television, newspapers provided a counterbalance, but now telejournalism techniques have been adopted by such large-circulation publications as *USA Today*, the most widely read nonbusiness newspaper.

The second important structural distortion of television news is a tendency to personalize everything, to tie issues and events to specific, readily recognizable individuals—using a version of the Hollywood star system to make us pay attention to a news story. The people whom reporters consider newsworthy come from a rather small universe; this structural bias ensures that alternative views and ideas will seldom receive national attention, even if they might add interest to the public debate. It also ensures that when something goes wrong, telejournalism has a tendency quickly to identify a newsworthy person as the focus of blame—to cite the ineptness of the chief dogcatcher when the problem may be too many stray dogs—rather than work to trace the roots of the problem, say, to a social climate in which too many families were encouraged to own pets.

Telejournalism's third structural bias is a disregard of long-term issues in favor of chasing "breaking" news. For the recent Cairo conference on population and development, a document of more than one hundred pages was produced. It examined the subject from a variety of viewpoints and made many recommendations, but even so careful a program as the *MacNeil–Lehrer News Hour* joined the journalistic crowd and devoted its coverage almost entirely to discussion of the single paragraph in the voluminous document that dealt with "abortion on demand."

Telejournalism's concentration on man-bites-dog stories and ignorance of the intricacies of complex matters focuses news audiences on the present and denies us the context of history. Me-too journalism, in which most reporting organizations follow the same stories in the same ways as their competitors, also contributes to the narrow vein of information and critiques available to the public through the media. Of relevance here is the shallowness of journalistic research in general, which seldom provides a solid basis from which reporters might evaluate the remarks made by politicians. In a study done for the Brookings Institution, reporters from print, radio, and television admitted to Stephen Hess that they used no documents in three-quarters of the stories they filed; they also considered plum assignments those in which they never had to look at documents but could rely on phone calls to sources for information; when any documents were consulted, they were most likely to be from a news organization's own morgue of old news reports, and least likely to consist of weighty basic research papers.[5]

"I used to get memos from the brass about the issues we should be covering," a senior correspondent for a network flagship station told me, "but now the memos remind me to smile more." Local news is the worst offender in erasing the line between entertainment and information. "Happy talk," in which anchorpersons chat amiably with one another in order to make viewers think they are a close-knit team, has been raised to an art and is augmented by an additional encroachment device, sensationalism in all aspects of a news broadcast, from the choice of what to cover to the style in which stories are covered. A 1993 *Washington Post* survey found that tabloid stories, defined as those featuring "crime, sex, disasters, accidents or public fears" about these matters, accounted for between 46 and 74 percent of late evening local news shows in Miami, New York, Chicago, Los Angeles, and Washington, with most of the remaining time taken up by weather and sports. Some stations used dramatizations of crimes to heighten viewership and tried to present such sensationalism as a public service that helps to catch criminals, while others made no bones about their willingness to range quite far from their own viewing area to feature items that arouse prurient interest. The news director of WSVN of Miami aggressively defended his methods and pronounced himself bored with critiques that failed to understand television as "an entertainment business."[6]

For articulate behavior, sensationalism and a tabloid focus are themselves disasters. Such reports tend to feature distraught and tongue-tied victims, inchoate bystanders, and monosyllabic policemen. The focus on sensational events also leads news producers to overlook other sorts of news, especially the sort whose impact may not be so obvious or so pictorial, and which might require valuable air time to elucidate.

"We've all gone Hollywood—we've all succumbed to the Hollywood-ization of the news," the CBS anchorman and evening news managing editor Dan Rather recently announced to a gathering of industry news executives:

> It's the ratings, stupid, don't you know? And they've got us putting more and more fuzz and wuzz on the air, cop-shop stuff, so as to compete not with other news programs but with entertainment programs (including those *posing* as news programs) for dead bodies, mayhem, lurid tales. . . . Hire lookers, not writers. Do powder-puff, not probing interviews. Stay away from controversial subjects. . . . Make nice, not news. . . . We put videotape through a Cuisinart trying to come up with high-speed, MTV-style cross-cuts. And just to cover our assets, we give the best slots to gossip and prurience.[7]

Rather's grasp of the problem is right on target. He also correctly identified two enemies, the fact-based tabloid programs that feature dramatic recreations of crimes and the broadcasts that are no more than public relations for the entertainment business. In terms of the number of their imitators, the most influential current programs are the syndicated broadcasts *Entertainment Tonight* and *America's Most Wanted*. However, Rather's much-discussed speech was at best a modest tongue-lashing in which his own and other reporters' culpability in pandering was left unmentioned and in which the only internal blame was placed on anonymous executives.

The faults lie far deeper, in the structure and practice of television news itself, and are intertwined with the adverse effects that television news has had on our articulate behavior.

About fifteen years ago, a student in my scriptwriting class wrote "Mayor Frank was emitted to the hospital today." Of course she meant "admitted," but the mistake intrigued me. As I learned from questioning her, it was not a spelling error and not a matter of poor hearing. She was literate, a native English speaker who had done well enough on her college placement tests to earn entry into a private university and who, before setting foot in my classroom, had already passed her freshman English courses. We jointly figured out that she had misperceived the word "admitted," having heard it many times from the mouths of television newscasters but evidently having never stumbled across it in print or else having never recognized in the printed word "admitted" the concept she understood as "emitted."

After tripping over many similar misperceptions in the speech and writings of my students, I reached the reluctant[8] conclusion that the majority of Americans are not only getting their news from the broadcasts of the television networks, they also appear to be obtaining from these broadcasts their notions of proper and effective ways to use language. To examine how language usage has changed in the past thirty years in television news, I decided to analyze it in a context that had otherwise maintained considerable stability during the period from 1963 to 1993, the nightly half-hour broadcasts of the *CBS Evening News*, as represented by examples placed into the collection of the Museum of Television and Radio.

The very first half-hour edition of the *CBS Evening News with Walter Cronkite* was broadcast on August 29, 1963, one day after the March on

Washington at which Martin Luther King, Jr., gave his "I have a dream" speech.[9] Prior to that date, the evening news had been fifteen minutes in length; this expanded edition was an experiment. In a newsroom, Cronkite reads directly from paper, and in the field, reporters do the same. There are few filmed action reports; almost no graphics are used; the atmosphere, language, and editorial attitudes are all print-based. The program begins abruptly with Cronkite reading a report of a statement made by France's President Charles de Gaulle to the effect that Vietnam ought to be free from foreign influences; Cronkite interprets this as a surprising and unexpected swipe by de Gaulle at the involvement of the United States in Vietnam.

Marvin Kalb reports from the State Department. He has interviewed a half-dozen people in Washington, but we do not see or hear them as he summarizes their reactions to de Gaulle's statement; Kalb quotes a phrase or two from each of several sources. He uses "elaborate" as a verb, calls de Gaulle a "taboo topic," allows that the French leader has produced "further disarray" and finishes by repeating the title of a song in the musical *The King and I*, "Tis a Puzzlement." In the reports of Cronkite and Kalb, as in Roger Mudd's from Congress, whence he speaks of the ratification of a nuclear test ban treaty, the sentences have dependent clauses and often run to 18–25 words. Each sentence contains such conceptual and abstract words as "unanimous," "reduction," "underdeveloped," and "colonial," and such phrases as "using the Sino-Soviet ideological dispute as a cover." Absolutely no pictures accompany these reports.

The first commercial, for a headache pill, is quite wordy, of about the same density of language as the news reports, a wall-to-wall narration accompanied by a few almost amateurish images. A second commercial, later in the broadcast, also leans heavily for its impact on words appearing on the screen; if you do not follow those words, you do not get the message.

The first true field report comes from a correspondent at Idlewild Airport in New York. He is covering the return to the United States of fifty college students who have gone illegally to Cuba; their passports are being confiscated. We see none of the action, but the reporter joins a pack of others to interview the returning group's spokesman, Philip Luce. Luce admits that "there is a privileged class in Cuba," but says it consists only of students. The CBS reporter immediately asks, "Is there any privilege of free expression?" and the ensuing battle of wits holds the screen for another minute. A second field report features a miner rescued after five days "at the bottom of a potash mine," who truculently says that he should have been dug out "manually," through the debris, instead of having had to wait for an "alternate shaft" to be drilled. His rescuer, also interviewed on site, contends that the rescuers did the best job possible, given the circumstances, and politely refuses to rise to the bait in response to the miner's charges. From Chicago, there is film of a mostly black group, home from the March on Washington, which has had to march again to a newspaper office to protest an editorial about the event. Allied is a film clip of Norman Thomas, the old lion of the Socialist Party, addressing a party gathering and commenting at length on the appropriateness of the tactics of the March as well as those used by some in his audience during a recent sit-in at the office of Robert F. Wagner, Jr., Mayor of New York City. Like marches, sit-ins ought to have definite goals, Thomas says, and he chastises his cubs for not defining theirs well enough in the Mayor's office. To complete a roundup on the subject of integration, in the studio Cronkite weaves together wire service reports of sit-ins and protests in several cities, connecting and contrasting the events verbally, without any visual aids.

The broadcast's most complex word usages are in a report about a "compulsory arbitration law . . . the first ever produced in peacetime." The reporter, Stanley Levy, contends that the railroad unions are worried that "the delicate equilibrium of collective bargaining, imperfect as it is, may have been thrown out of whack," but that "despite the protestations," some good might come out of it. The only gratuitous film and story presented are of a young and previously unknown actress about to play the role of Christine Keeler, a woman at the center of the scandal that had recently brought down a British Cabinet Minister. President John F. Kennedy's name is mentioned only once, in a brief filler announcement that he has gone on vacation in Hyannis, Massachusetts; not even a still photo of the President accompanies the story.

For the broadcast just reviewed and the others detailed below in this chapter, I compared the vocabulary range and word usage with the norms of that time, as displayed in standard use-frequency lists. There are principally two lists. One, compiled at Brown University, is based on a million words taken from a great many samples.[10] The second is that discussed earlier in this book, compiled for the American Heritage dictionary for children. Some of the words used on that premiere broadcast, such as "ideological," "equilibrium," "disarray," and "allegations," occur only two or three times each in the 5 million words scrutinized for the children's literature American Heritage corpus. They are not so "rare" as "protestations," which is not present at all in the AH corpus. However, all these words can be found from dozens to hundreds of times in the adult literature Brown Corpus, an indication that they are regular residents of a grownup's vocabulary.[11] Using these tools, I estimate the working, everyday vocabulary of this pilot Cronkite evening news program—and, by extension, that presumed to be the audience's—at 9,000–10,000 words, a range that might be expected of a well-prepared high school graduate. It is also the range encountered on the front pages of several of the following morning's major city newspapers, such as the Boston *Globe* or the *New York Times*, with which I also compared this broadcast's language usage. The television reporters' sentences are full, sometimes near to bursting from the effort of condensing information. Their sentences are also complete, have dependent clauses, and are highly grammatical; they are often longer than can be uttered with a single breath. This, too, compares well with the Brown Corpus, where the average sentence length of the "Informative Prose" sections was between 18.53 and 24.07 words. Moreover, the interviewees featured on the broadcast, from the rescued miner to the student back from Cuba to Norman Thomas, are all more than reasonably articulate; I suspect that their ability to express themselves is part of why they "made air."

The October 27, 1972, edition of the *CBS Evening News with Walter Cronkite* undoubtedly has a place in the archive because it was the first lengthy broadcast effort to put into perspective the unfolding Watergate scandal.[12] Immediately noticeable are the better graphics and visual aids, the more prominent images, and the presence of more film from various sources.

The Watergate report is teased, and then there are some brief highlights of other matters. Henry R. Kissinger is reported as negotiating with the North Vietnamese, over the objections of the South Vietnamese but with assistance from the Russians; "The strong impression here in Washington is that the Administration will not allow . . ." From Saigon there is film, labeled by a title over the screen as being brought in by satellite, and interpreted for us through such phrases as "Fact is, agreement is being imposed on Thieu." That these reports have been mostly grammatical and filled with complete sentences is made apparent only by contrast with the one filed by reporter Dan Rather. Standing in front of the fence around the White House, Rather jars the viewer by speaking in headlines: "Nine vetoes today, more promised tomorrow," he begins. His report about President Nixon's actions continues on in similar shorthand English; generic footage of Washington serves as background for a graphic list of the subjects of the vetoed bills. Beyond saying that Nixon has called the bills "budget-busters," Rather provides no analysis of the vetoes.

The commercials are more visual than those of 1963. They feature a good deal of movement, some moderately compelling imagery, and narrative drive, and less dense wording.

For the Watergate report, Cronkite stands in front of a display and emphasizes that what comes next will isolate and separately label fact, connections, allegations, and "conjecture." Film of the burglars being taken out of the paddy wagon is stopped at points to identify the participants, and these visual images are later graphically linked to others by lines that stand out against a black background. "The episodes grew steadily more complex." Daniel Schorr says, "We are asked to believe that . . ." and uses the words "illicit" and "conjecture," while other reporters employ such sentence formations as "There have been so far neither evidence nor allegations. . . ." These formations require an audience attuned to the niceties of written, composed English, an audience that can wait until the tenth or twelfth word in a sentence makes clear the intent of the earlier ones. There are interviews with a wiretapper, Alfred Baldwin, and with a man who was asked to commit dirty tricks by Donald Segretti—whose own name, we are told twice, is the Italian word for secret. In explaining their actions the interviewees speak in long sentences, mostly without hems and haws.

When the Watergate report is over, a truncated news of the day is resumed. I was struck by the absence of footage from the campaign trail or even mention of the Democratic candidate, George McGovern, since the election was only a few days in the future. Film accompanies nearly every report, and screen time is lavished on the closing one, the funeral of Jackie Robinson, an emotional milestone for the people of Harlem, which is well filmed and described in telling detail by Charles Osgood, who finishes by quoting an entire stanza from A. E. Housman's "To an Athlete Dying

Young," a poem he does not name, presumably because the audience would already know its title.

Comparing this broadcast with the word-frequency references, I find the vocabulary level slipping, except in the long Watergate report, which had clearly been in preparation for some time and showed evidence of a good deal of thought and revision in the writing. Throughout the program there is a diminution of verbal nuance, flair, and wit, and not simply because the subject of Watergate is too serious for invention. The words spoken are those that, in general, are among the more frequently used words of the Brown Corpus, the few exceptions being such words as "allegations" and "conjecture." In fact, most of the words are in the ballpark of the first thousand or so lemmas that account for three-quarters of the American Heritage Corpus. Complexity of sentence construction is also vanishing. Most of the sentences are one breath long, no more than fifteen to eighteen words, which for the most part precludes the use of dependent clauses or of the passive voice. In terms of sentence length, the broadcast sentences are coming less to resemble the Brown Corpus's "Informative Prose" and more to mimic the shorter and less complex "Imaginative Prose." Interviewees on the broadcast still speak at some length; their vocabularies are substantial and appropriate to the descriptive tasks.

The *CBS Evening News with Walter Cronkite* of March 6, 1981, was the last for which Cronkite served as anchor.[13] The set has been cleared of clutter and activity, and the backgrounds are single-colored for use in conjunction with the Chromakey, a device for inserting graphic material into a quadrant of the screen. The headline is the appearance of President Ronald Reagan in the White House briefing room for a press conference, one of the first held in his administration. Commentary focuses on the President's having picked the questioners ahead of time, by lottery. Reagan holds the screen, and his jokes are featured as prominently as his direct answers to questions about abortion rights. In the next report there is a quote from Labor Secretary Raymond Donovan and some comment on government statistics showing that there has been "improvement in the economy, but the changes were too slight to cause much optimism." In a third segment, "combat" is used as a verb, but otherwise the language is not memorable.

The commercials are more jazzy, with striking visual images, such as a large open desert area in which gasoline cans are lined up like dominos to be knocked over, to emphasize the good mileage obtained from the advertised car. The few words, uttered by a man carrying a can to insert into the line, support the image.

After the commercial, there are more excerpts from the press conference, centering on whether troops are being sent to El Salvador to fight or for some other purpose. "To stop destabilizing forces," Reagan says, and adds that their mission is no different from that of the troops previously dispatched there by President Carter. No one asks Reagan to define who or what he means by destabilizing forces. The President cites preelection fears that he would be "trigger-happy" and therefore dangerous in office, and quips, "I've been here more than six weeks and I haven't fired a shot." Though there is more to discuss on this complex topic, CBS uses the one-liner in the way that the President has perhaps intended, as a humorous end to discussion and as a lead-in to the next commercial.

Film and tape accompany and more obviously define three-quarters of the stories. Item: a convicted murderer who is scheduled to die soon, but whose execution is being contested by the ACLU, over the murderer's objections. "They ought to kill me while they've got the chance," the murderer says in a clip. That is followed by an ACLU representative objecting on camera to "official, ceremonious homicide." The murderer then repeats his plaint in virtually the same words he used earlier, and the story closes with the information that the ACLU has now given up its fight because it has no legal standing in the case. Next item: film of a California man just released from prison; wrongly convicted, he spent nine years behind bars before the same prosecutor who put him away found and presented evidence to overturn the conviction. Both reports are man-bites-dog stories, of interest mainly because of their novelty.

The most complex story of the day is about unusual activity recorded several months ago by a satellite off the coast of South Africa and suspected then as reflecting an explosion of a nuclear device. U.S. officials now contend the activity resulted from an anomaly in the recording device, possibly caused by a stray meteorite having struck the satellite. The viewer has to work hard to figure out that because the new Administration's views about South Africa are different from those of the Carter Administration, the interpretation of the satellite data may have been politically altered. The main feature of the report is the grilling of a government scientist who has to defend the far-fetched official explanation. This reduction-to-confrontation saps the story of context and displaces sorely needed additional analysis.

Cronkite closes with a finely worded commentary to the effect that too much has been made out of an ordinary passing of the baton, and that in the near future he will return to the air with documentaries.

The vocabulary of the broadcast seems further diminished, though some subtleties of wording are still present. I estimate the range as approximately 7,500 words, a smaller range than one encounters in reading the front pages of the following morning's major newspapers. "Forthcoming" is used to mean "readily available," rather than "about to appear," the more accepted and less archaic definition. Most of the stories feature simple declarative sentences; no more passive voice, "it has been learned" or other formal scaffolding. The compilers of the Brown Corpus have pointed out that the passive voice is harder to process semantically than the active voice, in which the noun and verb are usually close together.[14] Perhaps CBS News has adopted simpler usage in order to assist the audience's semantic processing. Occasional sentences still reflect a reporter's unwillingness to use small words when more descriptive larger ones are available: the Solidarity union "reacted defiantly to Soviet pressure that the labor rebellion be curtailed." Such words as "defiantly" and "curtailed" are not high up on the frequency-of-use lists, though they clearly fall within the category of vocabulary necessary for adult comprehension. The participants in the dramas of the day have been given more air time, while less has been reserved for journalistic explanation and evaluation of the events and the players. Many of the interviewees, with the exception of the jailed men, are more articulate than the reporters are permitted to be.

The *CBS Evening News with Dan Rather*, the edition of November 9, 1989, is in the archive, along with others from that month, which all deal with the collapse of Communism.[15] "The Berlin Wall is still standing, but it doesn't stand for much," is Rather's opening comment, over a photo of the Wall. This teaser is followed by the screen-filling animated logo. Since the Berlin Wall will forever stand for many things, among them the nature and proclivities of Communism, the frustrations of the Cold War, and the attempts of every tyrant in history to keep out the barbarians while fencing in his people, Rather's double-meaning headline is forced and off the mark. We are supposed to recognize it, however, as wit.

The language used throughout the broadcast echoes this opening salvo. "This may be the most important, most significant action yet" is the tenor of many of the lead-ins. There is a lot of telling you what we're going to tell you, and frequent instructing of the audience to be on the lookout for irony and to be impressed with the historic nature of the news and the report. The exuberant Rather employs other off-the-mark metaphors, such as "racing to stay ahead of the curve of history." He stands, not sits, in a sleekly modern set. At a map of middle Europe he uses his hands to point out how in past weeks East German refugees have had to detour through other countries in order to flee to the West. He is scriptless; there is no pretense at being tied to paper. When he says that the newly installed East German government has declared its nation's border open as of tomorrow morning, a line snakes down that border on the map, a graphic device that moves, even if it does not quite illustrate that the border will open.

There is videotape of the East German government voting to open the border and of the Bonn parliament's response to that action, in which the members spontaneously rise to sing the national anthem. Alan Pizzey, who has narrated these tapes, appears on a huge screen in the studio for cross-talk with Rather. The anchorman asks short and pithy questions: "Does this mean there's going to be an immediate mass exodus?" and, "Is re-unification closer?" Pizzey cannot offer much in response, though he tries; as both men must know, these questions are currently unanswerable; moreover, what can be hazarded the audience already knows from having scrutinized the reports just presented.

President George Bush's response, Rather says, is "cautious and sub-dued . . . low-keyed." To tell us "what's behind it," Lesley Stahl is summoned, and she repeats that the president is "low-keyed." Bush is shown at his desk in the Oval Office, flanked by James Baker, John Sununu, and other aides, and caught with his rhetorical pants down. His demeanor shouts that he wants to say very little, but he is prodded by re-porters into a bumbling reaction, "I'm not going to hypothecate that it may—Anything [that] goes too fast . . ."

Rather's pronouncement that for all intents and purposes "the Berlin Wall is obsolete tonight" leads into a retrospective that includes clips of John Kennedy's "Ich bin ein Berliner," Ronald Reagan's "Mr. Gorbachev, tear down this wall," footage of the Wall being built, and ten seconds of

Ted Sorenson's remembrance of the crisis that caused it to be built, then works around to the conclusion that "the system that held it in place has collapsed."

"No one is really sure of the consequences," we are told as prelude to ten-second reactions from Senators Bob Dole and Richard Lugar, both labeled with titles over the lower third of the screen that barely have time to register on the brain if one is also trying to pay attention to what the man on screen is saying. Next come juxtaposed eight-second clips of Secretary of State James Baker and a Soviet spokesman, Gennadi Gerasimov, who say virtually the same thing in the same words and, in case we did not understand the parallel, commentary reiterating that this is what they have done. "Neither superpower has faced the implications," we are informed; yet the very opposite notion, that the United States has given thought to the implications, can be deduced from the report of David Martin at the Pentagon, who relays Secretary of Defense Dick Cheney's statement that the NATO alliance will remain intact even though there is a lessened threat of war in Germany.

In the studio, Rather stands at a bar, leans forward on his elbows, and questions two experts opposite him about the end of the Cold War. "Could serious reform in East Germany keep people there?" and "Could this be a part of Gorbachev's plan?" and "What about the reunification of Germany?" These questions, too, cannot be properly answered at this moment in time. Brief, thoughtful responses suggest that there may be nothing left in East Germany for West Germany to reunite with and that events are beyond anyone's control, especially Gorbachev's.

The commercials are full of visual tricks. Each has multiple images that make for a continually busy screen.

"An alarming report today on the high cost of living longer" is the phrase used to introduce not a story about dollars and cents but a report about Alzheimer's disease, which turns out to be more widespread than previously assumed. The tape and commentary from the field constitute very good reportage, but there is very little attempt to interpret the findings or their implications; today, only the Berlin Wall merits analysis. Dan Rather closes the broadcast with a reminder to join him later in the evening for *48 Hours*, whose subject will be "Sex and Teenagers."

Except for such totemic words as "reunification," which had entered common parlance in the previous few weeks, the vocabulary is once more diminished. There is hardly a word in the broadcast that could not be found listed in the first few thousand of the American Heritage corpus. That is, a junior high student would be able to get virtually all there was to get out of this broadcast. Maybe the student would stumble over President Bush's "hypothecate," but not over the words used by any of the reporters. The range, estimated by the same methods used above, is about 6,000 words. Abstract words are seldom used; short and descriptive phrases predominate. Sentence length remains the same; otherwise we would be in the realm of grade school. However, sentence structure has been trimmed, almost cut to the quick. The style seems short and sweet but has actually become so simplistic as sometimes to make commentary or introductions misleading, as in Rather's preface to the report on Alzheimer's. CBS News seems to be slipping out of the realm of the written language, where a knowledge of about 8,000 words is required to understand an article in a newspaper, and to be entering the domain of the spoken word, a realm in which one word-frequency list compiler contends that 848 words account for 90 percent of all usage.[16] The broadcast piles headline upon headline, states and restates easily understood ideas, and features a plethora of colloquial phrases that are not always apt. Correspondents such as Stahl, Martin, and Pizzey, who are capable of sustained reflection and analysis, have no opportunities to apply those journalistic tools, because they are serving principally as funnels for quotes from officials. Baker and Lugar, men known to be erudite and articulate, do not have much air time in which to complete their thoughts, while the President is caught in the process of preparing his. Informed speculation about the future is limited to twenty seconds each per in-studio expert.

The November 15, 1993, edition of the *CBS Evening News with Dan Rather and Connie Chung* (which the author viewed at home) has as its lead the news that thousands of American and South Korean troops are "massing near the North Korean border" for an annual military exercise. "An exclusive report from the front lines" is promised. The tone is alarmist. Are we again at war? David Martin narrates film and tape of a mock attack "played out against a backdrop of the looming confrontation over North Korea's suspected nuclear weapons program." Martin insists that tensions between North Korea and the United States have "never been higher." Lest we dismiss this as hyperbole, Representative Gary Ackerman is brought on to advise that North Korea, which he visited last week, "has no touch with reality." This is balanced by the contention of an academic expert that the "nuclear issue" is being "used as a battering ram, if you will, against the United States' closed-door policy on investment [in North Korea] and on trade and aid." This tension-lowering notion is ignored during the remainder of Martin's report, which stresses potential confrontation in such terms as "dangerous game . . . if either side miscalculates . . . have to fight the final battle."

"Another final battle," Connie Chung announces, is the struggle to collect votes for and against NAFTA, the North American Free Trade Agreement. Before reports of this combat zone, we are given the results of a poll CBS has just commissioned; its findings show some rise in sentiment for the agreement, and, after a recent "debate," a drop in the popularity of H. Ross Perot. "But Perot was at it again today," Chung tells us in a preface to tape of a press conference near the Capitol. "Thirty pieces of silver was peanuts last night," the former presidential candidate charges, referring to a dinner at which President Bill Clinton wooed members of the House; "but even though Judas was in the room, they didn't get a single vote at the Last Supper." Perot's monumental rudeness in equating the president of the United States with Judas Iscariot (and himself, by inference, with Jesus Christ) draws no comment from CBS. In the following report, five or six Congressmen receive about five seconds apiece to state their "positions" and "reasons" for or against the bill. Most appear in tape clips that are the fruit of press conferences or photo opportunity sessions. Bob Schieffer does comment about the alliances among the representatives, but only to offer a safe, mildly cynical observation about politics making strange bedfellows.

"Homes are more affordable now than they have been in twenty years," Dan Rather says. He probably means that mortgage rates are low and many buyers are taking advantage of them. CBS does not mention that the "more affordable" conclusion flies in the face of well-known statistics that the average dollar price of a home and its price in relation to family income have risen dramatically in the past two decades.

Bob Simon reports about a Mideast "peace process under violent attack from extremists on both sides." There are images of rock-throwers, funerals, car windows being smashed right under the lens of the camera, settler tents afire, a placard with a photo altered to show Yitzak Rabin in an Arafat-like headdress, and an Israeli soldier on an ambulance gurney.

"A soldier on routine foot patrol gets a knife in the back, and another wound is dealt to the peace process." As with nearly all the metaphors and analogies on this broadcast, this one is askew and of questionable accuracy, but it *is* catchy.

In an effective use of contrasting visuals and supporting narration, Cuban defectors who flew to Florida in a crop duster and to whom asylum will be granted are juxtaposed with a group of Haitians who swam ashore near Miami and who are likely to be deported. Over tape of another gurney with a dead body, Rather touts a forthcoming segment, "A warning from the President: 'Fight crime now, or pay a steep price later.'"

After the commercial, Connie Chung announces a new interest in fighting crime "from the President on down, even as the body count continues to rise." Down, up—I get it. We see more gurneys with bodies. Chung continues to highlight the President's concern with crime as we see Clinton arriving to speak at an African-American Methodist church. "This past weekend," says Chung, "he warned that his ambitious domestic programs won't succeed if America's social fabric continues to unravel." The President at the podium: "Unless we deal with the ravages of crime and drugs and violence," he says, none of the things that society seeks to do can be accomplished. Chung's narration next tells us that the President argued that if Martin Luther King, Jr., could see the violent world of today's urban teens, he might think his fight had been in vain. Now the President says this in his own words: "The freedom to die before you're a teenager is not the freedom Martin Luther King fought and died for. . . . How would we explain to him all these kids getting killed and killing each other?" Then the images change to those of a conference of mayors and police chiefs in Chicago, and CBS's crime theme continues.

As was later made clear by many observers, what CBS did not tell us about the President's speech or let us hear from his lips was far more significant than what was excerpted from that speech or commented upon by Chung. The President was speaking from the pulpit in Memphis where King spoke the night before he was assassinated, and in the speech he took the role of King and imagined what King might have said today: "I did not live and die to see the American family destroyed. . . . I fought to stop white people from being so filled with hate that they would wreak violence on black people. . . . I fought for freedom, but not for the freedom of people to kill each other with reckless abandonment, not for the freedom of children to have children and the fathers of the children to walk away from them and abandon them, as if they don't amount to anything." Many major newspapers ran articles in the days following the speech, arguing that it was, as E. J. Dionne, Jr., characterized it in the *Washington Post*, "the most important of [Clinton's] presidency," one whose "straightforward" message was that the "United States has reached an entirely new turn in the struggle for racial equality, and it's time to be honest about both the gains we've made and the huge problems we face." The speech was an attempt to redirect the national debate on the issue of crime, from an emphasis on law-and-order solutions to an emphasis on the moral necessity of a society to face what Clinton dubbed "a crisis of the spirit," and to cleanse its own house. A few days after this broadcast, Anthony Lewis in the *New York Times* went so far as to congratulate the President for this "triumph" achieved by "passionate voice," in which Clinton broke out of "the expected and the calculated" mold of political speeches and spoke "as if from inside himself, responding in emotional terms" to today's wrongs, which, many people contend, is the thing above all else that Americans desire and need a President to do.[17] CBS did not quote *any* of the lines cited in this paragraph; instead, it excerpted the President's discourse in a way that made Clinton appear to echo CBS's own predilection for alliterative wisecracks; CBS reformulated and repackaged Clinton's entire appearance in Memphis to fit the Procrustean bed of its own clustering of stories.

Chung next tells us about the President's plans to fight crime, which will stress "personal responsibility, intact families, and jobs"—all themes struck in the speech, but not heard in the excerpts CBS chose—and contrasts Clinton's wish list with a "Senate that is pushing legislation that is top-heavy with punishment." This introduction, too, is not quite accurate, since the President is known to favor passage of the Senate bill. That bill and the previously passed House bills differ, the reporter Linda Douglas informs us, so if the Senate's is passed, there will have to be a compromise made. "The mood of the public is fierce, and Congress may not be allowed to go home for the holidays until it has agreed on crime-fighting legislation." One more catchy button line that is not quite correct, since public pressure has seldom kept Congress in session.

"The story that launched three prime-time television movies came to a real-life conclusion today," Connie Chung announces, though the sentencing of Joey Buttafuoco is far from the end of the sordid Amy Fisher affair.

"Pop star Michael Jackson has popped out of public view," we also learn. Dan Rather contributes a well-worded short paragraph about a new Supreme Court ruling on abortion. More air time is devoted to a CBS poll showing that nine out of ten people believe Lee Harvey Oswald did not act alone in killing John F. Kennedy; at week's end, CBS will broadcast a new documentary on the subject, Rather tells us. He also reports that this high percentage of skeptics represents a rise from past polls but does not mention that it may be attributable to the influence of Oliver Stone's revisionist movie, roundly criticized for its jumbling of fact and fiction. There is a long segment on the neo-Nazi movement in Germany, in which the CBS camera crew travels with a group as they break laws and evade the police, then interviews their spokesmen, who are articulate in English.

The daily "Eye on America" segment questions the safety of the chicken we eat; "the answer could very well be in your hands," Rather says. Frank Currier informs us that we are eating more chicken these days but "the dark side to this white meat revolution is food poisoning." As the report progresses, we understand in retrospect Rather's double meaning: If you touch uncooked chicken and get salmonella on your hands, then put your fingers in your mouth—as one interviewee unwittingly did, to lick off the barbecue sauce—you may get sick. Visual images for this segment rely heavily on quick, repeated cuts, of a cleaver smashing a barbecued chicken into pieces, and slow motion of uncooked chickens flying off a processing line. A critic of government inaction says, "You shouldn't have to treat a product inspected for wholesomeness like a toxic substance in your kitchen." There is good information for the audience on the need to turn chicken in a microwave during the cooking in order to prevent salmonella from surviving. A second part of the report, about the sacking of poultry processing line inspectors who are too tough, is promised for tomorrow.

In this last broadcast of our series, several previously latent trends have become startlingly overt, and each of them has an impact on the articulateness level of the broadcast. Only reports with film or tape attached are now worthy of more than a few seconds of air time. Narration continually tells us what we are about to see and hear, then tells us afterward what we have heard and seen, as though we cannot be trusted to figure it out for ourselves. Reportorial reaching for alliterative or cute phrases, for hackneyed contrasts, for analogies or metaphors where none are required and their presence may confuse the listener, has become rampant. Phrase-slinging has overwhelmed and replaced analysis and insight. For that matter, there has been a curious flowing together of the language of the reporters and that of the people who are filmed or taped: The desire (or need) to utter quotable statements has infected all the correspondents and seems now also to drive the discourse of interviewees, speakers at press conferences, and the President. All of them have learned it is such sound bites that are considered worthy of inclusion on evening news broadcasts. Otherwise, words do not matter much; they are used only in support of the more powerful communicator, images.

The vocabulary displayed in this broadcast has degraded only slightly from that of the 1989 example; CBS News is still around the seventh-grade level. With a few exceptions, all the words used on the broadcast can be found in the top fifth of the frequently used list in the American Heritage corpus compiled from children's literature. And broadcasts cannot go much lower in average sentence length than the twelve-to-fifteen word sentences typical of this broadcast, or else the correspondents will be speaking solely in headlines. My guess, and I must emphasize that this is conjecture, is that the sentences are coming more to resemble those used in what the Brown Corpus labels "Imaginative Prose," characteristic of fiction, than those of the "Informative Prose" characteristic of newspaper and magazine articles and nonfiction books. I believe this to be a consequence of a misperception on the part of media executives and reporters that the news is now required to compete with fictional programs and that news stories must be conceived as dramatic confrontations between clashing combatants, which mandates the use of language more appropriate to fiction. The language of the broadcast is tending toward complete union with the few thousand words that we utter in our everyday conversation. It refuses to consider as its base the much larger vocabulary of the written language—even of that vocabulary constituted by a dictionary recommended for use by grade-school students. Whereas the first Cronkite news of 1963 was clearly based in full literacy, this 1993 broadcast exists in rhetorical limbo, between the written language and the spoken language, between the literate-based language and the language of secondary orality. As a model for, and a great influence on, the language that Americans speak, it has become a reflection of the not-very-good, where it was once a reflection of the best.

* * *

On an Oprah Winfrey broadcast, when a young doctor confessed that he was something of a romantic, he reportedly received 40,000 letters from women wishing to share his life. While not every talk program can generate that amount of attention, collectively talk shows have an enormous audience, as many as 80 million viewers daily, and as the doctor's story makes clear, it is an audience that pays close attention to what is being said on the programs. To learn more about how language is being modeled for us on talk shows, on November 9, 1993, I spent the day watching and listening to snippets of eight mainstream syndicated talk shows.

At nine in the morning in New York, while NBC and some other channels carry game shows and cartoons, and while Mr. Rogers holds forth on public television, there are three talk shows in head-to-head competition: Jane Whitney on CBS, Montel Williams on the Fox network, and Regis Philbin and Kathie Lee Gifford on ABC.

Jane Whitney features a man whose problem is that he has two girlfriends. Tina and Jim are the guests in the first segment. She is angry about the situation, while he seems as contented as the cat who swallowed the cream. We later learn that Jim called the program and offered to appear with his two girlfriends, ostensibly to resolve their predicament. Jane Whitney's questioning demonstrates that she knows the terms "psychobabble," "avoiding commitment," "relationship," and "monogamous," but most of her queries are monosyllabic: "Some people, like, sleep with only one person at a time."

Jim's two lovers have never met. Now, to applause, the second young woman emerges from behind a curtain, and then, under Jane's questioning, the two comment on how they are and are not alike.

JANE: Do you feel you have anything in common with her?
SECOND: Him.
TINA: How do you know he loves you? He loves me!
JANE: You're playing, like, seniority here. Like, bookends.

Montel Williams's guests are six couples made up of older women and younger men. Each woman introduces her young man, using such terms as "hunk," "sex appeal," and "perfect specimen of humanity," and making sure to announce his birth date, for the men are a decade or two younger than the women. The couples behave as though they are in the first flushes of affairs. We learn that the Montel Williams show arranged and taped a party at which these people were first introduced to one another, in exchange for promises to appear on the program. The basic subject of the program is sex. Queried by the host, one young man speaks of "not having to work for it" and another confides about older women, "they tell you what they want," which prompts an admission from one that "we want a little pleasure for ourselves." Titles over the screen inform us that "JOHN/ Likes women of all ages" and "NICK/ Loves older women." The snickering quotient of the program is high. At the transition to commercials, footage of the mixer party is followed by a snippet from tomorrow's show, "Two sisters, one man. . . . You'd be surprised at how often this happens." At least one set of sisters are twins. During a later segment of the broadcast, a ponytailed male therapist comments on the couples, using such phrases as "comfort . . . not expected to last . . . emotional ties are suspended." The therapist is then questioned by the panel, which induces Montel to tell about his own experiences with older women. A billboard asks us at home, "Are You a Mom Who Wishes Her Son Would Stop Dating Tramps?" Those who can answer "yes" are to call the show.

"Born to Be Unfaithful," Jane Whitney's next program, will feature people who have been unfaithful and are the offspring of unfaithful parents. The subject after that is "Mothers who allow their teenage daughters to have sex in the house"; on videotape, one such mother says she prefers her daughter and the daughter's boyfriend to have sex at home "where I know that they're safe."

Barbara Walters visits Regis and Kathie Lee to impart backstage chatter about the celebrities she has interviewed for her latest special, to be broadcast that evening. In a clip, Barbara tries to learn from Julia Roberts whether the movie star thinks her husband of a few months is ugly or just differently handsome. Julia opts for handsome. In the studio Barbara and Kathie Lee brush cheeks and make hand motions to convey that they must phone one another for a lunch date very soon.

Fred Rogers visits a pretzel bakery. In an apron and baker's hat, he observes the various processes of the assembly line and kneads some dough with his own hands. His conversation with the bakers, aimed at an audience of preschool children, employs almost as large a vocabulary as that of the nine o'clock talk shows.

Not yet ready to make conclusions from such a small sample, later that day I watch segments of five more talk shows: Joan Rivers on CBS and, on NBC, Jerry Springer, Maury Povich, Sally Jessy Raphael, and Phil Donahue.

"How going back to the trauma of birth will help you clear up present problems" is the way Joan Rivers touts the subject of her program, but before discussing that she chats with a gossip columnist about the recent birth of Marla Maples's child, in which "aroma therapy" was used, and welcomes a pair of married guests to talk about "past-life therapy." The couple maintains that they were actually married in a previous life. The wife says that through reliving and understanding an incident in Roman times, she has been cured:

GUEST: All that anger drained away. . . . My heart got tender. I got compassionate.
JOAN: All this is one session?

A billboard advertises a 900 number for the home audience to call. The charge is 95 cents per minute to obtain Joan's personal schedule or information on future programs or to tell your own story in the hope of becoming a future guest. Then we are finally introduced to a female "prenatal psychologist." To investigate "early traumas . . . impressed on the psyche," this woman helps patients to go back to the moment of birth, even to the moment of conception. She has brought along some patients, whom Joan Rivers introduces: "My next guests have all been reborn, not through religion." These guests include another ponytailed male psychologist, who has been rescued by regression therapy from suicidal impulses, and a mother-and-daughter pair, similarly rescued from allergies. We shortly see a videotape of a volunteer who has gone through the therapy backstage. After the tape is shown, the volunteer comes onto the set and comments on reliving the attempt to get out of the birth canal: "I was engaged in some sort of battle."

From Boston, Jerry Springer features several trios, each consisting of a grandmother, her teenage daughter, and the daughter's infant. The infants have been born out of wedlock, one to a girl who became pregnant at twelve, the others to girls who were thirteen and fourteen. The teenagers had all considered abortion but had decided against it. Jerry asks about birth control. One new mother says, "He figured that if he pulled out, I couldn't get pregnant." A new grandmother allows that in retrospect she does "feel guilty" at not having given her daughter birth control instruction. "At thirteen, I didn't think she was going to be—you know—actively having sex with her boyfriend," who was nineteen; "I was in denial." Jerry Springer nods, and in general his treatment of an important subject, the epidemic of teenage pregnancies, is even-handed. He questions the women sympathetically and with dignity, although he never refers to them by their names but says "Mom" and "Grandmom." He asks a woman in the latter category if the sensation of becoming a grandmother could have been a proud one, given the circumstances. She says, "I don't know; it's like, I was in the delivery room with her, and it's like—'Memories.'" Audience members express their belief that the fathers should be arraigned on charges of statutory rape, but the new mothers and grandmothers all agree that would not help anyone. A 900 number is provided so that the audience at home can respond to Jerry's billboarded query, "Are you now or have you ever been in an unusual relationship?"

Maury Povich has gone to Texas for "Return to Waco: Answers in the Ashes." In front of an audience of former cult members and Waco residents, Povich questions Mark Breault, who left the Branch Davidians in 1989; Breault's complaints to the authorities have been blamed by some survivors for instigating the raids. One such survivor charges from the audience that Breault is personally responsible for the deaths that ensued. Breault says he told the authorities that David Koresh was abusing children and relates here that Koresh instructed mothers to obtain larger sanitary napkins for their daughters and to use them to enlarge the girls' vaginal canals so he could penetrate them. The story is hotly contested.

The government's lead pathologist then summarizes his team's findings about the thirty-two people who died in the bunker. In the most literate language I have heard all day, language that is compassionate, direct, and precise, he details the manner and cause of death: So many had gunshot wounds, so many died of asphyxiation; a gunshot wound in the mouth may have been self-inflicted, but a wound in the back of the head almost certainly was not. His findings, being made public for the first time, devastate the people in the audience and on the set whose relatives died in that bunker—as we at home are forced to learn because the cameras focus on their faces so that we become privy to their emotions. While the pathologist tells his story, Maury Povich approaches one panel member whose face fills the screen and asks, "Is this what you think, Stan, happened to your family?"

"Could your sex life use a pick-me-up?" asks the announcer of the Phil Donahue show. Then voice and tape display aphrodisiacs, love potions, and an acupuncturist at work, and a panelist comments that "I'm getting turned on just by watching."

That, of course, is just what was intended.

Sally Jessy Raphael's program on November 9, 1993, deals with two 1986 cyanide poisoning deaths in the Seattle area, for which the wife of one of the victims was convicted and imprisoned. Of all the programs of this day, it is the worst exemplar in terms of use of language. First, Sally encapsulates the story for us in emotional kindergarten language: "Some family members say Stella was railroaded. 'She's innocent. Poor Stella.' Some say her daughter Cynthia was really the mastermind behind the deaths." A journalist has written a book about the case. He has corralled the guest panelists, but during the course of the program he must frequently interpret and augment what these guests say, for the guests prove remarkably unable to present their thoughts coherently or even clothed in words that aptly convey their meaning.

STELLA'S NIECE: I didn't think that—there wasn't enough problems that would institute her to kill my uncle . . .

STELLA'S FRIEND: She was somebody that would've taken a gun and shot him point-blank, instead of being sneaky and committed murder in the way that she was convicted.

When one guest is entirely unable to convey her meaning, Sally is forced to correct her in order that the audience can understand the story:

FORMER HOUSEMATE: She used me as a scapegoat.

SALLY: As a screen.

AUDIENCE MEMBER: Maybe Cynthia was child-abused.

As with my student's use of "emitted" for "admitted," these poor grammatical, vocabulary and word-usages are evidence of the sort of misperception of language that can only come from learning language in a secondarily oral way. Pop psychology terms aside, the discourse of the moderators, the guests, the experts, and most of the studio audience members of all these programs mixes grade-school vocabulary and grammar with a leavening of naughty language. Granted, there is no pretense of trying to be articulate, but neither are there many accidental instances of felicitous phrasing. Vocabulary levels are depressingly low, more in line with the spoken-word corpus than might be presumed, since parts of the programs are scripted, and since the guests and stars of these programs are not speaking in private but in rather public circumstances, in front of viewing audiences numbered in the tens of millions.

Talk show language has become almost completely detached from the literate base of English. It is as though the program-makers have concluded that literate English has nothing to do with the emotive, real-life concerns of human beings, and therefore cannot be used to describe or analyze them. As a result, talk shows exist in the realm of vocabularies limited to the few hundred most commonly used words in the spoken language, augmented by a few terms pirated from the sublanguage of therapy. To talk of "Mothers who allow their teenage daughters to have sex in the house," or to inquire "Are You a Mom Who Wishes Her Son Would Stop Dating Tramps?" is to speak down to the audience, not even to address the audience on its own level. These lines employ a vocabulary not much beyond that of a nine- or ten-year-old; the facts show that the daytime viewing audience is chronologically older and better educated than that. Most of these programs are broadcast during hours when children are in school, and as for the educational level of the watchers, the statistics are that in this country three-quarters of people twenty-five and older have completed high school. But the programming elites seem to have nothing but contempt for their audiences composed of average Americans—for "the people we fly over," as one executive called them. Rather, the programmers embrace the fuzzy McLuhanesque belief that a world dominated by new electronic media will wholeheartedly share tribal emotions.

Walter Ong asserts that the culture of secondary orality may mean a return to the primacy of the unconscious for those within it.[18] That culture's gestation period is being shortened by the practices of today's news programs and talk shows, which encourage the audience to acquire information principally through images, and through a lexicon that mimics the oral rather than the literate language. The limited vocabulary, constrained syntax, unknowing or deliberate misuses of language, affectation of minor wit, constant reference to base emotions, and chronic citation of pop cultural icons in attempts to bond with the audience—these characteristic elements of news and talk programs constitute an enfeebled discourse.

The antidote is well known, since most of the people who create news programs and talk shows are themselves literate and fully capable of using the literate-based language. That antidote is to use the power of words to haul these programs back up to a literate level they once attained. Purveyors of talk shows currently reject such a goal as not commensurate with their objective of gaining the largest audience. However, there is no evidence of which I am aware that demonstrates any inverse relationship between the shows' popularity and the vocabulary and articulateness levels of talk show hosts and hostesses (and that of their carefully screened guests). Precisely the opposite may be true: Articulate behavior is part of the hosts' and hostesses' attractiveness. Phil Donahue and Oprah Winfrey are articulate as well as charismatic people. Rush Limbaugh's ability to deflate liberal icons and to create telling puns—"femi-nazis" for strident feminists—have attracted him a wide following. All three, and many others among the talk-show stars, possess good vocabularies, but they have yet to employ them to best use. All too often, they reach for the simple instead of using their tremendous abilities to make complicated matters exciting and understandable. Given these stars' large talents and capacities to enthrall, audiences would undoubtedly follow them up the scale of literacy as gladly (and in just as large numbers) as they have followed them down the scale.

As for news broadcasts, the transformation could be even simpler. News broadcasts need to take a pledge to not only convey information but to set aside time in the broadcast to have that information illuminated by the minds and vocabularies of the reporters. Permit reporters once again to do the tasks of synthesis and analysis of information, as well as the job of being on the spot to collect it. Utilize television's fabulous educative ability. Employ vocabularies that may once in a while send an audience member scurrying to a dictionary—or, better yet, set a goal of encouraging the audience to incorporate interesting words into their own vocabularies. During the Gulf War, millions of Americans learned a new word when Peter Jennings of ABC News spoke of oil as a "fungible" commodity, which he explained meant that a unit of it from one source was essentially the same as a unit of it from another source. Network news divisions could improve the articulateness levels of their viewers by raising the vocabulary and sentence-structure levels of their own broadcasts and by taking the pledge to use "fungible" and other such marvelous if unfamiliar words when they are clearly appropriate. How about one new word a day? Such a practice would be unlikely to provoke viewers to turn away from their favorite newscasters and to the competition.

We need for our broadcasters once again to champion and employ the power of words as well as the power of images. This is not only in the public interest, but in their own. Informative broadcasting relies, in the end, on an audience that places some premium on the value of ideas. If its discourse is increasingly impoverished, then the audience will retreat from information-based programs into the wholly pictorial realm of video games and interactive fictional programming, where the audience has the illusion of deciding what happens. Then there will be no more market for television news or talk shows. What the informative shows are doing by embracing images and diminished language is the equivalent of a restaurant slowly poisoning all of its customers.

A PAUSE FOR REFLECTION: WHAT IS BEING LOST

*C*ertain qualities are being lost in our headlong rush toward an inarticulate society. Though these qualities are falling through the cracks of the processes of our educational system, their absence can be most clearly sensed in the products of the overentertained culture. They will be equally visible in later chapters on the political culture.

The most evident matter is *the majesty of the language* itself. Precise, perceptive, graceful, incantatory English is disappearing from mass entertainment products because the literate language is being pushed aside, considered an inadequate tool for moving people to laughter or tears. This is not merely a matter of refusing to book the film version of a Shakespearean play into a thousand multiplexes because it is assumed incapable of reaching a large enough audience; rather, it is a matter of refusing to consider germane to any mass audience the writings and dreams of thousands of would-be Shakespeares, a matter of allowing marketplace pressures to force their aim downward, away from full employment of the literate-based language. Scripts that are shorter on dialogue and longer on quips, and that celebrate the semiliterate, reinforce the trend.

Associated with the loss of majesty in the language is *the ability to express our thoughts well*. On screen this loss is often seen and heard in the form of characters incapable of reflecting verbally on anything other than emotional subjects. In the film *Poetic Justice*, when a character whom we are to believe capable of writing good poetry (actually the work of Maya Angelou) has a falling-out with her lover, she and the lover go their separate ways, not with sentiments well expressed but with epithets traded back and forth until they have reached the point of absurdity. Comparisons, metaphors, extrapolation, induction, and other facets of analytic thought are seldom found in mass cultural products and appear less and less in the discourse of those whose lives have reference to no other sort of cultural products. Too much watching and listening to these entertainments accelerates the decay of conversation, which, as discussed earlier in this book, is already on the wane in the home and in the schools. Up until very recently in the history of the world, most people entertained themselves principally by talking with one another and by discussing subjects other than their own emotions. Now the hours of the day in which private discussions used to be held have disappeared, replaced by time spent in the company of an entertainment product. As with the alliance celebrated in *Beavis and Butt-head*, friendships today are often based on a shared taste for a particular mass entertainment—we both like the same rock groups and MTV programs, so we must be compatible and will be able to chat about them. Unfortunately, when the condition of being co-audience members is removed, conversation itself is compromised. Moreover, the mass media products do not provide much fodder for conversation anyhow, because they contain very little in the way of challenging content.

The next most significant loss is *quiet*. The dictionary lists as definitions of quiet: calmness, stillness, inactivity, freedom from noise, a peaceful quality, freedom from turmoil or agitation. Yet agitation, turmoil, and noise are the very qualities associated with today's entertainment products, and their direction is toward more frantic movement, rollercoasters of emotional ups and downs, volcanoes of visual and auditory sensations. The concomitant of overentertainment is overstimulation. Just as the newest audio-visual aid in school must use a greater variety of color, image, and sound, the next action feature film must be more densely battle-packed than the last, the next music video more spectacular, the next recording more overwhelming to the ears. Aural and visual noise drown out other stimuli, and when they do, quiet decreases apace. The fifty hours a week we spend watching television, listening to the radio or recorded music, and going to the movies effectively displace awareness of other aspects of the world, to a degree whose completeness is staggering. Forced to hear music in elevators, clamped into a museum audio tour, isolated by wearing earphones while jogging, we are deprived of the immediate experience of place and increasingly forgo the possibility of conversation with strangers. We congratulate ourselves on being in control of our personal environment in these matters, but our choice surrenders rather than enhances our individuality, since we implicitly agree to be limited by the options available to us as consumers of packaged mass entertainment.

According to Max Picard, whose poetic book about *The World of Silence* is a classic examination of the subject, silence is "nothing merely negative," not the "mere absence of speech [but] a positive, complete world in itself." Silence has to do with the inner soul, with aspirations, with things larger than man, Picard contends. It does not fit into our lives today because it "does not fit into the world of profit and utility . . . it cannot be exploited."[1]

"Dead air" is the term used to describe a moment in a broadcast when there is suddenly no talk, no music, no sound effects to command the viewer's or listener's attention. Dead air is not a deliberate pause but the sort of silence that, like a vacuum, is abhorred. Picard, writing about this phenomenon in the age before television, suggested, "It is as if men were afraid that silence might break out somewhere and destroy the noise of radio."[2] Producers fear silence almost as greatly as they do an absolutely still screen; either might provoke a consumer to change channels or to become restive. But perhaps the producers of entertainments are wise to bombard us continually with visual and auditory stimuli, because as an audience we show every sign of liking them. Not satiated by the mass media products we already have, we seek greater stimulation, embrace the latest technological advances, desire more cable channels delivered to our homes and channelsurf restlessly among them by means of a remote control device. We watch more hours of television today than we did five years ago and eagerly await the new total wraparound drug of virtual reality.

Ferraroti has charged that we are addicted to television. We welcome our addiction, a fact reflected in our misunderstanding of quiet as unfilled time or space. Not only the entertainment producers but we people in the audience no longer recognize quiet as a distinct and valuable experience, the context for contemplation, quiet as the source of most important thoughts. Thomas Merton wrote of the "desires of solitude," of entering a monastery in which silence "enfolded me, spoke to me, and spoke louder and more eloquently than any voice" and produced epiphanies of insight that changed his life.[3] These days, when the flood tide of noise and visual activity recedes, we are left not with the possibilities of the contemplative context but with the sense of a hole that needs to be filled.

The fourth consequence of being overentertained is our increasing *passivity*. Recognizing this, perhaps, the very newest trend in mass media entertainment is touted as countering passivity by championing interactivity. Such "activity" as that promulgated by a home shopping network, however, differs from the inactivity of the couch potato only in that the home shopper is invited to push the buttons of a phone in order to buy something. Most interactivity devices allow only for halting an ongoing video display in order to receive further information. In an experimental classroom, you can click on a key word to learn more about how Columbus introduced the horse to the Americas, but you cannot engage the computer/television-teacher in a free-ranging, actively participatory discussion.[4] The "data superhighway" in which the information streams and capabilities of telephone and cable television lines and the processing possibilities of desktop computers will soon be combined, is touted as interactive heaven. Announcing the proposed merger between Bell Atlantic and TeleCommunications Inc., a company that hoped to provide many of the lanes on that data superhighway, TCI chairman John C. Malone envisioned a single box on top of a home television, acting as a steering wheel that "will allow us to control all the communications needs of a household with one device." Adding the telephone's switching capabilities to the computer screen will, for instance, enable a customer in one home to play a video game with a customer in another home far away from the first.[5] For the most part, however, the new technology will merely provide people with greater capability of reacting to the screen, while at the same time increasing our physical separation from each other, a condition not usually conducive to active participation.

To be an active rather than a passive audience member, whether at home or in a school, one must do more than push a button or seek information. Active in the best sense means to be curious, skeptical, reticent, individual, and/or imaginative in relation to what is being proffered. Oldtime radio earned the appellation "the theater of the imagination" because it required that sort of active audience participation. In the live theater, a joke may fall flat if an audience member decides that it does not strike him or her as funny and refuses to laugh. No such possibility is permitted in television. To make us slip into laughter, banana peels called laugh tracks are inserted under our independent decision-making processes. These encourage us to join a supposed crowd of chortling revelers, just as, in other scenes, mood music is used to remind and to seduce us to perceive what we see and hear as romantic, dangerous, or happy. By such devices, individual, skeptical, and active responses to a television program are discouraged. As important, the responses that the producers want us to have and so reinforce by those devices are always in the emotional realm—the gut reactions, not the cerebral. We are not to think but to sit there and laugh, cry, or sneer along with the (unseen) crowd. Dispersed audience members cannot be trusted to remain pacified and passive, hence there is a tendency among advertising producers to ratchet up the sound volume so that their commercials are louder than the programs around them and, more recently, to differentiate the commercials visually from the body of the program by means of deliberate pictorial distortions and simulated video glitches. We are not to change channels or visit the refrigerator or the bathroom when it is time for the commercial. We are to remain positioned properly in the direct path of the data superhighway until given permission to leave our homes, or to push another button, in order to buy the advertised soapsuds, *Jurassic Park* dolls, classic video releases, or overly expensive sneakers.

There is no need for us to be skeptical or curious or to indulge in mental gyrations, because all potential mysteries are cleared up for us by our favorite sleuth, our friendly game show host, our authoritative anchorperson. Nothing is left to our interpretation; we are expected to be satisfied that what has been transmitted is all the information essential for us to know. That has not always been the case with the news. At one point during Walter Cronkite's reign at CBS, he considered adding a line at the end of the half-hour news broadcasts advising viewers that for information beyond the headlines and the regrettably brief summaries just presented, they should consult their daily newspapers. The idea was never implemented. It would have invited viewers to turn to a competitive advertising medium, and—even less desirable and more alarming to the network—to think. By encouraging his audience to read, the anchorman might have moved them from passive to active! No wonder Cronkite's unintentionally radical notion was quickly scotched.[6]

While reading, one can be quiet—indeed, must be quiet—but one cannot be truly passive. Even the most trashy of books requires more of its readers in terms of intensity of attention and mental engagement than the equivalent lightweight television program, mainstream movie, or rock video. The best books have the feel of personal communication between the author and reader. They engage our mental abilities. In response to the 14.79-second sound bite of a presidential candidate on the news,[7] we do not reach down inside ourselves to formulate a searching question that might illuminate the candidate or the issue; in response to a nostalgia question on *Jeopardy*, we do not muse about the possible relationship between the knowledge displayed and the contestant's background; nor in response to attending a rock concert or to viewing a music video do we attempt to conjure in our heads the architectonics of the music. Instead, we sit there and vegetate, stimulated to contemplate only the next opportunity to consume. And to feel bad about ourselves. Mihaly Csikszentmihalyi's research demonstrated that people engaged in such active pastimes as gardening felt better after doing them, but that "after watching TV for a few hours, self-esteem and most other indicators of the quality of experience decline. . . . Most people, when carefully surveyed, report feeling depleted and depressed after watching television for hours."[8] This is behavior consistent with the pattern of addiction. Low self-esteem, depletion, and depression are also noted in addicts when they come to the end of a "high" caused by drugs or alcohol.

When we are passive, our viewing, listening, and learning skills degrade until they are nearly devoid of moral perspicuity. Soon, if we are not careful, our transformation will be complete: from watchers into voyeurs, from listeners into eavesdroppers. The ultimate television screen in our homes will have the shape of an enormous keyhole. As we become more glued to that keyhole, our passivity increases and spills over into other areas of our lives: We become passive in the face of political upheaval, emotional nuance, and employment of the language where it requires concentrated (and thus active) thought.

Through that keyhole, even more so than at present, we shall view a world in which *history is eclipsed*. Television has been touted as a mirror of our surround or as an open window on it, but the window is mostly closed, the mirror a distorting one. As Gerbner has documented, television brings us a world in which reality is seldom transmitted untransformed. What we see and hear is chopped, blended, and sweetened to fit into the categories (and air time constraints) of news programs, talk shows, sitcoms, game shows, dramas, soap operas, and sports extravaganzas. Even when the coverage is "live," we are seldom permitted to evaluate it ourselves, but must perceive it through slow-motion replays and the interpretations of a commentator. By such means the context of any incident or fact is removed, a process that virtually ensures the death of the complex and the triumph of the simple. Happy endings, the polar opposite of what actually happened, are attached to docudramas, as in a recent made-for-television movie starring Oprah Winfrey as the mother of a poor Chicago family in a public housing jungle. In the reporter's book that was the basis for the movie, the mother's bad actions at the end of the story vitiated much of the good she had done earlier in it; on screen, that ending was scrapped and a suitably uplifting one that celebrated the mother was substituted. Whatever in the real world does not hold the screen pictorially or emotionally is considered to be boring and is eliminated from what is broadcast.

Whether the content is drama, commercials, news, or any other programming, television transmits the same set of coherent common images and messages into every home. For many people, this becomes the only reality, and it is a reality that overwhelmingly exists only in the present. One could posit a commercially successful sitcom set in a feudal lord's court, but American television has nothing approaching that. The most successful historical series have been in the mold of *Happy Days* and *M*A*S*H*, both set in the 1950s, or Westerns set in a romanticized version of the mid-nineteenth century. *The Waltons* competently mirrored the reality of the Depression years, but is the exception that proves the rule. In popular entertainment, history is mostly alien and uncharted territory. The distant past seems to date to 1929 (the year when talking pictures were introduced and the stock market crashed) and to extend back tens of thousands of years to the dawn of recorded time.[9] What audiences do learn about history from popular entertainment products is cartoonish or boorish and gives them no sense that people ever existed in any interesting way anywhere on this planet prior to the landing of the hillbillies in Beverly Hills. On television and in music, and to a lesser degree in films, the setting, the people, and the action are all contemporary. Even more distorting, most of the characters populating this present-tense landscape seem to have no personal past or to possess only fragments of their own history—unless they happen to be Vietnam veterans or to have been abused in their childhood, in which case their past becomes a cliché, a plot device akin to a ticking time bomb that waits to go off until the appointed moment in Act III.

To live without history is to exist on the same level as an animal. Among the qualities that define us as human beings is having a sense of the past, an understanding that goes beyond our own immediate knowledge to include those events and personalities we have never personally experienced. Among the attributes separating adults from children is that grownups act in reference not only to the wider world but also to the deeper world that includes the past. That wider and deeper world is antithetical to the purposes of mass media, the journalism professors Kathleen Hall Jamieson and Karlyn Kohrs Campbell suggest. They view the primary function of the mass media as the attracting and holding of a large audience for advertisers; in pursuit of that goal, they argue, any messages and information transmitted to an audience through the mass media must be "transient or ephemeral, here today and gone tomorrow; intended and useful only for the immediate moment; tied to a particular time and place, then thrown away."[10] The very transience encourages consumption habits at the same time that it discourages deep thought, which might get in the way of our concentrating on what the next commercial has to tell us. Equally contributory to the entertainment's ephemeral nature is that we in the audience now seem more sensitive to, and usually prefer, materials that reach us in familiar and comfortable forms. We do live in the present, of course, and most people have strong feelings that our era is radically different from all those that preceded it, but the media through which most evidence of the past now comes to us, filmed and videotaped reports, augment that feeling. Moving pictures give an exciting aura of "actuality" to events that have been preserved. The fiery end of the dirigible *Hindenburg* is familiar to millions of people because the film of the disaster has been endlessly broadcast; the torpedoing of the passenger liner *Lusitania*, whose effect on world history was greater in that its sinking helped to precipitate the Great War, was not well captured on film, so that catastrophe is less familiar to the general public—which contributes to the public's misperception that the loss of the *Lusitania* was of less importance than the crash of the *Hindenburg*. The new principle in history is, out of sight, out of mind.

In *War and Peace*, Tolstoy raised a central question about history: Is what happens to the world a result of the actions of men like Napoleon, or is it a consequence of the clash of great movements to which the leaders are as much in thrall as their followers? When the evidence is distorted in favor of the available images, as it is today, the answer to the Tolstoyan question comes decisively down on the side of the man—not because that is the truth, for the question will never be resolved, but because our impression of history has become hostage to the photo opportunity.

Moreover, the selection of what is chosen to be preserved is skewed toward entertainment figures and toward the most recent events. While we have enough film and tape of Carol Burnett to permit a visitor to the Museum of Radio and Television to watch and listen to her performances for a week on end without repetition, we have only one scratchy voice recording and a few yards of newsreel film of Woodrow Wilson. Our archives and memories retain all too many image-records of matters not germane to historical understanding, such as President Gerald Ford's physical mishaps or the materials from which are fashioned endless fanciful speculations about the deaths of Marilyn Monroe and John F. Kennedy.

Images crystallize memory, as Aristotle taught. He considered this a positive process, but in our time it has turned to a negative one, because we are so weakened in the use of our memories that we are no longer able to recall very much of our personal lives without the aid of images. Moreover, and similarly, the overload of information that comes to us through the television set serves to erase public memory.

As we are encouraged to let history slip from our grasp like sand through the fingers of an idle child on a beach, our connection to the past is further weakened by mass media attempts to focus attention on individual facts, usually of dubious significance. The "trivial pursuit" conception of knowledge degrades history to nostalgia—a commodity that is more marketable. More people today probably know the precise date and year of Elvis Presley's birth than know the precise date and year when Grant and Lee met at Appomattox Courthouse; a recent survey discovered that most of the students queried could not even place the latter date in the correct half-century. That the people of the United States would buy three hundred million Elvis Presley stamps in the first few months of issue is the reflection of a market force that cannot be denied; Postmaster General Marvin Runyon defended the choice of Presley for a new stamp by maintaining that the pop singer "did change our culture . . . more than many, many other people depicted on stamps. We need to . . . put images on our stamps that mean something to this country."[11] Meaningfulness, at least to some people, is now a concomitant of popularity and a quantity capable of being measured by the ability of a person's image to sell products for others. Indeed, the Post Office is already using these popular images as sales tools. A booklet of twenty stamps includes, in addition to Presley, depictions of Otis Redding, Buddy Holly, Dinah Washington, Bill Haley, Clyde McPhatter, and Ritchie Valens; by means of a coupon in the book, purchasers are enticed to buy, through the mail, a CD or audio cassette recording of their songs, which have "never before [been made] available together."

The enforced displacement of real history directly and adversely affects articulate expression in ways that produce three additional losses. First, it *removes a galaxy of articulate heroes* whom we might study as models. Encouraged to think of heroes mainly in terms of athletes, movie stars, and talk-show guests whose exploits will continue to be recycled because they exist on film and tape, we ratchet down our potential admiration for the articulate figures of the past, especially for those who had the misfortune to live before the age of electronic reproduction. Second, it *removes complexity*. To be complete, a historical explanation must take into account the interplay of social forces, the personalities of leaders, and the economic, geographic, and even meteorological conditions that impinge on an event or an era. To encompass all this requires a fair amount of time and more than a few words. If we happen to know the Appomattox date, April 9, 1865, we are prepared to make the proper answer to a quiz show query, but if we cannot set that date in context, say, by means of an understanding that the surrender of Lee to Grant took place in Confederate territory, after four years of war, a winter of hiatus in the fighting, and a springtime of Union military victories, and when the Confederacy was pressed at sea and running out of supplies—among other important factors—the date itself is almost meaningless. Third, it *suppresses history's reverberations*. History makes the greatest impact by demonstrating in unmistakable ways the parallels or contrasts between the past events being chronicled and contemporary matters. History forces the mind of the audience member to think of connections, to conduct a dialogue with itself as well as with the material being presented. Absent the stimulation of real history, that most important of all colloquies can only be banal and vapid.

Chapter 6

LAND OF THE WORD

$\mathcal{T}$he 1992 campaign for the presidency of the United States of America was distinguished by a new wrinkle in election strategy, the repeated appearances of all three major candidates on a large variety and number of television talk shows. As indicated above, the level of language usage of these programs is unusually low, while their emotional content is high. Moreover, those programs are the flashpoints in which the ability to express thoughts well is being lost and history eclipsed. President George Bush, the incumbent; the Democratic challenger, Bill Clinton; and the independent, H. Ross Perot, sat separately for Larry King of CNN, Katie Couric of NBC, Phil Donahue, and other "soft" questioners, and on their shows fielded carefully screened questions from the home audiences, but they avoided *Meet the Press* and *Face the Nation*, where panels of seasoned reporters are the interviewers.

In terms of the meanness of public speech, this was the worst campaign season in memory, even exceeding the level of the subsequent 1994 campaign. How closely the meanness of the 1992 campaign was linked to talk show appearances cannot be precisely ascertained, but the conjunction is disturbing. The rancor was more evident nearer the bottom of the ticket than at the top. Outrageous racial appeals were made by the former Ku Klux Klan official David Duke and by the New York senatorial candidate Al Sharpton. There were also diatribes from the televangelist Pat Robertson and the columnist Pat Buchanan. At the Republican convention in Houston in August, Buchanan announced that there was "a religious war going on in this country for the soul of America" between God-fearing Americans whose beliefs matched his own and those who disagreed with him. He described the earlier Democratic convention as a "giant masquerade ball [where] 20,000 radicals and liberals came dressed up as moderates and centrists in the greatest single exhibition of cross-dressing in American political history." Robertson contended in a letter to supporters in Iowa that the Equal Rights Amendment, which he opposed, "encourages women to leave their husbands, kill their children, practice witchcraft, destroy capitalism and become lesbians."[1] Most mainstream Republicans rejected what Buchanan and Robertson said even as their extremist appeals received national exposure and certification through television and newspapers.

The first televised presidential candidates' "debate" was thus awaited with more dread than eager anticipation. The October 11, 1992, joint appearance was marked by the *ad hominem* attacks of Bush and Clinton against each other and by Perot's folksy jibes at both of them. The vice-presidential forum on October 13 was even more acrimonious. Admiral James Stockdale, the third-party candidate, was so appalled by the verbal brickbats launched by the men on either side of him that he was unable to speak, and even though an intelligent man who has been articulate in other situations, he came across to the television audience as stupid. For the second presidential candidate encounter, on October 15, 1992, a new format was devised that, it was hoped, would promote better debate. The Gallup Organization selected an audience of 209 uncommitted voters in Richmond, Virginia, who, for the first time since candidate debates had been televised, were to take the place of journalists and ask the questions; the format would resemble a television talk show.

Questioning started off reasonably well, with audience members trying to pin down Perot on specifics of his broad proposals and receiving from Perot short answers and promises that he would reveal more details in his half-hour "infomercial." Then an audience member expressed the sentiments of many by observing that "the amount of time the candidates have spent in this campaign trashing their opponents' character and their programs is depressingly large" and asking, "Why can't your discussions and proposals reflect the genuine complexity and the difficulty of the issues?"[2]

"I'm not going to sit there and be a punching bag," President Bush answered as prelude to insisting that he had to speak about character because it was important, and then he reiterated charges that Clinton had dodged the draft and would "turn the White House into the Waffle House." Clinton's response indulged in a similar though less strident personal attack. The audience grew restive, and the next questioner, a pony-tailed man who said he was a "domestic mediator," pleaded, "Can we focus on the issues and not the mud? . . . Could you make a commitment to the citizens of the United States to meet our needs, and we have many, and not yours?"

Somewhat chastened, for the remainder of the ninety minutes the candidates responded cogently to questions about issues and to requests from the audience to provide specific details on their proposals and positions. Audience members appeared informed about the issues and asked good questions about them. They introduced personal concerns without insisting on them, and did not insert themselves as personalities into the context, as journalists in previous televised debates had done. The evening was a triumph for the audience in controlling the tone of the discussion, a victory for an electorate that wished to hear issues seriously discussed.

One might dismiss this as puffery but for objective evidence that the audience paid close attention to what the candidates said. While the televised debate was going on, across town in Richmond 104 randomly selected undecided and "weakly committed" voters, whose tentative support was divided equally among the candidates, watched the forum in a special way. This panel was able to register its approval or disapproval of what each candidate said, as it was being said, by means of hand-held electronic devices hooked up to computers. On the panel's dial boxes 1 was the lowest rating, 7 the highest, and 4 was neutral. A telling set of panel responses was recorded during the candidates' answers to a question about term limits. When President Bush forcefully asserted that he supported such limits, the meter readings went up to 5.48, a score well above average. Governor Clinton then began his response by saying, "I know they're popular, but I'm against them," and the meter readings turned immediately negative, to 3.17. However, as Clinton explained what he favored instead, a plan for strict limits on candidate and political action committee spending, coupled with a requirement that candidates appear in open debate forums, a plan he insisted would place incumbents and challengers on more nearly equal footing, the meter-readings started going up and soon reached 5.38. "The pattern of rising and falling support," the designers of the experiment later wrote, "suggested an audience that was grappling with difficult issues and who, while having opinions that shaped its initial reactions, was open to reasonable counter-arguments." In the wake of the forum, nearly half of the meter-wielding panel's members said they had changed or made up their minds about the candidates as a result of what they had heard. A substantial fraction of the uncommitted panel moved toward Clinton, less so toward Perot, and still less toward Bush, about three weeks before the election.[3]

The ultimate significance of the October 15, 1992, debate and the electronic monitoring of the listeners' panel lies not in its accurate prediction of late vote shifts but rather in the clear implications for speech and debate. They revealed that voters fed up with inadequate political discourse demand better attention to the issues and to improving the language of the political arena, listen carefully to candidates who rationally present positions on issues, and change their minds based on what they have heard. This is the lesson of the 1992 campaign: Voters want the candidates to aim higher, and as audience members are prepared to do so themselves, that is, to consider complex issues in complex ways.

This is good news for political rhetoric and for America. Unfortunately, during the remainder of the 1992 campaign such possibilities were soon obscured by a return to earlier practices of personal attack and obfuscation. On the eve of the election, a medical economist, asked to assess the rival Clinton and Bush health care plans, glumly painted them in phrases applicable to virtually all of the 1992 campaign discourse: "They tell you very little, they leave things very vague and they play to an electorate that cannot stand the truth."[4] In short, the October 15, 1992, debate remains today a lone reminder of what might have been.

Adult articulate behavior is taught in large measure through the use of models. Since political figures are extremely prominent in American life, and even though they are not universally admired, the style and level of the politicians' articulate behavior has an equal if not greater influence on the population's speech than do the products of the entertainment industry. Unfortunately, the excess commodification that has seriously compromised entertainment and television news products has also affected politics, in large part because politics can no longer be conducted without the use of the same modern communications technology that transmits entertainments and news broadcasts.

Classical rhetoric consists of four elements: the language used, the context in which it is used, the nature of the audience, and the personality of the speaker. In this and the next two chapters, modern political rhetoric is examined by means of this four-part schematic, for each of the four are contributing to the decline in articulate behavior within politics and, by extension, in those who model their discourse on what politicians do and say.

The context for political oratory in the United States has a great deal to do with the country's history and system of governance. Fighting battles with words instead of resolving them through the use of brute force is a hallmark of a truly democratic country. The constitution of the former Soviet Union proclaimed it a democracy, but all issues there were settled by authoritarian means. There is an intimate, fundamental relationship among dialogue, debate, and democracy, one that has been cogently summarized by the philosopher Kenneth Burke. He calls democracy "a device for . . . setting up a political structure that gives full opportunity for the use of competition to a cooperative end. Allow full scope to the dialectic process, and you establish a scene in which the protagonist of a thesis has maximum opportunity to modify his thesis and so mature it in the light of the antagonist's rejoinders."[5] By this analysis, the most democratic of decisions is the compromise agreed to after thorough debate.

From the time of the Pilgrims to the eve of the Revolutionary War, open if not entirely freewheeling debate thrived in local governance in the American colonies, partially because of the colonies' rural nature and remoteness from the authority of the European kings. Tolerance for the voices of many varied and competing religious doctrines was also among the practices that distinguished the colonies from the European mother countries. Since the most grating aspect of British tyranny was its refusal to permit the airing of ideas that might contradict its own edicts, it was logical for the colonists' profound distrust of the monarchy to transmute into a demand that *all* opposing voices be heard—not to let a single opponent speak for any others, but rather see to it that many disparate viewpoints and ideas be permitted to compete for acceptance. If all men were created equal, then all deserved an equal chance to express their opinions. The colonists were seeking not the sort of shuffling of leaders that had been the outcome of many European revolts, but to accomplish a far more radical change, to come of age and debate among themselves the proper structure and leadership for their own government. They had confidence in the power of words to build a government that would not depend for its existence upon any individual, neither George III nor George Washington.

Unlike other periods of upheaval, the American quest for independence exhibited what an early historian called "a strife of ideas: a long warfare of political logic; a succession of campaigns in which the marshalling of arguments not only preceded the marshalling of armies, but often exceeded them in impression on the final result."[6] By their exhortations, Samuel Adams, James Otis, and Patrick Henry scorched the old order and cleared a path for the nation-nurturing eloquence of Jefferson, Hamilton, Madison, Paine, and John Adams. Continuous, often vitriolic debate is the story of the ratification of our Constitution, with those opposed to its adoption vociferous enough to balance the power of those who wanted it to become the law. The debate over what the Constitution would say was as full and tough as any debate ever recorded. From that process the ultimate compromise was wrung, one that finally assured the ratification of the Constitution: the Bill of Rights. In those ten amendments, the fashioners of our democracy sought to guarantee freedom of speech, not only for the purposes of championing the press, individual liberty, and self-expression but, just as important, for the purpose of permitting citizens to engage in political debate. When adopted, the First Amendment had as much to do with protecting debate as it did with protecting newspapers and the right of free assembly. The fact that the notion of free speech as participation in the political process has since been obscured does not obviate it as a necessary component of American democracy.

One fortunate result of the torturous debate over the precise wording of the Constitution was that after ratification very little skirmishing continued between the opposing camps. Europe marveled that Americans were a people who talked out matters of importance to the citizenry until they were settled, a people who upended previous practice by making rule subject to reason and consensus.

Fifty years after the Declaration of Independence, on July 4, 1826, former presidents John Adams and Thomas Jefferson died; in a eulogy to both men, the most famous orator of the 1820s, Senator Daniel Webster, identified the source of their power as the intimate connection between their articulate speech and their actions. Their eloquence, he said, "was bold, manly and energetic; and such the crisis required." Jefferson and Adams made policy and carried it out; according to Webster that was their principal glory; rhetoric served mainly to elucidate and further their policy. That was why Webster could conclude, in a generalization that would itself be much quoted: "True eloquence . . . does not consist in speech. . . . It must exist in the man, in the subject, and in the occasion."[7]

In Webster's day the men, the great subjects, and the occasions for eloquence were still plentiful, though the context had changed. The smaller towns of the country practiced a highly participatory form of democracy. In the evenings and on the many public holidays, townspeople would listen to speeches about the great questions of the day and would then discuss the issues. To do so was the style of life and a social requirement: Americans were argufiers and retorters, a vocal citizenry who valued eloquence and aspired toward it. Touring the United States just then, Alexis de Tocqueville noted the tendency for its citizens to be involved in matters of public importance. He wrote, "If an American should be reduced to occupying himself with his own affairs, at that moment half his existence would be snatched from him; he would feel it as a vast void in his life and would be incredibly unhappy."[8] That was most true on a local level. On the national level, participatory democracy had been overtaken by the sheer size of the country and by the success of the Federalists in convincing the citizenry that the proper basis of central government was representative rather than full participatory democracy.

Following Aristotle, Alexander Hamilton and James Madison argued that ordinary citizens could have only limited knowledge of the wider world, could not govern people and provinces that were different from themselves, and could never be as properly inclined as their representatives to do what a strong central government must, such as aggrandize the power of the nation in international affairs and protect the rights of individuals from the tyranny of the majority. Following Hobbes, these Federalists insisted that once the populace had invested their sovereignty in the national government by means of their votes, they must let the elected representatives govern them and stop trying to do the job themselves. After the Federalists' victory, Joshua I. Miller, a student of early democracy, suggests, "the hallmark of democracy came to be elections and the protection of individual rights, instead of the actual rule of the people through participation in governing."[9]

Even as quasi-representative democracy replaced and amended direct participation, however, the citizenry continued to show tremendous interest in the actual debate of the men in Congress and in the speeches elected officials made when out on the hustings. During the period from the Revolution to the Civil War, Michael P. Kramer writes, "Americans realized that their experiment in self-government put an extraordinary burden upon public opinion and hence, upon the dissemination of information and political debate."[10] Speeches made in and beyond Congress were the main source of citizens' information, and the influence of the speeches was magnified by newspapers that reprinted them and critiqued their degree of eloquence. For several decades in Congress, Daniel Webster, Henry Clay, and John C. Calhoun launched oratorical missiles at one another's positions and during every salvo provided the audience with intellectual excitement as well as fireworks.

Momentous and troubling questions for the republic had to be addressed by those orators in the period between the War of 1812 and the start of the Civil War: What to do with the lands to the west, on what basis to admit new states to the Union, the correct role for the Bank of the United States, whether to go to war with Mexico, what rights states held versus the authority of the central government, and how to deal with slavery—all questions that bespoke the widening economic and political gulf between the North and the South. Perhaps as important, debates on those questions were held in the context of the communality of language that existed among the participants and in their wider audiences. That communality did not derive solely from the more homogeneous state of American society in that day; rather, the debaters agreed on the meanings of the words they used and used them only in agreed-upon ways. It was possible for an audience to weigh and choose among the arguments without first having to figure out if what Calhoun meant by "liberty" was the same as what Webster meant by that word.

Public appetite for congressional debate was matched by public delight in the oratory of the trial; on court days in many rural counties, people flocked to the clash of celebrated lawyers, "the eloquence of the speakers often receiving as much attention as the facts of the case," Barnet Baskerville, a historian of oratory, concludes.[11] Also in great demand were speeches on ceremonial occasions—the Fourth of July being the most favored moment for patriotic flights of language; printed collections of such speeches sold very well to the public. Those books served as more than reading matter; the printed speeches were widely used as pieces to be declaimed and as models for composing one's own.

Perhaps more than the Revolutionary era, the period on the eve of the Civil War was the time in the history of the United States when debate itself was democracy's cutting edge, when the system of governance heard many voices and tried to cull from their clash a consensus on important matters. America, land of the word; America, country of the ideal combination of elements for debate—large issues, eloquent advocates, an intensely interested and enlightened audience.

The importance of that keen audience to the level of the debate cannot be overstated. Aristotle had noted that to be effective all rhetoric must make of the audience an active and participating partner. In any era, what the philosopher Harold Barrett has styled "the good audience" exhibits social awareness, an acceptance of the civility necessary to reasoned debate, and a willingness to be moved by what is said.[12] For many years after the country's founding, those qualities of the good audience informed debate and provided part of the good context for rhetoric. Special emphasis must be placed on the nineteenth-century audience's civility, which the social historian Richard Sennett reminds us has to do with the duties of citizenship. It is "the activity which protects people from each other yet allows them to enjoy each other's company. . . . Active expression requires human effort, and this effort can succeed only to the extent that people limit what they express to one another."[13] Civility as cognizance of the limits on behavior dictates that reasoned debate can occur only within boundaries recognized by all sides. Erase those barriers of politeness, and the audience may be hearing many different sorts of speeches and harangues, but the discourse will no longer constitute the true debate that Kenneth Burke identified as the essence of democracy, in which each speaker is constrained as well as encouraged to temper his or her argument in the flame of another's.

The golden age of oratory and debate coincided with and drew its strength from an important recent enlargement of the base of citizens. States were overturning earlier laws that had made property ownership a prerequisite for voting; redefinition of citizenship instantly gave the vote to hundreds of thousands of people whose advent was for the most part celebrated by those already on the rolls. Although citizenship was no longer to be confined to the elite, the educational gulf that had separated the elite from the newly enfranchised masses was recognized as being in need of bridging before the masses were fully ready to cast discerning ballots and participate in the country's political life. Where earlier the elite had explained things to the wider and less elite circle, now education would assume that function. It was felt that the more the public knew, the higher would be voter interest and involvement in the great issues that were at stake. During President Andrew Jackson's terms, among the causes arousing fervent concern were prison reform, temperance, women's rights, states' rights, free education, trade unionism, better care for the insane, and the abolition of slavery.

To meet the demand for educated discussion of these issues, as well as the general desire in the land to hear great speakers, the American lyceum was born. The lyceums became what their historian, Carl Bode, labels town meetings of the mind. The purpose of the original lyceums, begun as local associations in New England, according to their founder Josiah Holbrook, was "the improvement of conversation" in the hope that talk about important subjects would "take the place of frivolous conversation, or petty scandal, frequently indulged, and uniformly deplored, in our country villages."[14] Though partisan politics and religion were barred as subjects because they were considered too divisive, all the great causes were presented and discussed in the lyceums. Consideration of the issues in the lyceums fed into debate on them in Congress and in state legislatures, with the response in the deliberative bodies often dependent upon audience reaction in the lecture halls. Lyceums were central to community-building, the creation of a like-minded group of people who agree on what course of action is proper in regard to a particular issue; classical rhetoric holds that speakers have no effect beyond theatrics unless and until they create some coherent audience community of interests.

The lyceum at Concord, Massachusetts, featured Emerson, Thoreau, Webster, and the Harvard scientist Louis Agassiz; lyceums in other cities were hosts to the likes of the educator Horace Mann, the publisher Horace Greeley, and the visiting British satirical novelist William Makepeace Thackeray. The Cooper Union in New York, the Franklin Institute in Philadelphia, and similar institutions in Baltimore, Washington, and hundreds of smaller cities served as forums for wide-ranging intellectual stimulation. Audiences paid close attention for hours at a time and seemed to appreciate the niceties of the exordium and the peroration. The lyceum movement fared better in the North, where a larger percentage of those eligible to vote were literate, than in the South and the West,[15] but overall it achieved great saturation and success. Attendance at lyceums was socially approved and indulged. Big cities had a few attractions to rival them—concert halls and theaters—but small towns and the rural countryside had no other acceptable public diversions. Lyceums were the virtually unchallenged purveyors of a heady mix of education, exhortation, and entertainment.

The lecture circuits soon became commodified, were turned into a business. By 1845 the occasional lecturer Henry David Thoreau was re- marking on this transformation to his diary: "Curators of lyceums write to me, 'Dear Sir: I hear that you have a lecture of some humor. Will you do us the favor to read it before the Bungtown Institute?' . . . What a grov- elling appetite for profitless jest and amusement our countrymen have." Oliver Wendell Holmes, one of the most popular lecturers, worked with that appetite; trying to explain why his own offerings had recently become more lightweight than when he had started on the circuit, Holmes wrote to Ralph Waldo Emerson, "I am forced to study effects. You and others may be able to combine popular effect with the exhibition of truths. I cannot."[16] Comical lectures began to command larger audiences than purely serious ones, and it became known that the addition of music to an evening's platform—choruses, soloists, Swiss bell ringers—boosted sales of lecture tickets. By the eve of the Civil War, lyceum programs were almost wholly transformed and had more to do with pleasing and amus- ing the crowd than with edifying potential voters.

The appetite for impassioned debate of serious issues was still acute, however, as was demonstrated by the behavior of orators and audiences in the seven "joint discussions" held by two Illinois senatorial candidates, Abraham Lincoln and Stephen Douglas, in the late summer and fall of 1858. The subjects were the thorniest of the time: slavery, popular sover- eignty, and states' rights. The audiences often exceeded 10,000 people per session. The crowds stood—sometimes in the rain—to listen to an open- ing argument of an hour, a ninety-minute response, and a half-hour rebuttal, three hours in all. Lincoln and Douglas were both accomplished speakers, diametrically opposed in philosophy and worthy opponents. Their appearances featured a good deal of scurrilous personal attacks and many misrepresentations of facts and of each other's positions, but overall the debaters addressed the issues in massive detail. Though far from perfect, the Lincoln–Douglas discussions were the high point of a society that believed in the efficacy of debate.

The Civil War was the first American event that had the characteristics of mass politics. The involvement of the populations on both sides of the Mason-Dixon line, rather than simply of two opposing armies, was new, a mass phenomenon; eventually, the larger mass strength of the North overwhelmed the South.

The war was a watershed in the history of articulate expression in the United States. It changed the debate-and-compromise pattern by altering the balance of power between the legislative and executive branches. Citing the exigencies of the emergency, Lincoln arrogated to the executive more authority than it had ever held, and in the process took powers away from Congress; after the war the former balance was never restored.[17] The changed deliberative atmosphere deeply affected the character of the post–Civil War Congress, to the detriment of the oratory that had once been its flower. Another factor affecting quality of debate was the system of advancement. In Great Britain, elected representatives rose to prominence and executive positions primarily through competence and persuasiveness in legislative matters. As a result, debating ability and force of argument continued to be highly valued by Members of Parliament, with considerable energy expended in honing the skills necessary to do well on the floor of the House of Commons. In Congress, where the non–merit-based seniority system was the only way to the top, there was little reason to value eloquence and no incentive.

As for the audience, Reconstruction was a time when the attention of the public at large turned inward, to the achievement of personal financial independence, and citizen interest in subjects of national import flagged. With farms and mines to be settled in the West, railroads to be built, and manufacturing and merchandising enterprises to be established, the business of politics became the support of business, an arrangement in which money spoke louder than words. No wonder, then, that in the quarter-century after the Civil War grandiloquence supplanted eloquence and speeches seemed designed as much to obfuscate as to illuminate issues. And this, when two of the greatest examples of brevity, clarity, and deep meaning ever achieved in formal speeches were before the public, Lincoln's address at Gettysburg and his second inaugural.

Lincoln's plain-speaking masterpieces embodied the old understanding that eloquence consisted in more than the ability to handle words well. As Kenneth Cmiel suggests in a study of language, before the Civil War eloquence "involved larger concerns about audience, personality and social order. Eloquence was civic."[18] After the war civility began to break down, as it often does in a postwar climate; in the belief that the old order of society has proved unworkable, people devalue many things that the old order has cherished. Eloquence became a synonym no longer for excellence but for bombast; empty oratory, the rodomontades of the windbag, became the order of the day and the subject of parody and scorn. *The Nation* called 1872's crop of July Fourth speeches "synonymous with blatant nonsense or platitudes in thought, tawdry rhetoric in diction, and crude, egotistical chauvinism in spirit;" the editor of *Scribner's Monthly* grumbled, "There was a time when a lecture was a lecture. The men who appeared before the lyceums were men who had something to say. . . . Now a lecture may be any string of nonsense that any literary mountebank can find an opportunity to utter."[19]

No longer could a distinction be drawn between the performer on the lecture circuit and the politician on the stump. In consequence of this distressing convergence, Richard Sennett writes, politicians "began to be judged as believable by whether or not they aroused the same belief in their personalities which actors did when on the stage."[20] That condition caused the public—now routinely referred to as the audience—to take an increased interest in the content of the politician's life and a decreased interest in what causes or ideas he espoused.

Decay in regard for a politician's ideas was exacerbated by a serious change in the content and the process of American politics. In the postwar era, Congress had more bills per session to consider and less time to debate each one. Action was transferred from the floor of the public chamber to the committee room, where debate was quashed by the crack of the party's whip. Power, rather than a speaker's persuasiveness, became the weapon for changing opinions—though on the main issues there was very little difference in principle between what the parties sought for the nation. James Russell Lowell suggested in the *North American Review* that "a speaker in Congress addresses his real hearers through the post-office and the reporters. The merits of the question at issue concern him less than what *he* shall say about it so as not to ruin his own chance of re-election." "All over the country," *The Nation* reported, there was "a growing impression that Congressional debates are farces intended to amuse or befog the country people." Angry clashes between members in the House of Representatives were as carefully orchestrated and falsely emotional as stage duels.[21]

Such charades took place while the problems facing the nation were complex and troubling: what to do with the burgeoning arrogance of the railroads and the trusts, how to respond to dozens of strikes, how to counter an economic depression that lasted an entire decade, how to deal with political corruption so pervasive that it reached to the stolen presidential election of 1876. Evidence that the public still hungered for debate over such issues comes in the simultaneous rise of the Chautauqua.

The Civil War had silenced the American lyceums, but the yearning for enlightenment they expressed was still there. James Redpath, a former newspaperman, had watched Charles Dickens and his manager struggle through the 1867–68 lecture season and thought he knew better how to organize tours; his clients soon included Mark Twain, Josh Billings, Wendell Phillips, William Lloyd Garrison, and Julia Ward Howe—entertainers all, but also the promulgators of ideas. They soon had to compete with the new Chautauqua movement. Begun in 1874 as a summer institute for training Sunday school teachers, by 1879 the Chautauquas encompassed hundreds of local assemblies in which thousands of people eagerly attended series of what we would now call adult education courses. By the mid-1880s the brown canvas tents were pitched in several thousand communities each year; they stayed a week at each stop, during which, according to the movement's historian, Joseph C. Gould, the lecturers and performers "presented a fantastic variety of offerings subsumed under the general rubric, 'culture' . . . and helped give discipline and direction to angry and inchoate movements of social protest. . . . It was, fundamentally, a response to an unspoken demand, a sensitive alertness to the cravings of millions of people for 'something better.'" Among the lecture subjects: conservation of natural resources, the eight-hour work day, women's suffrage, pure food and drug legislation, national forests and parks, slum clearance, city planning, direct election of United States Senators, the Boy Scout and Girl Scout movements, and regulation of interstate commerce. Although the serious stuff was sometimes fleshed out with bagpipers, trained dog acts, and jugglers, audiences understood Chautauqua tent lectures to be important and responded to them as such. Although the lecturers and entertainers did receive money for their labors, the nonprofit, nonbusiness status of the Chautauquas and the presence of clergymen on the platform at nearly every program helped give the Chautauquas moral and hortatory authority. From the 1870s through to the Great War, traveling Chautauqua, Gould writes, "brought to the attention of millions of Americans an impressive number of new ideas and concepts, many of which might never have [otherwise] received the popular support that guaranteed their acceptance."[22]

It is important to note that the summer lectures were augmented by the reading circles and correspondence courses that were a concomitant of the Chautauquas. The lecture was not simply an entertainment to be attended and forgotten; it was part of an individual's continuing involvement in public affairs and in an ongoing, lifelong educatory process. Those in the audience at a summer Chautauqua could be counted on to attend Redpath bureau lectures in the winter. The Chautauqua was initiator, template, and continuing prod for articulate expression. Its essential experience was of words shared, first by the lecture audience that together heard the great man or woman impart the ideas; later through the communal discussions carried on by the residents long after the tents had left town; and still later as the audiences reformulated the ideas in their own thought and speech.

After a quarter-century of political doldrums, in the 1890s there was an awakening of sorts to significant new political speech in America, and it led to a decades-long colloquy about the country's direction. If a precise moment for the revivification can be pinpointed, it would have to be William Jennings Bryan's speech before the Democratic convention in 1896. In that speech Bryan cogently expressed the two economic theories that would underlie political discussion from then on and warned that Americans must soon choose between them. The Republicans, he said, believed that "if you will only legislate to make the well-to-do prosperous, their prosperity will leak through on those below," while the Democrats held that "if you legislate to make the masses prosperous, their prosperity will find its way up through every class which rests on them." Nearing the end of his speech, Bryan steered to the topic of the day, silver coinage. He pledged that "the producing masses" of this country would not permit the gold standard to be imposed on them, and ended with these phrases, by which he is now most remembered: "You shall not press down upon the brow of labor this crown of thorns, you shall not crucify mankind on a cross of gold."[23] The speech so electrified the delegates and so swayed them in their opinion on the most proper solution for the country's economic crisis that they awarded the presidential nomination to the thirty-six-year-old. Twice more he won the Democratic nomination, and he also became one of the most popular Chautauqua speakers, asked to repeat the "cross of gold" speech thousands of times from the lecture platform.

And if a last eloquent moment can be pinpointed, it would have to be the presidential campaign of 1912, which involved a half-dozen of the greatest speakers in the country: the socialist candidate Eugene V. Debs, the Democrats Bryan and Governor Woodrow Wilson of New Jersey, and the Republicans Senator Robert La Follette, President William Howard Taft, and former President Theodore Roosevelt. Not since the Founding Fathers had such a cohort of great articulations held the American political stage.

LeFollette capsized his own candidacy with a single fumbling speech on the night of February 2, 1912, before the Periodical Publishers of America annual meeting in Philadelphia, which he began with a diatribe against the eight hundred journalists in the audience. Bryan lost a long battle for the nomination to Wilson but then became an important campaigner for him, in the months before the election, making an average of ten speeches a day. Debs was so persuasive a speaker that even in a year when there were three major candidates in the field, as a fourth-party candidate he garnered 900,000 popular votes and swept more than a thousand Socialists into local, state, and national offices.

Wilson was a refined speaker in the old mode, one who appealed to reason and asked his audience to reason with him to the logical conclusion. Roosevelt was of a newer mode, what was coming to be known as a spellbinder, a speaker who saw his objective as rousing the audience, often in a frankly illogical, thoroughly emotional way. In a letter to a confidante, Wilson outlined the differences between himself and Roosevelt as personalities and as orators: "He appeals to their imagination; I do not.

He is a real, vivid person, whom they have seen and shouted themselves hoarse over and voted for, millions strong; I am a vague, conjectural personality, more made up of opinions and academic prepossessions than of human traits and red corpuscles."[24]

Roosevelt, who coined the phrase "Speak softly and carry a big stick," spoke very loudly and frequently, in a high, squeaky voice, as he redefined the primary power of the presidency as "the bully pulpit." A single speech demonstrated that he had truly reentered the fray and would seek a third term as President, a speech to the Republican convention in the summer of 1912. In it, he attempted to turn his party from its retrograde ways and toward progressivism. As he spoke, the crowd was swayed, and followed him, applauding his points, roaring as he roared. Roosevelt ended his address with phrases ever afterward associated with his name: "We fight in honorable fashion for the good of mankind; fearless of the future; unheeding of our individual fates; with unflinching hearts and undimmed eyes; we stand at Armageddon and we battle for the Lord."[25] Though the delegates gave their overwhelming approval to the speech and to Roosevelt, they acted on the bosses' instructions and voted to support Taft for reelection. In reaction, Roosevelt formed the Progressive Party, the party of the Bull Moose. Taft, who could be an eloquent speaker when the spirit moved him—as it did in later years, when he was a champion of the League of Nations, and when he became Chief Justice of the United States—decided in 1912 not to be moved. He chose to run from the Rose Garden, leaving the field to Roosevelt and Wilson, both of whom he believed would out-poll him no matter what he did. Wilson and Roosevelt, agreeing with that estimate, identified each other as the main opponent.

In Wilson's basic campaign address he told his audiences that the big businesses against whom Taft and Roosevelt supposedly worked were in fact their partners and were running the country; the United States was heading to ruin and was about to forget

> . . . the ancient time when America lay in every hamlet, when America was to be seen in every fair valley, when America displayed her great forces upon the broad prairies, ran her fine fire of enterprise up over the mountainsides and down into the bowels of the earth, and eager men were everywhere captains of industry, not employees; not looking to a distant city to find out what

they must do, but looking about among their neighbors, finding credit according to their character, not according to their connections.[26]

After the votes were counted—Wilson 6.3 million, Roosevelt 4.1 million, and Taft 3.5 million, with Wilson's 435 electoral votes giving him a huge majority—the newly elected President summed up a campaign of extraordinary eloquence on all sides. Standing on the porch of his seaside New Jersey home, he solemnly told supporters, "There is so much to reconstruct . . . that a generation or two must work out the result to be achieved. . . . I summon you for the rest of your lives to set this government forward by processes of justice, equality and fairness."[27]

Before the Great War, the brown tents of the Chautauquas had featured ideas; one of the most popular lectures was "Responsibilities of the American Citizen," as outlined at various times by Debs, La Follette, and the muckraker Lincoln Steffens. The boast of the tent circuit's organizers then was that no serious idea in the United States was barred from the platforms. But tent Chautauquas began to die out after the war. In 1921, President Warren Harding summoned the country's populace not to activism but to "normalcy," and Americans, as they had done after the Civil War, turned to building businesses and achieving individual prosperity. Large issues still needed to be addressed, among them the changing relationship of labor to management, the safeguarding of the stock market from manipulators, provision for the increasing number of elderly people whose survival into old age was made possible by advances in medicine, and the degree to which the United States would participate in international war-prevention activities—but those were not seriously debated in Congress during the 1920s, and for the most part they were absent from the lecture platform.

Radio at first tried to copy the Chautauquas with weekly discussions and long addresses by prominent people. However, what characterized the Chautauqua tents—the sense of a community taking in, discussing, and sharing among themselves the speaker's thoughts, achieved through the intimacy of the tented arenas and the small towns—was not present with radio, whose audience consisted of isolated individuals, listening in the privacy of their homes and unable to effectively talk back to the speaker or to transform the speech into anything resembling a debate. Radio produced commonalty in the audience, not community.

While ostensibly augmenting political debate by enlarging its audience, radio was simultaneously eliminating or rendering superfluous many usual occasions for making political speeches and the need for the audience to hear them in person. As Robert and Helen Lynd noted in their study *Middletown*, in the 1920s listening to the radio began to take the place of family attendance at great political rallies, "or the trips by the railroad to the state capitol to hear a noted speaker or to see a monument dedicated that a generation ago helped to set the average man in a wide place."[28]

The peak year in Chautauqua attendance was 1924: tents in ten thousand towns, reaching 40 million paying customers—10 million more Americans than voted in the 1924 presidential election. But the underlying rot had already set in, and it was not all due to the introduction of radio, which had not yet hit its stride. Internal commodification factors came into play ever more strongly. Since the war, in attempts to achieve what the central office called quality control, local Chautauqua managers had been told to report audience reaction after each performance. If a performer did something that the local manager did not consider "safe," that performer received a strongly worded "suggestion" from the central office. Popularity and ease of acceptance became the criteria by which the offerings were judged. Serious advocates of causes, once the staple of the Chautauqua platform, were eliminated, because they might offend someone. After 1924 the falling off in attendance was steep. By the late 1920s the tents could be booked into only a few hundred towns. The causes of the decline were first thought to be technological: the radio, which allowed people to stay at home for entertainment and uplift, the advent of the movies, and the simultaneous improving of the roads and the cheapness of automobiles, which permitted people to go farther from home to seek entertainment. The more culpable factor was the attempt to produce ever bigger crowds and larger receipts; in that pursuit, entertainment was stressed over education to such a degree, Joseph C. Gould concludes, that "the once-vigorous Chautauqua movement . . . drowned in a flood of pap."[29]

So it was that at the start of the era of mass politics and mass entertainment in America, the time when Governor Al Smith, running for the presidency, could wonder at the new power that radio afforded to reach the electorate, and while there were many important subjects to be debated, the context that had supported great speech in the political arena was already seriously compromised.

Al Smith liked the increased ability to reach the public that radio gave him but insisted something was missing from a radio address—the microphone never nodded approval or dismay, never let the speaker know if it was restless, never recognized sarcasm with appreciative murmurs. What Smith noted in this analysis was the decreased possibility for interaction between speaker and audience. Radio changed the context of American political discourse by physically separating the speaker from the audience.

The audience neither sought nor welcomed the separation, a fact made manifest as the Great Depression took hold and there was a desire on the part of the citizenry to hear more frequently from their political leaders. Franklin Delano Roosevelt's victory in 1932 was fueled by his ability to take advantage of that yearning and to speak well on the radio, which he also used well throughout his years as President, for instance, in the well-remembered fireside chats.

A great public speaker, Roosevelt nonetheless dealt political oratory a blow from which it has not yet recovered by becoming the first President to assemble and make regular use of a stable of speechwriters. The practice of accepting help in composing major speeches dated back to George Washington, a fine thinker and writer whose ego was not beyond obtaining assistance from Jefferson, Hamilton, and other agile phrase-turners; in the case of Andrew Jackson, such assistance was sorely needed and readily at hand; during the hundred years following, even Presidents not generally acknowledged as orators, such as Warren Harding, wrote most of their own speeches. Franklin Roosevelt, too, was a reasonably adept writer of speeches, but the exigencies of the day as well as his own temperament pushed him to use a behind-the-scenes team that included Judge Sam Rosenman and the playwright Robert Sherwood. Here, too, the context had changed: The demand for speeches had become large enough that writing them threatened to take up too much of the President's time, so Roosevelt discussed his ideas with aides who prepared drafts, which the President would then revise and annotate before delivering as addresses. "We have nothing to fear but fear itself," a phrase indelibly associated with Roosevelt, was a late addition to his inaugural address from his aide, Louis Howe.

Subsequent Presidents many times increased the number of aides devoted to speechwriting, until by the 1960s virtually none of a President's speeches were being written by the President without assistance, and virtually all were composed by speechwriters, often from drafts made by competing teams. The practice soon encompassed speeches written for members of Congress, governors, and candidates running for public office. The first formal course in speechwriting, introduced at American University in Washington, D.C., in 1952, provoked alarm from Walter Lippman, who equated failure to write one's own speeches with failure to write one's own love letter: "The truth is that anyone who knows what he is doing can say what he is doing, and anyone who knows what he thinks can say what he thinks. Those who cannot speak for themselves are, with very rare exceptions, not very sure of what they are doing and of what they mean." Kathleen Hall Jamieson, citing Lippman's reasoning, suggests that "ghosted speeches have done to politicians what Hallmark cards have done to the relationships between lovers and live-ins, mothers and children. With a ready-made expression available for $1.00, we are no longer disposed to express our own feelings with pen on paper."[30]

How a mass electorate recognizes or reacts to the falsity of emotion in the uttering of a ghosted speech is a factor that has not yet been quantified, but it is a likely contributor to the electorate's well-known distrust of politicians. At best, a speechwriting team assists a busy President in elucidating his views. William Safire described his relationship to President Richard Nixon as one in which Safire helped "to refine a point of view, to fit into a framework, making allowance for political compromise, then to clothe that point of view in the most dramatic and persuasive words that came to mind, and then to help promote, project and advance the man and the Administration that I was a proud part of."[31]

Even when we grant that the speechwriter is in appropriate service of the speech deliverer's ideals, the separation of the conceptualizer from the deliverer, an almost inescapable consequence of the rise of speechwriting, exacerbates the troublesome distinction that always exists between the speaker's private and public personae. The sociologist Erving Goffman argued that a public persona is a matter of almost pure image, not of substance. Successful political figures put on masks when they take part in the public arena; they become more like icons and less like ordinary human beings.[32] A speech was once a counteraction to the wearing of masks by political figures. So long as the speech was written by the political figure, it reflected his or her own thought processes, had an important connection to personality, and could serve as a window for the audience onto the essential nature of the speechmaker. When the speech delivered by the politician is almost entirely written by others, the dynamic is changed. A ghostwritten speech forces the deliverer toward the rigidity of the mask and makes of the speechmaker an actor, whether or not he or she is or wants to be one. In this contextual change, the act of performance comes close to displacing the act of thought, and the quality of thought suffers.

Scripting now encompasses many more tasks than the drafting of speeches. Much has been written about the influence of the "debates" of the 1960 campaign between John F. Kennedy and Richard Nixon on the outcome of the election; what has been overlooked is how that context affected political discourse and the relationship between the speaker and the audience. According to Sig Mickelson, then president of CBS News, the details of format were worked out in a series of a dozen meetings between network executives and the candidates' representatives.[33] Mickelson proposed that the candidates make opening statements and then question each other—in other words, have a real debate, where the clashes of idea and opinion would be clear and the audience would be able to judge the questions, the answers, the retorts, and the ways in which the candidates replied to or evaded each other's queries. Both Kennedy's and Nixon's men rejected that idea, saying they did not want their candidates to appear too prosecutorial, or, on the other end of the spectrum, to pose questions in too polite a manner for fear of not appearing civil. The participants finally settled on a format that had a *Meet the Press* type of panel asking questions, and limited the answers of each candidate to two-and-a-half minutes per question. By rejecting mutual questioning and long answers, the candidates nullified the possibilities of a debate. What the public saw, in essence, was joint press conferences. During one, the candidates were actually a continent apart, but the backdrops had been decorated to preserve the illusion of a joint appearance. The prescribed time for the answers and the great variety of issues to be covered in each program vitiated any attempt to discuss a subject in meaningful detail, much less to analyze and refute the opponent's contentions. Most of what Kennedy and Nixon said was well rehearsed, sometimes word-for-word repetitions of stump speeches they had previously given. Between 80 million and 100 million people watched the "debates," and the popularity of the programs overwhelmed any potential objections to the format, especially later, when analysts credited Kennedy's performance with tipping the balance of the election in his favor. Part of what tripped up Nixon was his attempt actually to answer the questions put by the panelists, which made his responses less coherent than Kennedy's. The Senator merely used the journalists' questions as jumping off points for what he had already decided to say. In television terms, and in terms of helping the winner, those non-debates were successful. The pattern they established has been followed, for the most part, ever since 1960.

As many as fifty people in the White House now contribute to and argue over drafts of a presidential speech. Teams of writers were made necessary because the occasions on which a presidential speech is called for have multiplied. Roosevelt's fireside chats were few in number and, except during campaigns, he limited his public speaking to one or two addresses a month; his news conferences—another opportunity, in more modern times, for scripted speech—were mostly off the record. In the television age, with its demands for continual display of leaders and heightened appetite for presidential comments on all sorts of subjects, Jimmy Carter averaged one address a day every day of his entire four-year term. Bill Clinton appears to be on track to exceed that record. Speechwriting staffs for members of Congress, Cabinet officials, and myriad other official positions continue to expand.

At the dawn of this country, political rhetoric was uttered in support of policy. That was the quality Daniel Webster celebrated in his eulogy of Adams and Jefferson. Today, as Samuel Kernell has pointed out, the formulation has been inverted, so that policy serves rhetoric.[34] As we shall discuss in the next chapters, this is most blatantly evident in election campaigns. It is this last change in context that, according to the analyst Roderick P. Hart, has now caused presidential speechmaking to "become a tool of barter rather than a means of informing and challenging the citizenry." A speech is a play for votes, and any other objective for it is a distant second. One consequence, Hart suggests, has been to engender a loss of respect for the president's words; no one takes them seriously, now—not presidential colleagues and opponents, not the media, not the public, not even the Presidents themselves.[35]

If this loss of respect characterizes Presidents' speech, it is even more the case for the words of lower-ranked elected representatives and officials. And if the change is bad for the cause of informing and challenging the public, it is worse for debate itself, which requires participants who demonstrate their understanding of the opponent's arguments as prelude to making syntheses and compromises with them. So the politicians, no longer seeing any gain in striving for the grand argument, the telling phrase, the brilliant retort, become less eloquent while audiences grow disenchanted, and true debate, that foundation of democracy, continues to wither. We arrive at the sad, pale mockery of democracy encapsulated in the image repeated endlessly on C-Span cable television: the lone legislator speaking in trumped up passion to a House entirely empty of other representatives.

Chapter 7

POLITICS AND LANGUAGE

In order for discourse to be substantially changed—and that is what we are referring to in examining the decline in articulate behavior—all four elements must alter. In the previous chapter, I argued that the *context* for political discourse, so readily sponsored and championed in the eighteenth and nineteenth centuries, was weakened by commodification pressures of the sort that gutted first the lyceums and later the Chautauquas, and by the various factors that pushed political leaders to lower the level of debate and oratory. Although it touched on the relationship between speaker and audience, that chapter did not have much to say about the *change in the language* itself.

The English language has altered more rapidly in the twentieth than in any previous century, and more rapidly in the last third of the century than in the earlier thirds. Although many people now feel constrained by the language and sense that its possibilities have diminished, the opposite is true, because more words are being added to the lexicon than are being subtracted from it.[1] Many additions are entirely new words—"quark," for example. An equal number are borrowings from another tongue, words formed by alterations of old meanings, or words compounded or derived from already extant words. Those follow the same route to general acceptance. They arise first as spoken words or phrases, most often in a defined subculture—rocket scientists, jazz musicians, professional athletes—that uses the new terminology to describe and characterize processes and objects familiar to the in-group; sooner or later the new words work their way into everyday conversational usage, then begin to be written down in specialized publications, and afterward in more mainstream publications. Only when the words have accumulated enough documentable citations are lexicographers likely to include them in the next edition of a dictionary.

Henry Kucera, an expert on the number and type of English words in use, contends that if we wished to get along by understanding 80 percent of the English communicated to us, "we could manage with a vocabulary of less than 3,000 words and could dispense with dictionaries." In fact, of the hundred most frequently used words on the list that Kucera helped compile, the Brown Corpus, the "function words" (articles, prepositions, pronouns and auxiliary verb forms such as "be," "have," or "do") account for the places from 1 to 32. The first real content word, "say," appears at 33, and the first noun, "man," not until 44. The first hundred words on that list account for nearly half of all those used in everyday speech and writing. However, Kucera writes, the list includes many thousands of less frequently used words, and the 20 percent of communication made up of those latter words "turns out to be crucial in the process of comprehension."[2]

That is to say, the less frequently used words are those in which the language of politics is always based. Moreover, the preponderance of the words being added to the lexicon are just those longer and more rarely used words that deeply affect comprehension.

Raymond Gozzi, Jr., who studied the additions to English made between 1961 to 1986, suggests that when our interpretations of words no longer fit with our experience, we invent words and give new meanings to older ones to reconstruct and revise our definitions of reality. According to Gozzi, the words that emerged during the last quarter-century tell "stories of a culture becoming more complex, contentious, and confusing."[3]

Gozzi has chosen his adjectives carefully. Complexity comes in part from the fact that the largest source of new words (45 percent) is science and technology. Chemists, engineers, and medical specialists tend to speak a language that is often impenetrable to outsiders. While words like "autologous" or "neutrino" enrich the lexicon, they do so in a way that widens the divide between the few who use them easily and the many who cannot. Complexity also comes from the substantial quantity of new phrases used to describe the increasingly subtle variations of our world, for instance, the 24 percent of the additions that have to do with life-styles—"shopping mall," "junk food," "junkies," "turned on." A great deal of contemporary experience has been politicized, with areas of life that never previously carried the freight of ideology now made to do so. It is descriptive to term some edibles "junk food," but it is commenting on social conditions to call people "junk food junkies" or to extend the definition of the term "binge" to a spree of eating as well as to overindulgence in drink. Gozzi observes that addiction has become a source of many new words and a metaphor for a lot of modern experience. Moreover, descriptive terms such as "turned on" can acquire a political edge when they connote a quality that one group finds desirable but another considers undesirable.[4]

The increasing politicization of our society causes us now to construe in political terms many matters that were not previously in the political realm. Consider the problem of properly describing a man who is in prison after being convicted of assault. A skilled and careful novelist might build up a portrait from the details of the person's existence. For those who are not novelists, however, description is often politically colored. Some people might label the prisoner a "psychopath," others call him "a victim of poverty," still others "a sinner to be redeemed," while in the language of a fourth group he might be considered "an example to be punished." Because our language now insists that an observer adopt one or another of the categorizations, and because each conception contradicts the others, it has become unlikely that any describer will view the prisoner as he really is. Hannah Arendt reminded us in her 1963 book *On Revolution*: "In politics, more than anywhere else, we have no possibility of distinguishing between being and appearance."[5] In the past thirty years the difficulty for both speakers and audiences in separating what actually exists from how it is made to appear has only gotten worse. According to the philosopher Murray Edelman, any entity whose meaning is not incontrovertibly fixed sooner or later becomes politically up for grabs. "The characteristic of problems, leaders and enemies that makes them political is precisely that controversy over their meaning is not resolved." Edelman construes politics as "a meaning machine," and the strife between competing ideologies as a war in which each side tries to impose on the population its own interpretations of words.[6] Politicization of nearly every aspect of culture and society may be the inevitable result of this grab over meanings.

Gozzi found predominantly negative connotations to many new words, for instance, to most of those that involved communication: "shoot down," "zing," "zapped," "put down," "cheap shot," "blindsiding." He was struck by the "paucity of terms for honest communication." Contentiousness, which even more closely reflects the politicization of culture, showed up in the 11 percent of the new words that describe social and economic conditions and in the further 7 percent that refer to types of people and action, because nearly all the terms are derogatory, for instance the "mutually denouncing vocabularies" of what became known in the 1960s as "freaks" and "straights." Contention and confusion are reflected by the many new terms and metaphors having to do with deception, mystification, social pressures, "psychobabble," and combat. "If the trends in the vocabulary continue," Gozzi concludes, "we can predict a social reality of increasing stereotypes, ideology, and social conflict . . . and we will increasingly define communication in combative terms."[7]

Confrontational discourse of the kind that increasingly characterizes the exchanges among Congressional representatives or among the panel members on *The McLaughlin Group* decreases the likelihood of articulate expression. In the past, one politician could criticize Senator X as "too intelligent for his own good," a phrase that emphasizes that X's condition has a positive aspect—and a phrase that, if said directly to him, leaves him room to respond in a civil way. Today, if a rival Senator labels the latest reincarnation of Senator X a "nerd" or a "dweeb," the characterizer is using a more negative and stereotyped phrase, one that more irretrievably differentiates Senator X from the speaker, one that lays down an ideological challenge to which Senator X will be most likely to respond in kind, thereby raising the temperature. When people scream at one another, anger displaces articulate expression. If the initial function of language was to bring people together, the most recent additions and changes to English are pushing them apart by wedges of complexity, contention and confusion.

Popular language has always contained taboo words. In a study that also covers the quarter-century from the 1960s to the mid-1980s, Kenneth G. Wilson, a college administrator and professor of English, notes two contradictory contemporary trends in regards to such taboo words. The first is a much increased use of sexual and excretory expressions. Wilson points out that some but not all of them were formerly considered obscene; a few body-descriptive terms were once used in polite company but have been exiled since Victorian times. Wilson concludes from such evidence that there is no real logic to what is considered obscene; if violence were the measure of obscenity, "rape" would be our most offensive swear word. In recent decades, because of the breakdown in manners, so many more "curse words" have deeply entered the popular usage lexicon that Wilson believes the taboo against their being voiced or written in public and private situations has been gelded, which he does not find particularly heinous. The second trend is that while new dictionaries downplayed the awfulness of curse words, the same tomes increasingly flagged what Wilson labeled "worse words," a whole phalanx of offensive racial and ethnic slurs. Dictionaries cautioned against their use, Wilson writes, because "Sensibilities have become much more tender over the past twenty years, and not just minority sensibilities, either."[8]

Epithets of all sorts are so frequently used now that some people are unable to speak without resort to them, so it is important to stress that the use of expletives in daily speech is more than a substitution of words, it is a diminution of the language. We shall explore the expletive categories one at a time, "curse words" first, and then "worse words." The most diligent encyclopedist of "maledicta,' Reinhold Aman, has shown that the vocabulary of curse words may be colorful, but it is small. Most are copulatives, which have replaced the favorite naughty words of an earlier age, whose most insulting epithets were variations on the theme of condemning someone to damnation.[9] It is not the words themselves but the use to which they are put that is of the essence. The researcher Vivian de Klerk determined that men use more obscene words per conversation than women, and men in such all-male bastions as locker rooms do so more than males in other settings. In certain situations, de Klerk writes, the use of expletives enjoys a "covert prestige value," because it masquerades as power speech, with its "assertion of dominance, interrupting, challenging, disputing and being direct."[10] Perhaps speech in the Senate and house cloakrooms and closed committee sessions has always had such a character, but when it spills over into the more public political arena—as it did, most notably, in the Watergate tapes made public with their expletives only transparently deleted—public discourse is degraded. A clue to the real reason for the use of obscenities is provided by the work of another research group, which investigated how obscenities are bandied about in domestic arguments. It concluded that the use of obscenities is an indication of the exhaustion of the participant's discriptive powers; obscenities are attacks on someone's self-concept, not on his or her position on an issue. During disagreements between spouses, it is just such "argumentative skill deficiencies" that regularly lead to violence.[11]

Exhaustion of descriptive powers and substitution of epithets is what we heard in a Senate 'debate" in which Senator Alphonse D'Amato of New York sang "with a pork-pork here and a pork-pork there" to describe what he found wrong with a bill awaiting passage, to which Senator Frank Lautenberg of Newaystiony responded that D'Amato's antics resembled the odor of what comes out of a pig in a barnyard. It stands to reason that as the level of verbal violence in a conversation increases, its articulate content deteriorates. Moreover, in a situation where the coin of the conversational realm is obscene attack words, no other verbal currency has as much value.

Now, to "worse words." Studying the history, number and characteristics of ethnic slur epithets, as well as the moment when particular ones entered American English, Irving Lewis Allen found that these terms are integrally related to cultural conditions. They arise from cultural contact between immigrant groups, especially in cities, and are "aggravated by inequality, perceptions of competition, and the forces of market society." Allen, a historian of language, contends that American English has always been burdened with an oversupply of terms of opprobrium; moreover, the United States' history of incorporating successive waves of immigrant groups from disparate backgrounds makes for an unusually large residual repertoire of ethnic slurs, which combines with English grammar and word patterns to make American English "particularly conducive to vocabularies of prejudice." Allen's numerical studies revealed that the number of nicknames for broad racial entities is largest for the minority population that has been here the longest and is the largest—the African-Americans. He also discovered that established slurs are transferred and applied to newer immigrant groups as they displace older ones as the focal point of anger; whereas Negroes were once derogated as "lazy," that epithet was increasingly applied to Hispanics as their number here soared. Similarly, Jewish immigrants were once excoriated as "cunning" or "money-grubbing;" in more recent years, those same nasty terms have been applied to the newly successful among Asian immigrants. Extending his analysis into sociology, Allen writes that for the majority, name-calling of minorities is an attempt to control them and to justify "inequality and discrimination by sanctioning individious cultural comparisons." He also contends that ethnic slur words serve some purpose for minorities in terms of group cohesion and demarcating the boundary between the majority and the minority.[12]

While these last conclusions may be unduly speculative, there is no doubt that slurs in the mouth of the majority accomplish the purpose of closing the mind: there is no reason for further consideration if blacks are stupid and Hispanics are lazy.

Kenneth G. Wilson's studies also led him to look beyond individual words to how language was being used now in ways that were different from those of a quarter-century ago. Philosophical about some matters that upset other English professors, such as the erosion of the subjunctive, a form he considered to be of limited use anyway, Wilson was disturbed by imprecision in word usage. Although "less" specifically refers to quantity and "fewer" to number, and the two words are not interchangeable, today's students frequently substitute one for the other, thereby muddling the meaning of both. In similar losses of precision, abstract nouns are being stripped of their pejorative connotations: "enormity" is now used to denote something large, not something monstrous, and "notoriety" is equated only with fame, not with being unsavory. Language uses abstract words to widen descriptive horizons and to provide added possibilities for insight. Diminished precision in abstract modifiers results in sentences that are vague and generalized rather than cogent and potent.

The transmogrification of nouns into verbs, and strong verbs into weaker ones, has been taking place for centuries. "Clout," in the fourteenth century a strong and active verb meaning to hit a hard blow, as in "she clouts him," is now either a transitive verb or a noun whose synonym is political power. "Huddle," a formerly strong verb—as in Emma Lazarus's line about "huddled masses yearning to breathe free"—has seen its old connotations of disorder stripped by football jargon, so that today "huddle" is a noun that stands for the orderly circle or patterned row of linesmen that faces the quarterback before each offensive play. To use "huddle" today as it was once used is to risk being misunderstood.

Kenneth Cmiel reminds us that there were plenty of linguistic errors in the popular speech of the nineteenth century in the United States, and that some observers saw them as revealing "a deep cultural illness. . . . The unstable tongue was indicative of the American ethos. Americans were restless, hostile to the tempering of tradition, almost mindlessly committed to innovation." While Cmiel ridicules the contention of cultural illness as elitist cant, he nevertheless charges that the ultimate victory of the nineteenth-century champions of popular speech harmed good discourse, because "the language of the common people lacked the breadth and perspicuity needed to house true eloquence."[13] Fullness and insight are made possible by the plethora of abstract words that English contains, but today such words exist only at the rarefied upper reaches of the frequency-of-use lists: very few people use them regularly.

The last study to consider in this brief survey of the inroads made into the modern language is a 1990 examination of "conversational narcissism," which documents how Americans routinely turn conversations from topics of general interest to themselves. This tendency, the authors of the study contend, is pervasive and rooted in our culture of individualism, a pattern that leads to self-absorption. Analyzing a series of conversations held in various settings, they find conversation increasingly characterized by the overuse of "I" statements, by boasting, by the tactic of asking questions only in order to demonstrate the questioner's superior knowledge or to top the other person's story with one's own, and by continual shifting of the conversational focus to the self. The most frequently used written word in the language is "the"; but the most frequently used spoken word, the authors remind us, is "I".[14]

While imprecision is leaching out of the language properly descriptive words like "enormity" by stripping them of their pejorative meaning, and while words like "lazy" and "cunning" are increasingly proscribed in our vocabulary—removed, as it were, by force, because they have accumulated too many negative connotations having to do with the flashpoints of ethnic and racial prejudice—our language is increasingly infiltrated by epithets, ethnic slurs, expressions of personal feelings, and combative constructions. Politicians, who feel keenly the need to reach the broadest number of people, have embraced rather than rejected these diminutions of language. Their discourse suffers accordingly—and so do all of us who hear it.

In the early 1920s, when H. L. Mencken wrote his classic study *The American Language*, he thought the greatest danger was that American

English would become a separate language from British English and would thereby lose a good deal of its linguistic heritage. He savaged such abominations as slang, jargon, expletives, and terms of abuse, but when it came to euphemisms, Mencken was—by today's lights—curiously restrained:

> The American seldom believes that the trade he follows is quite worthy of his virtues and talents; he thinks that he would have adorned something far gaudier. Since it is impossible for him to escape, he soothes himself by pretending that he belongs to a superior section of his craft, and even invents a sonorous name to set himself off from the herd. Here we glimpse the origin of . . . *mortician* for *undertaker, realtor* for *real-estate agent, beautician* for *hairdresser, exterminating engineer* for *rat catcher,* and so on.[15]

Mencken decided that the most awful offense was the substitution of phrases like "passed away" for the more realistic "died" and decried all similar attempts to avoid the unpleasantness of death. Mencken's uncharacteristic blandness when it comes to euphemism becomes understandable only when we realize that his study was written before the heyday of the Nazi and Soviet regimes, whose totalitarian language usages have greatly affected the language of politics, not only in their own empires but also in the United States and in much of the Western world.

When the armies of the Great War were still mired in trenches and the outcome was in doubt, President Woodrow Wilson made a bold pass at altering the map of Europe by using a phalanx of charged words (rather than the armies in the field) to try to overthrow tyrannical governments. His goals were to end the war and at the same time to install democracy in Germany and other monarchies. He articulated his appeals in leaflets that were dropped by airplanes directly to the soldiers and civilians of the enemy nations, a tactic that bypassed the heads of state with whom negotiations between countries had traditionally been held. Those printed speeches amounted to one prolonged call for revolt, couched in a rhetoric that declared war on all autocracies. Shortly the German people overthrew the Kaiser and his minions, and several Balkan states engaged in similar revolutions. The success of Wilson's inflammatory appeals in overthrowing the established order made deep impressions on the fledgling Communists taking over Russia and on the German army corporal Adolf Hitler and his comrades, who would soon form the nucleus of the

National Socialist party. Both the Soviet Communist and German Nazi regimes sought to change language radically in the service of their goals, to paint simplified pictures of the world that construed their actions as good and everything else as bad.

Whereas Woodrow Wilson had used language whose meanings were already widely accepted, Hitler and Josef Goebbels changed language to accomplish their purposes. This process was given a name, *sprachlenkung*, a word that survived World War II and was later used to describe similar attempts at language manipulation in the Communist-led German Democratic Republic. In linguistic terms, Goebbels and Hitler swallowed the Sapir–Whorf hypothesis whole and used it to their advantage. Using the (now discredited) notion that our thoughts are conditioned by the language in which we think, they twisted language to twist thought or, more precisely, to reduce the public's capacity for thought. *Wer denkt, zweifelt schon* (he who thinks has already doubted), a Nazi slogan proclaimed; doubting was forbidden, because it led to independent conclusions. According to John Wesley Young, literary and social critic, the ultimate aim of Nazi language alterations was to produce a citizen who, "partly because of his constant exposure to the emotional and manipulative rhetoric of the Party and his addictions to dogmas and catchwords, would never— could never—exert himself to think critically about the regime and the manner of society it was creating." Hitler wanted people to embrace not a philosophy, a word that suggests activity of the mind, but Nazi viewpoints whose basic lines were to become, as he put it in *Mein Kampf*, "unforgettably branded in his memory."[16]

The Nazis recognized that even the most innocuous discussion could provoke questions and answers that might challenge their dominance. According to the philosopher Michael Foucault, participants in a discussion accept that they and everyone else involved in it have the right to speak; Foucault contends that the Nazis could not win on that sort of level playing field, so they refused to allow any real discussions. The very opposite of the willing participant in a discussion, Foucault writes, is the propagandist or polemicist, "a parasitic figure . . . an obstacle to the search for truth" that characterizes real discussion. Jacques Ellul has written that propagandists of any stripe try to produce three effects. First, they attempt to suppress the critical faculties of the hearers and to substitute collective passions. Second, propagandists try to provide justification for their listeners' actions. Third, propagandists attempt to create a new sphere of the sacred, placing entire categories of people and ideas beyond criticism—which is to say, not subject to debate. Foucault contended that the propagandist tries to "abolish" those with differing viewpoints. He identified an integral connection between the speech of totalitarian regimes and their excesses of political power: their language of "anathemas, excommunications, condemnations, battles, victories and defeats" might seem on the surface to be merely manipulation of words, but, Foucault wrote, we must remember that those words "are also ways of acting which are not without consequence."[17]

On assuming power in 1933, one of Nazis' first actions was to eliminate communications channels that might carry opposing viewpoints. Simultaneous with their efforts to capture the press, they published authorized dictionaries that expunged from the official lexicon such words as *Pressfreiheit* (freedom of the press) and passed ordnances forbidding writers from using certain words and phrases in their articles. "Red," for instance, was virtually banned from the language because it was identified with communism. In a determined thrust toward the irrational, toward emotionalism and the promotion of "counterfeit faith," Young writes, the Nazis invoked the *volk* and blood-and-soil imagery, creating from the mix "a whole emotional sublanguage, a vocabulary of the anti-rational." The Nazis also tried to legitimate their regime by employing archaic words and by referring to Hitler as the equivalent of Christ and to his followers as "the chosen." Pope Pius XI was so enraged by Nazi usurpation of Christian mythology that in his 1937 encyclical he wrote: "If they do not want to be Christians at least they should forgo enriching the vocabulary of their unbelief from the Christian treasure of ideas."[18]

Hitler's worship of the brutal, first expressed in his prison writings, carried over into the extraordinary savagery of the words and metaphors of the Nazis. Repeatedly they used adjectives that connote violence and sadism, "ruthless," "fanatical," "brutal," "brazen," "tough," "hard," "granite," "inflexible," "relentless," and particularly violent verbs, "finish off," "annihilate," "exterminate," "cut down." In their metaphors the Nazis also militarized speech, in the 1930s calling a peace offering a "peace offensive" and—still before the outbreak of actual war in 1939—congratulating themselves for having already fought "a battle for autarchy, a grain battle, a battle against mice, a battle against unemployment" and having begun a "battle of the cradle" that would lead to "world domination" by the Aryan race. Nazi speeches referred to monumental ideas like "destiny" and "fate," and featured sentences that hinged on such adjectives as "conditioned" and "predetermined" in order, Young writes, to "evoke an image of an individual devoid of free will and frozen into one spot in an unchangeable cosmic pattern." The culmination of these usages was a lumping together of all enemies into one phrase that employed newly created or hyphenated words because a single one could not properly describe the enormity of the foe. Hitler started the practice of compound epithets in *Mein Kampf*, which castigates the "tearful pacifist professional female mourners." Upon his taking power, the enemy became "the international world Jew," a phrase that encompassed both those Jews presumed to have influence in the West and other Jews presumed to have influence in the U.S.S.R. Goebbels expanded the net of opprobrium to include all of Hitler's enemies as the "plutocratic-Jewish-Masonic-Marxist-Communist System" and later in the war, when the siege of Stalingrad was going badly for the Nazis, the enemy became the "Jewish-bolsho-pluto-democratic International." No wonder Goebbels confided to his diary his pride in his "lexicon of abuse."[19]

The Nazis also sired a lexicon of euphemisms. In order to prevent civilians from objecting to the onset of war when Nazi armies invaded Poland, Germans were told it was a "police action." The same fear that the German populace would see through what the Nazis were doing spawned many other circumlocutions. The withholding of money from workers' paychecks was touted as "voluntary contributions" to the unemployed, while the razing of a Protestant church that had been a focal point of opposition to the government was "urban renewal." The SS did not arrest people and confiscate their belongings, they took citizens into "protective custody" for the purpose of "securing their property."

While euphemisms softened some government actions, others were toughened by purposely skewed language uses. "We are all steel and iron/ We are all prime material," the Hitler Youth sang, as if they were not and ought not to be human beings. Dehumanizing imagery emphasized to the German people that they could be "tempered like steel, charged like batteries, or synchronized like watches or stoplights." Nonhuman terms served to deride the Reich's enemies, who were regularly called dogs, subhuman vermin, "international maggots and bedbugs." Areas of a city were made *judenfrei*, a process that stamped out the Jews in the way that an exterminator would stamp out roaches. To speak of the Reich's objects of disdain as more like bugs than people made it easier to act inhumanely toward them.[20] In many and varied ways, the Nazis' alterations of language did influence if not always control thought, for it led directly to the rationalization, and to the acceptance by the German population, of the worst excess of the Third Reich, the extermination camps in which 6 million Jews and several million other people were put to death.

Max Horkheimer, founder of the Frankfurt Institute for Social Research, had written convincingly prior to the Nazi era that the principal challenge of the mass culture industry to civilization lay in its assault on the capacity to engage in critical thought. When the Nazis overran Germany, Horkheimer, concerned about their language distortion processes, came to believe that a Nazi battlefield triumph would result in the demise of reason itself. "When the idea of reason was conceived," Horkheimer wrote, "it was intended to achieve more than the mere regulation of the relation between means and ends; it was regarded as the instrument for understanding the ends, for *determining* them." Lacking the words and the thought processes to understand the ends, therefore to express notions contrary to the ruling power, people in a Nazified future would be unable to resist or even intellectually countervail that power.[21] Though the Nazis did not prevail, the threat that Horkheimer identified in their language distortions—the extermination of reason itself—survived the war, and not only in Germany.

Lenin stated that the Communist Party's most important task was "the selection of language." Russian Communism, more theoretically based and doctrinaire than National Socialism, was more dogmatic in its insistence on controlling language and had many more years of absolute power in which to affect the minds of its people. Whereas Hitler never hid his totalitarianism, Lenin, Stalin, and their successors consistently cloaked their harsh regime in the verbal garb of its opposite—extolling representative democracy while rigging elections, ruling in the name of the workers while forbidding strikes, thundering against exploitation while perfecting systems of forced labor, championing independence while holding half of Europe in vassalage.

According to *Pravda*, the goal of the Party was to be "the only master of the minds, the only expresser of the thoughts and hopes, the only leader and organizer of the people." Communist language in support of those goals had three distinct functions: to fan mass enthusiasm for the Party and its policies; to distort reality and impose a Marxist-Leninist *mirovozzreniye* or world outlook on the masses; and to foster in the masses "an uncritical intellect, a reduced mental condition in which they can do little more than assent to their complete domination by the state."[22]

Communists verbally divided the world into the good Communist camp and the bad capitalist camp. Heaven was life under communism, and hell was capitalist society. This either/or, all-or-nothing view was further accentuated by the common practice of combining each negative word applied to the enemy, such as "lackeys," with a pejorative adjective like "imperialistic," "reactionary," "counterrevolutionary," or "petit-bourgeois" to make certain the audience understood how inky the blackness really was.

The aim of name-calling was to so ingrain certain phrases in the minds of Communist audiences that just mentioning the phrases would produce knee-jerk reactions. According to Aleksandr Solzhenitsyn, for centuries the word *kulak* had meant "a miserly, dishonest rural trader who grows rich not by his own labor but through someone else's"; the word was permuted by Stalin so that it came to stand for crafty peasants who worked against the interests of the state. Once that definition had replaced the old one, Stalin could announce that whole areas had to be "de-kulakized" (*raskulachivat*) to rid them of undesirables—when, as Solzhenitsyn insists, the real kulaks were desirable because they were independent and represented the strength of the people. Many such words were put into circulation, Solzhenitsyn writes, "and although they meant nothing they were easily remembered, they simplified matters, they made thought completely unnecessary."[23]

The Party was the monolith to be worshiped, continually extolled for its "unity," "strength," "leadership," "wisdom," and "superior understanding." Such words could no longer be applied to individuals other than when they spoke directly for or through the Party. Official spokesmen so frequently used "struggle," "comrade," and "solidarity" that these words dropped all nuances of meaning beyond those assigned by the Party. Though it was logically inconsistent for a "peace-loving" regime to use violent or harsh words, Young suggests that caustic words dotted Communist discourse because the Party encouraged the hating of opposing institutions and ideology. More so than the Nazis, the Communists used euphemisms to subvert one of the main purposes of any language, the identification of things in the world. While Nazi euphemisms attempted to disguise the intent of the speaker, Soviet euphemisms tried to force the adoption of the speaker's point of view that something known to the hearer to be bad was actually something good. A puppet regime was a "people's democracy," the Berlin Wall an "anti-fascist dike," and the Soviet empire a "fraternal family of socialist countries." Lukewarm allies were upgraded to "brothers," while enemies' appelations became resonant with layers of meaning: "capitalists-imperialists," "reactionary tools" or "lackeys of the capitalists," "socialists who played into the hands of the imperialists," or—even more hated—"traitors to the Party."

These linguistic devices, which in the West seem easy to parody and include ironic quotation marks, pejorative prefixes, and the use of phrases like "so-called," were more difficult for the audience inside the Iron Curtain to discern or challenge. For them the phrases served as mnemonics and directives. After the former diplomat Arkady Shevchenko defected from Russia, he could look back and write that his Communist upbringing had conditioned him "to speak in formulas without reflection or vacillation."[24]

The mnemonic, reflexive character of both Nazi and Communist speech echoes the cardinal split that Walter Ong has identified between the oral and the literate societies. For Ong, an important aspect of that divide has to do with the different ways that oral-based and literate-based populations have of knowing about the world. He uses the phrase the "oral noetic" to describe the manner in which oral populations acquire, formulate, store, and retrieve knowledge. Interpreting Ong, the speech communications professor Frank Dance draws attention to a handful of such oral knowing devices: mnemonics; formulaic expressions; the standardization of themes; the "epithetic" identification of classes or individuals; the cultivation of praise and vituperation; and the "formulary, ceremonial appropriation of history." The frequent repetition of such phrases as "running dogs of capitalism," a favorite Communist slogan, is not only formulaic but also a labeling that turns individuals into cartoon characters that are easy to hate. The oral way of knowing, Dance writes, is the opposite of analytic; it is "empathetic and participatory rather than objectively distanced."[25]

In other words, by imposing oral ways of knowing and paths of thought, the Nazi and Soviet tyrannies were attempting to force their captives toward ways of behaving that preceded the introduction of the written word—to bomb them verbally, as it were, back into the thinking modes of the Stone Age.

Having worked assiduously to bring about the defeats of both the Nazi and Soviet regimes, the people of the United States have in too many ways adopted the totalitarian empires' villainous underminings of language. We are in danger of becoming what we heard and once despised.

In 1948, when George Orwell's novel *Nineteen Eighty-Four* was first published, "doublespeak" and the empire it reflected were considered an attack on totalitarianism, especially the Soviet kind. Doublespeak's main feature was the eclipsing of all possibilities of reason, so that the only version of reality known to the public would be that promulgated by the government. Thought itself was to be narrowed so that the only mental gyrations possible would be in areas the state considered safe. The official language of Oceania is Newspeak, which, Orwell writes, "was designed not to extend but to *diminish* the range of thought."[26] Less remarked at the time was that Orwell's conception of doublespeak was also an attack on the steady diminution of the English language by nontotalitarian enemies. Orwell identified those enemies in his other writings, for instance, decrying the ever wider adoption of "cablese," the shorthand in which newspaper and radio wire services communicated between the field and the home office, and excoriating the euphemistic language of bureaucrats.

In 1989 the American National Council of Teachers of English issued a volume that examines "doublespeak in a post-Orwellian age." The editor, William Lutz, suggests that the parodist "would be surprised at the new and ever more sophisticated and effective misuses of language which have been developed since [1948]. He would also be surprised at the pervasiveness of language misuse; at how it has spread from the language of politics to the language of business, of education, and almost all aspects of life."[27]

Lutz is undoubtedly correct, but he has not identified the reason the misuses have spread. The Nazis and Soviets believed every element of society had to be infused with political meaning; we are in the midst of a similar though less calculated transformation by language, one that reflects the extension of the marketplace ethic into every arena of American life. This commodification exercise has as its goal the avoidance of blame and the euphemistic encapsulation of all matters that if bluntly named might provide the mass audience with reason to dislike the speaker. Hugh Rank, a communications professor, provides an important clue about the new language uses. In the old days in politics, he suggests, it was possible to distinguish the essence of advertising, the pitch, from the essence of political appeals, the pep talk. While the pep talk had been designed "to organize and direct the energy of a group toward committed collective action" by having the political speaker ask the group to join a party or a particular political movement, today's politicians no longer ask people to join a cause. Rather, Rank contends, they "toss the pitch," that is, they ask us to make a onetime purchase and to give them our votes. Even when pitch-makers are not at that very moment running for election, Rank says, the pitch is still the essence of their discourse.[28]

In the political arena, the pitch has led to decades of slippery language, from the locutions of the Vietnam era—phrases like "protective reaction strike"—to the equivocations of the 1980s and early 1990s—such as President Ronald Reagan's "mistakes were made" phrase in answer to charges about trading arms for hostages, and that phrase's echo in candidate Bill Clinton's apology for off-the-cuff remarks about Italian-Americans and the Mafia, "wounds were caused." Who caused the wounds? Who made the mistakes? The Clinton and Reagan responses deliberately begged these questions in order to evade personal responsibility for the misdeeds.

Politicians as well as corporate chieftains speak today of "restructuring" and "downsizing," of mergers that will "eliminate redundancy." Repeated many times, these words eventually pass unremarked into our everyday lexicon, but they are still attempts to disguise what can often be the harsh reality of firing wholesale lots of people to achieve better bottom lines. Schools used to refer to their charges solely as students, but to some schools and to the government's educational bureaucracy they are now known as "clients"; educators and bureaucrats also speak of "success" and "accomplishment" rather than the process of learning. Such substitutions are not innocuous. In them, communicative and precisely descriptive words are eclipsed and replaced by words that reflect strategies—in this instance, drastically changed strategies. The difference is this: While a student or pupil is in school to be educated, a client is there to be served. Strategic shifts of intention have similarly surfaced in the language used by health care and the arts, as professionals and government bureaucrats increasingly encourage medical and artistic institutions to conceive of themselves as producers and marketers of commodities to be consumed by their respective customer bases.

Many alterations of language by nonpoliticians that are essentially political are not as focused or as consciously employed, but they nevertheless incorporate some of the tactics and even the precise phraseology of the totalitarian regimes. When Gloria Steinem tells Oprah Winfrey and a television audience of tens of millions that "it is no accident" that American society is still dominated by white males, I cringe at her echoing of a Communist stock phrase, one that in the nations dominated by the Soviet Union served to introduce contentions designed to be reflexively affirmed rather than examined to test their validity. It undercuts Steinem's message to use words so heavily freighted with totalitarian baggage. It makes it difficult to evaluate her conclusions on their own merits. More chilling are the language uses regularly adopted by political partisans that bifurcate the world as the Nazis and the Soviets did—"you're either with us or against us"—or echoes of the way areas were made *judenfrei* and the Jewish "problem" was "solved" by the Nazis, as when the construction of "drug-free zones" is advocated as a way to "solve" the drug "problem." To label enemies, Jews, drugs, poverty, particles in the air, or preschool day care as a "problem" is always a strategic act—a political act—although speakers may not be aware of speaking strategically when they use such frames of reference. The recent national brouhaha over "health care" provided a cornucopia of phrases and labeling for strategic purposes. One group spoke of "preferred providers," by which they meant doctors who would sign contracts to offer care at low unit cost, rather than doctors who were so highly qualified that patients would prefer them to any others. A second group spoke of "universal coverage" when they meant that poor people would be able to go to doctors even if unable to pay for their services, and that tax dollars would pay for such visits. Nearly every term used in the debate over health-care was equally loaded with political meanings, to the point that the contest seemed to be waged between competing sets of euphemisms. So widespread are strategic uses and misuses of words today that they are seldom recognized as political attempts to modify the ways in which an audience thinks about the world.

It has become difficult for audiences to know when communication is honest and properly descriptive and when it is not. Rank suggests that language must always be analyzed in context with the whole situation; when this is done, it is possible to separate hurtful euphemisms from those whose purposes are mostly banal.[29] Mencken to the contrary notwithstanding, to say that a person has "passed away" instead of that the person died is to employ delicacy of phrasing that may serve to assuage a grieving relative. Similarly it may be helpful (or at least banal) for us to refer to "mental hospitals" in preference to "lunatic asylums," because the change in wording assists us in understanding that the people confined to such places are human beings who can and should be treated for illness, not necessarily dangerous and irrational monsters who bear no resemblance to normal people.

On the other hand, by Rank's test it was surely more hurtful and deceptive than banal for the Department of Defense to refer euphemistically to civilian casualties of bombs dropped on Iraq in 1991 as "collateral damage," because the phrase has been designed to prevent the hearer from immediately recognizing that the words mask violent and unwanted deaths.

The issue is not always clear-cut. In 1984 our State Department dropped the word "killing" from its annual reports on the status of human rights abroad and substituted "unlawful or arbitrary deprivation of life." One view of this particular language substitution is that it was an infusion of legalisms not particularly designed to obscure, but William Lutz was moved to write that it was a maneuver that permitted State to avoid discussion of the "embarrassing situation of government-sanctioned killings in countries that are supported by the United States" and employed phrases "designed to mislead, to cover up the unpleasant . . . to alter our perception of reality."[30] Confusion is often the result of attempts at political language use. Were the Contras "freedom fighters," "guerrillas," or "terrorists"? At the time the Contras were fighting the Sandinista regime in Nicaragua, each of the three labels was regularly used by a different political group in the United States, the first two by groups that supported the Contras, the third by those who did not. In such situations the public's difficulty in figuring out which label might be the most accurate is compounded when a government phrase that has been initially viewed with skepticism by the press becomes routinized through repeated use, accepted and repeated by the media without further questioning.[31]

Sympathetic with the Contras or not, we must agree that attaching a label like "freedom fighters" to a group opposed to a regime is not a communication designed to convey the essential truth but a comment on the truth. That sort of comment on the truth, a forcing of the language away from direct expression, is one of the ways that tyranny always employs to eclipse true eloquence. In an important analysis, the dean of the Annenberg School of Communications, Kathleen Hall Jamieson, contends that true eloquence can thrive "only when the forum is open and freedom of speech is the norm," because when free speech is circumscribed, its place is always taken by "forms of communications better able to protect their rhetors."[32]

Protecting the rhetor is the basic function of political euphemisms, that staple of modern American political language. Some analysts believe that euphemisms are the only linguistic strategy appropriate for dealing with the enormity of the atomic age. Just as atomic bombs exceeded previous understandings of explosive power and destructive effects, they also defied and confounded the descriptive powers of language, Richard Ohrmann suggests. Those factors led to a misuse of language not confined to any particular administration or in response to any particular crisis; rather, Ohrmann writes, an "accumulated legacy of concept and language" has been passed from one administration to the next because we have been "carrying on daily life with the bomb in our midst."[33]

Even in the post–Cold War era, our language continues to be corrupted in totalitarian ways. We have applied dehumanizing and demonizing labels in situations where we have not been at war, for instance when American hostages were taken in Iran and when Kuwaiti oil fields were seized by Iraq. To equate Saddam Hussein with Hitler as President Bush did may induce patriotic feelings among Americans, but such tactics serve to prevent us from obtaining a full, many-sided understanding of the conflict involving that leader.

The end of the Cold War provides an opportunity to reassess our use of language during it. Between 1945 and 1990, were we in the West accurate in contending that the entire world was divided into the same either/or, mutually exclusive categories that were used to bifurcate it linguistically by the rulers of the U.S.S.R.? Did our use of words in this period push us to focus too much attention on our disputes with the Soviets and thereby to prevent us from turning our resources to countering the economic wars being waged against us by the resurgent economies of Germany and Japan?

Euphemisms and their cousin, jargon, often serve to demarcate boundaries between an in-group and everyone else. Again, there must be distinctions drawn between hurtful and banal uses. "Autologous bone-marrow transplant" may be an impenetrable jargon phrase to those outside the medical profession, but to physicians considering a treatment for a certain kind of cancer, it is a very specific reference. We seem to have more jargon today than in the past, and much of it has come into existence for the purposes of excluding, confusing, and misleading outsiders rather than for facilitating the communication of insiders. Nowhere has this trend been more apparent than in the communications of bureaucrats. Consider the words of Alan Greenspan, when as chairman of President Reagan's Council of Economic Advisers he testified before a Senate committee about possible changes in Social Security benefits: "It is a tricky problem to find the particular calibration in timing that would be appropriate to stem the acceleration in risk premiums created by falling incomes without prematurely aborting the decline in the inflation-generated risk premiums."[34] A specialist in economics might extract the meaning from this statement, but it was probably not understood by the committee and was certainly not squeezed out by the lay public. Greenspan's statement is language that only pretends to communicate; it is euphemism combined with jargon for a nefarious purpose: not to clarify but to obscure, so that no one would be able to disagree with the proposed action (or nonaction) because no one would be able to grasp it. Such deliberate opacity exemplifies what Orwell had in mind when he observed: "The great enemy of clear language is insincerity . . . a gap between one's real and one's declared aims."[35]

In the centuries preceding the introduction of the printing press, those who held power reinforced it by uses of language that mystified the powerless and kept them subservient. Even more so in today's world, power is inextricably tied to the use of language, and today's priesthood of professionals in many fields employs jargon-fueled mystification. That is a political use of language that deliberately excludes the "powerless" lay audience from participation. The doctor whose technical terms confuse, no less than the politician whose equivocations obfuscate, the lawyer whose terms intimidate, and the accountant whose explanations obscure, is taking advantage of audiences through what are called "gatekeeper" uses of language. They include euphemisms, jargon, and other devices designed to prevent rather than augment the free flow of knowledge. Lawyers have been particularly egregious in this practice. Writing of language in the legal process, Brenda Danet charges:

> Members of the legal profession publicly claim to deal with truth and facts but are actually preoccupied with elaborate rules governing the flow of talk and silence and have evolved a highly esoteric professional language, incomprehensible to those whose fate is at stake, that dominates the courtroom. To varying degrees, all these uses of language in legal settings reveal a preoccupation with language [as] the source of mystification. It obscures the referential function in language, the function that informs us about the world.[36]

Gatekeeper language also frequently masks what physicians do especially in circumstances that can be fraught with emotion. A relative of a cancer patient, seeking straight and hard informational answers to questions— how bad is the situation, how much time does she have left, is there any hope—was informed by her doctor that his relative's cancer was "treatable" and her prognosis was "guarded." A month later, after the patient died, the relative braced the physician again and was told that technically the patient's disease had been treatable—all conditions can be treated, some more effectively than others—and that in the context "guarded" meant simply that the patient's deterioration toward death had been carefully monitored. Charles Weingartner, a language analyst, deconstructs what happens in situations like that one, where the information provided by the speaker is "bad." While the doctor's discourse contained no deliberate lying, it was full of disinformation and semi-information. Weingartner defines "disinformation" as "utterances that do not easily permit the assignment of any meaning with any degree of assurance . . . [with a] conscious purpose of diverting interested parties from the pursuit of information." "Semi-information" comes in partial bits, some of which are accurate, "but none of which are adequate for the purpose of understanding either the matter involved or its possible consequences."[37] These "bad information" tricks are political uses of language, and while the doctor may have thought of them as banal, the patient and her family experienced them as hurtful.

The philosopher Jürgen Habermas provides an insight into the political nature of gatekeeper uses of language through his identification of the "scientization of the public sphere," a process now occurring in many societies. In this trend, elites effectively disqualify members of the public from being able to participate in policy discussions by insisting that only specialists can really understand what is going on.[38] When politicians come to believe that only they can understand what is going on in the high councils of government, and that their job is to translate it for us and to protect themselves in the process, the language they aim at the electorate takes on more and more aspects of purposeful deceit.

Political correctness has been seen as part of the continuing debate between conservatives and liberals. It is more precise and perhaps more helpful to regard political correctness as having its roots in gatekeeper language and other language uses that have their most virulent predecessors in the excesses of the Nazis and Soviets.

Most politically correct words and phrases are euphemisms, and as is the case with other euphemisms, there are helpful/banal ones, and provocative/destructive ones. Politically sensitive language that helps us to be civil, to curb racial and ethnic epithets, and to accommodate ourselves to our neighbors ought not to be casually lumped together with more severe and detrimental misuses of language. When a young gentleman of my acquaintance, whose birth certificate name is William, wants to be called "Bill," not William, Will, Willy, or Billy, I believe it is important to us both for me to address him by the name he chooses, and not by any other name. When Americans of African descent choose to be called "African-Americans" rather than blacks or Negroes or Afro-Americans—appellations previously considered acceptable—to give them proper respect I must change my behavior to meet their wish. Although there may be a political agenda in "African-American," I consider the term benign and must use it or else risk no longer being civil in my discourse. I also accept that stigmatization is most sensitively judged by those who feel they may be stigmatized, and that as an outsider I may very well have to curb my behavior to avoid unwittingly giving offense. Even though I am technically free under the First Amendment to use any name I may choose to apply to a particular group (or person), I acknowledge, as do most Americans, that this freedom of speech is not absolute and is and should be constrained by the boundaries of civility.

Unfortunately, civility and sensitivity take one only so far. In Kenya, a visitor is judged by how he or she pronounces the name of the country;

the British say KEEN-ya, while black Africans say KEN-ya. A visitor can choose which pronunciation to use. Sometimes, no matter what one may want to say, potential sensitivity is deliberately blocked. During Nelson Mandela's tour of the United States following his release from prison in South Africa, many T-shirts were printed with maps of the African continent, Mandela's likeness, and the words, "It's a black thing. You wouldn't understand." Who wouldn't? And why not? Are whites excluded by birth from possible understanding? This latter implication offended Dr. Johnetta B. Cole, the African-American scholar who is president of Spelman College. She told an interviewer that she hated the choice of words on those T-shirts and would have had them read, instead, "It's a black thing. You must try to understand."[39] Cole's rephrasing returns us to the civility that all sides must observe during the continuing dialogue of public life and reiterates the point that when civility is broached there begins a downward spiral of language that becomes increasingly difficult to halt.

Full civility becomes harder for outsiders to maintain when not everyone in a definable group agrees what decent and respectful conversation requires. Among the large and disparate population of Americans whose families have come from Spanish-speaking countries, some are willing to be called (as the census now labels them) "Hispanic," but a large percentage prefer "Latinos" or "Latinas." Sandra Cisneros refuses to have her writings included in any anthology that uses the word "Hispanic" and explains the difference between Hispanic and Latino: "To say Latino is to say you come to my culture in a manner of respect," she told an interviewer, while she contends that for an insider to refer to oneself as Hispanic "means you're so colonized you don't even know for yourself or someone who named you never bothered to ask what you call yourself. It's a repulsive slave name." According to a recent survey, most people of this background would rather be known as "Colombian-Americans," "Mexican-Americans," and so on—terms that are more specific to their country of origin—or the term preferred by many of the second generation who were born in the United States, simply "Americans."[40]

Very soon after the boundary line of civility is passed, we descend to the level where the requests for labeling changes are less benign and more likely to result in distortions that diminish the language. While I recognize that it is no longer fully acceptable to some females for me to refer to "mankind" in speaking of all the human beings of the world, I am not yet ready to scratch that reasonably descriptive word out of my lexicon. The first substitutes listed for it in the thesaurus are "human race" and "humanity"—both of which, women might point out, are also encumbered with the unfortunately phallocentric word "man." Similarly, while I am willing to put "crippled" on the shelf because I have accepted the reasoning that the word offends and unduly stigmatizes some people (especially those whose impairments were evident at birth), it gives me pause to be asked to substitute the phrase "differently abled" or "physically challenged" when referring to people whose abilities have been impaired. Are we not all differently abled one from another, all physically challenged in various ways—for instance, by age? To be required to strike out of my vocabulary the word "disabled" is to cut into my ability to describe. Recently the Los Angeles *Times* put out guidelines that banned or restricted the use of 150 words or phrases, among them some ethnically offensive ones— "Chinese fire drill" and to "welsh"—but also some that are precise and descriptive, such as "stepchild" and "crazy."[41] This diminution of the descriptive possibilities exacerbates and furthers the hidden political agenda, tipping the balance in such uses from banal into hurtful.

Descriptive possibilities are being assaulted from all sides, for instance, in the killers' attempts to substitute the phrase "ethnic cleansing" for the word "genocide" in press reports about Bosnia. Granted, "genocide" itself is a heavily freighted word, but it is descriptive; to adopt (without outrage) the newer term "ethnic cleansing" in regard to the destruction of Muslim populations is to turn a blind eye to evil, to refuse to accept the lessons of history irrevocably associated with "genocide" and—not incidentally—to support the political agenda of the killers. Other examples demonstrate that to use a word overlayered with historical significance when it is inappropriate to the situation is just as wrong. When a Hasidic Jewish driver accidentally killed an African-American child in the Crown Heights section of Brooklyn in 1991, and in reaction there was a riot in the African-American community during which a visiting Australian rabbinical student was killed, some politicians—former New York City Mayor Ed Koch, and then-mayoral candidate Rudolph Giuliani among them—called the riots a "pogrom." That was a deliberately inflammatory use of a word previously understood as applying only to state-supported mass murder. In the process of attempting to pander to the Jewish vote, the misusers of the word actually affronted people whose relatives had died in real pogroms.

Politically freighted language is disemboweling our attempts at ordinary description. In Los Angeles, a place dubbed by the columnist Joe Klein during a recent election season "the city of euphemisms," the roving bands of people and the fiery destruction of neighborhoods that took place in the wake of the acquittal of police officers in the first Rodney King trial were referred to by some public officials as "events" and by other leaders as "uprisings" or "insurrection" in order to avoid using the word "riot." Representative Maxine Waters of South-Central Los Angeles told Klein, "Well, if you call it a riot, it sounds like it was just a bunch of crazy people who went out and did bad things for no reason. I maintain it was somewhat understandable, if not acceptable. So I call it a *rebellion*."[42]

To describe or label something as complex and many-sided as what happened in Los Angeles after the Rodney King verdict by any single word, no matter what particular word is used, is oversimplification—another characteristic language technique of totalitarian regimes. But oversimplification is the order of the day. "Just Say No" is a wonderful slogan for a campaign designed to help children stay away from the pernicious influences of illegal drugs; the danger comes in mistaking the slogan for the only instruction necessary to accomplish the goal. No single phrase can replace the complex set of instructions and understandings of drugs and human nature that workers in the field know is needed in order to provide children with strategies for refusing to use drugs. To refer to members of one political party as "tax-and-spenders," and members of the other as "trickle-downers" is to oversimplify and distort by cutting out subtle distinctions and shades of difference. Those who believe all life is sacred and therefore that women ought not to be permitted to have abortions want their position to be known as "pro-life," a positive term, but their opponents would rather call them "anti-abortionists," while reserving the term "pro-choice" for their own belief in a woman's right to obtain an abortion if she wants one. In fact, all extreme positions on any issue are easily and quickly caricatured. To finely differentiate the various stances cutting out subtle distinctions and shades of difference adopted by dozens of more moderate and central political stripes requires lots of abstract concepts and words. Oversimplification goes hand in glove with the impulse to denature the abstract words on which subtleties of explanation often depend. Politicians today prefer simple, short, and straightforward words. But when longer words are entirely avoided, the result is to push us farther toward the sort of oversimplified world views that Hitler and Stalin decreed for their subjects.

The perceived need to advance sociopolitical agendas continues to subvert and destroy useful and descriptive words and phrases throughout society. The tennis professional Pam Shriver was quoted as saying that the playing of Zina Garrison-Jackson (her partner when they won a Gold Medal at the Olympics in Seoul) in a particular match in England in the spring of 1993 was "stupid"—and Garrison-Jackson, an African-American, said that the use of the word had racial overtones and demanded an apology, which was immediately forthcoming.[43] But every practitioner of every sport plays some matches stupidly and others intelligently. Must "stupid" now join "lazy" and "crazy" as forbidden words? Does it merit inclusion on a list of words not to be uttered by white persons lest they be construed by African-Americans as negative? Already some African-Americans contend that while they are permitted to use the word "nigger," a white person may not do so; I appreciate the sentiment behind that notion, but I am more in agreement with the feelings of those who are revulsed by hearing the word come from anyone's mouth.

When certain words are reserved to be said only by the in-group, and many other words are proscribed by in-groups, that is a political process, precisely the one employed by the Communist Party in the Soviet Union to capture language from the people. That sort of capture enabled an organization called the National Stigma Clearinghouse to persuade the John Deere Company to stop a series of advertisements that used the theme "the world's first schizophrenic lawn mower," because the Clearinghouse successfully contended that the use of "schizophrenic" in a nonmedical context was inappropriate and demeaned those who suffer from that particular mental disease. The Clearinghouse's cofounder was also recently reported to be upset over a syndicated Doug Marlette comic strip, *Kudzu*, in which a character joked, "I can't decide which feature I like best in 'Modern Depression' magazine . . . the monthly column 'What's the Point' . . . or the 'Suicide Notes to the Editor.'" Nora Weinerth explained her dismay over those jokes to a reporter, Michael Winerip, by saying "I've known too many women who've lost family to suicides."[44]

Have we entirely lost our sense of humor, or must we now engrave the words "suicide" and "depression" into our endangered/proscribed/do-not-use list? Too much in our society has become politicized, and the process has weakened our language. A number of previously acceptable words are now in the process of being newly stigmatized and readied for removal from general use. For instance, some homosexuals and lesbians object to the term "sexual preference"; for them, the term implies the existence of a choice in sexual orientation, when they believe there is no choice involved—they are convinced that sexual orientation is genetically controlled, a contention backed up by some biological research but not confirmed by other research. In other words, even though the facts are not settled, these groups want to settle the issue by controlling the words with which the issue is discussed.

Totalitarian language uses, gatekeeper language, political correctness: These are all attempts to change meanings by narrowing them, and it becomes increasingly important to understand the narrowing phenomenon. One way to look at it is to see the narrowing in a slightly different light: as reification. To reify is to regard an abstraction as a thing, and reification is rife in contemporary culture. When a child comes to define "milk" only as a creamy white fluid that comes from a carton, that is reification—a reduction of the abstraction of milk to that which comes in a container bought in a supermarket. Milk is deemed an abstraction because it is a single-word symbol that stands for the entire complex of meanings that adults can associate with that word, meanings that range from the creamy white fluid as a reflection of motherhood to the creamy white fluid as a product of the ways in which a cow fits into her environment. Milk has a multitude of connotations and denotations; the word ought not to be constrained to the way a city-bred child might explain it. When we are too young to understand all the meanings, or when we are socialized to think of the word "milk" in too narrow a way, we lack the ability to use the word in broader, more abstract contexts, as in the phrase "the milk of human kindness."

Throughout our society, words are becoming reified. It is happening because speakers with political agendas are pushing them in that direction. The reification emphasizes literal meanings and cuts out metaphorical ones. To be adult in one's thinking is to be capable of shifting from the literal to the metaphorical meanings of a word, and to know the distinction between the two. The metaphorical dimension of words is precisely what is needed for people to expand their understanding of meaning—to expand from the simple notion of milk as what comes out of a carton to the wider understanding of milk embodied in the phrase "the milk of human kindness." Normal human mental growth may well be defined as the process of ripening the mind through discovery of meaning—a broadening in which, as the individual matures, ever more subtleties, shadings, and understandings of language are reached. The psychiatrist Patrick de Gramont has studied what happens when an individual becomes mired in literalness and cannot realize new meanings. He reports that many seriously neurotic patients are unable to "play" with words; they are stuck in literal meanings and therefore incapable of engaging in the type of thought that permits improvement in the ways that they relate to the world. The way in which psychoanalysis heals, de Gramont writes, is by helping the patient "dereify" the world—a process of helping the patient retrieve the capability of enlarging, instead of continuing to narrow, his or her metaphorical dimensions of language.[45] The distortions of meaning in political speech—and throughout society—mimic the distortions that characterize mental illness. They come about, de Gramont suggests, as a result of capture of the language in ways that push speakers and audiences toward literal rather than metaphorical or symbolic understandings of words.

This capture, de Gramont insists, is for the most part ideological, which is to say, deeply politicized. The psychiatrist suggests that such capture serves to reverse or short-circuit the process of growth toward a multilevel understanding. Meanings are defined *for* us rather than *by* us; meanings are imposed *on* us by some outside power. Someone who has had a certain meaning of a word imposed on him or her from outside might, for instance, come to understand "struggle" only as the Communist Party defines it, "welfare" only as the liberals define it, "good" only as Christian fundamentalists construe it.

The meanings of such concepts as struggle, welfare, or the good are relative and should be subject to argument. By removing from the individual the possibility of arguing over them, we too narrowly fix their meaning.

We accept and expect that society will impose some basic meanings on children's understandings, because we must all be socialized in order to live in a densely populated world. For instance, we impose the meaning of a warning signal on a red traffic light to help children stop when they see a red light and thereby prevent them from getting hurt. But the imposition of meaning on the abstract words used by adults is a danger-filled process that serves to interrupt the lifelong maturation thrust toward distinguishing shades of gray and to push us toward seeing the world only in black-and-white terms. And that is a process more characteristic of the tyrannies that we have long opposed than it ought to be of the democracy we espouse.

When concepts are oversimplified so that words are defined more literally than metaphorically, more narrowly than broadly, more concretely than abstractly, an individual's ability to think for himself or herself diminishes apace because that person is no longer "free" to use those words to the fullest extent, for the purposes of making and extending meaning. To be free, therefore, we must insist on extending meaning. We must all resist the temptation to define narrowly; we must all settle on the best words and not the shortest words or those whose intent is euphemistic, so that we may properly and fully express ourselves and our political understandings of the world.

Chapter 8

"WE, THE AUDIENCE OF THE UNITED STATES"

Abortion is one of the most divisive issues of our time, and the terms in which it is usually addressed reflect what has happened to modern American political discourse. Researching a decade's worth of writings, speeches, interviews, and other communications of pro-choice and pro-life groups in one Midwest state, Marsha L. Vanderford traced how each side attempted to discredit its adversaries "by characterizing them as un-genuine and malevolent advocates" rather than as "good people with a difference of opinion." In time, each side came to believe that the other was "un-American," their tactics "dictatorial" and their discourse full of lies. Instead of using rational discourse, both groups used what Jacques Ellul would have called propaganda tactics that attempted to suppress the hearers' critical faculties, gave the hearers justifications for their courses of action, and created a coterie of ideas that were sacred and therefore not subject to discussion. The end result of a decade of "mutual vilification" rhetoric, Vanderford writes, was that "both pro-lifers and pro-choicers considered [further] discussion between the groups as fruitless" because neither side believed the other exhibited any willingness to compromise.[1]

Such failures of debate—and there are many in modern America—promote widespread disillusionment among voters. When Michael Huspek and Kathleen E. Kendall studied the political participation of lumberjacks in the Northwest, they found that although the loggers claimed to know little about politics and detested what little they did know, they actually had strong opinions about many issues but did not voice them in political settings, because they believed saying what they believed would do no good. They refrained from going to community meetings held by politicians because, they said, they did not want to indulge in "crybaby talk." Huspek and Kendall concluded that the loggers' "withholding of voice" was an active choice to stay out of the political process. When the Roosevelt Center for the Study of American Policy examined twenty political participation projects in various states, they found that nonparticipation could not be easily ascribed to apathy or alienation; rather, it had to do with the feeling expressed by various groups, most of them minorities, that they had no reason to engage in the political process because they had less than adequate access to the information and resources that make participation possible.[2]

Stanley A. Deetz writes that many potential participants are simply forced out of the deliberative process. Some are denied access to the forum of discussion outright; in consequence of feeling excluded, they have no urge to vote and feel no responsibility to do so. Others, like the lumberjacks, believe meaningful participation is denied to them and they are permitted only to vent their spleen in a powerless forum. A third group, Deetz charges, feels shorn of its right to speak by a system that insists, in order for a person to be heard, that he or she be an expert.[3] Many of us felt that we were members of this third group in regard to the complex issue known as health care reform. The rise of "mutual vilification" rhetoric, the "withholding of voice," and what Deetz calls "discursive closure" are alarm bells sounding a significant and deleterious change in the character of those who hear and are expected to respond to American political discourse.

The number of nonvoters has become larger than the number of Republicans or Democrats. In 1988 the most popular candidate in preelection polls was "none of the above." Although 1992 figures showed a 5 percent increase in the number of voters since 1988, the Committee for the Study of the American Electorate concluded that the United States still had the lowest rate of voter participation of all of the world's democracies. The committee estimates that about 20 million former voters no longer bother to cast ballots.[4] The democratic system of governance depends on the informed consent and participation of the governed.

As that participation dwindles, we must ask what has happened to the American public and its relationship to political speakers and to the political process itself.

"Truth is the proper and sufficient antagonist to error, and has nothing to fear from the conflict," Thomas Jefferson wrote, unless human interference "disarmed" the truth of her "natural weapons, free argument and debate." Jefferson described a universe for political discussion and participation that he and his contemporaries took for granted and which was based on the Biblical injunction that "the truth shall make you free." Political discussion was a joint search for the truth conducted by speakers and hearers with the objective of arriving together at a conclusion to which more than a simple majority could agree. Reason and persuasion were the most potent weapons of this discursive realm; it was assumed that the speaker's superior elucidation of the truth would, in the minds of all fair-minded hearers, overcome lesser or error-filled argument and would persuade all hearers to come to his side. In such a context of mutual respect between speaker and hearers, political discussion helped bring forth documents in which such phrases as "We, the people of the United States" not only sounded good but also caused heads to nod in agreement because of the unanimity of sentiment and logic that the words expressed.

The Jeffersonian view of the relation between speaker and public held sway through the time when the Federalists successfully transformed the governance of the United States from direct democracy to representative democracy. In the 1820s and 1830s, Tocqueville wondered what would occur if that bond were materially changed and worried what would become of America if citizen interest flagged and if Americans' tendencies toward individually were simultaneously to go unchecked. He foresaw:

An innumerable multitude of men, all . . . incessantly endeavoring to secure the petty and paltry pleasures with which they glut their lives. Each of them, living apart, is as a stranger to the fate of all the rest. . . . He is close to [his] fellow citizens, but does not see them; he exists only . . . for himself alone. Above this race of men stands an immense and tutelary power . . . absolute, minute, regular, provident and mild. It would be like the authority of a parent if, like that authority, its object was to prepare man for manhood; but it seeks, on the contrary, to keep them in perpetual childhood: it is well content that the people rejoice provided that they think of nothing but rejoicing . . . it everyday renders the exercise of the free agency of man less useful and less frequent. . . . Such a power does not destroy, but it prevents existence, it does not tyrannize but it compresses, enervates, extinguishes and stupefies a people.[5]

The absence of citizens continually and actively involved in the public life of the country would precipitate such a tyranny. Tocqueville did not expect to see it come to pass in America.

By the second half of the nineteenth century, the climate of political debate and discourse in the democracies was changing. William Gladstone, four times Prime Minister of Great Britain in that era and among its most eloquent men, said then that the successful orator's choice "is to be what his age will have him, what it requires in order to be moved by him." In Gladstone's universe, the weight was shifting from the speaker's obligation to truth to the speaker's obligation to tell his hearers something that would move them in the ways Tocqueville had identified, ways that enervate, stupefy, and extinguish independent thought and reaction to the speaker's message. The universe of political discourse has altered still more radically in the mid-twentieth century, as is summed up neatly in Kenneth Burke's aphorism: "Only those voices from without are effective which can speak in the language of the voice within."[6] In the Jeffersonian universe, the hearers constituted an active public that took part in the discussion and had to be persuaded to agreement by the speaker; in Burke's universe, the hearers have become considerably less than a public—a passive audience best appealed to by means of emotion. This change from a public to an audience is alarming and reflects that the American political arena is moving steadily away from the search for truth and the exercise of legitimate discourse, toward a realm in which coercion replaces persuasion and achieving victory is more important than any other purpose.

To coerce requires the use of force, whereas to persuade is to cause someone to believe something by reasoning rather than by force. The psychologist Harold Barrett contends, "Persuasion depends on a positive and free response from the audience, while coercion may succeed with power alone. . . . Caring people persuade; uncaring people coerce."[7] Coercion also entails less regard for the hearers' views than does persuasion. Coercion on the part of the speaker and passivity on the part of the hearers combine to form the lifeblood of demagoguery. This chapter contends that if our political speakers are moving toward demagoguery, the fault lies not in our stars but in ourselves—in a public transformed into "We, the audience of the United States."

For what reasons does a political speaker act as though his or her hearers are an audience and not a public? Most politicians have come to believe that to reach and move the broadest possible spectrum of the citizenry, they—no less than the entertainment producers—must aim low. Less than half the adult population surveyed in a four-year study conducted by the University of Texas for the federal education office was considered able to understand a simply written paragraph; moreover, a large proportion of the semiliterate could not read an airline schedule or address an envelope for mailing. In the 1920s, when the phenomenon of low voter participation was first noted in the United States, it was chalked up to lack of schooling, and the hope was that the spread of public education would soon increase voting. However, even after a huge increase in public schooling up through the 1950s, participation remained low. The next likely culprit identified was lack of information about the candidates and the issues, and the hope was that television would provide that information and thereby increase participation. Perhaps in response to television's publicizing of campaigns, the elections of the 1960s did show a slight, satisfying rise in voting. That rise soon vanished again, and despite having an electorate that received a tremendous amount of information relevant to political candidate choice through television, newspapers, and radio, the fraction of the electorate that voted in the 1984, 1986, and 1988 elections was smaller than it had been twenty years earlier. Information alone, then, could not be the key. Research showed that the demand for political information from voters was also in decline. In 1980 an estimated 72 percent of the households whose television sets were on between six and seven o'clock did watch ABC, CBS, or NBC news; by the late 1980s, only 62 percent did so, and the fall-off could not be accounted for by a rise in CNN viewership.

Robert Entman, a political communications scholar, suggests that for some time now the majority of the American population has had very little interest in what goes on in the political arena. In a 1956 poll 45 percent of the populace could not name any of the Congressional candidates in their district; in a similar poll taken in 1984 that fraction had enlarged to 68 percent unable to name their own district's candidates. Research conducted by the Michigan Center for Political Studies found that in 1980, 42 percent of people surveyed did not know if candidate Ronald Reagan was a liberal or a conservative, and an additional 8 percent thought he was a liberal; about the same fraction of those queried—that is, half the people—were ignorant of or dead wrong about the political stripe of then-President Jimmy Carter. Four years later, after innumerable headlines and television news stories detailing Reagan's conservatism, 43.5 percent of those questioned once more either failed to identify Reagan as a conservative or said he was a liberal. Just as astounding, most of the people queried in Michigan did not know which political party controlled the House or the Senate, nor whether control had changed in recent times. Similarly, a Markle Foundation poll conducted throughout the nation in 1988 reported that 49 percent of those queried could not identify Lloyd Bentsen as the Democratic vice presidential candidate, and 37 percent could not identify Dan Quayle as the Republican candidate for that post.[8]

Having dismissed access to information as the key factor in voter participation, researchers focused on two other possible explanatory mechanisms, poverty and literacy, because those at the bottom of the frequency-of-voting scale in the United States are today, as they have been for the past seventy years, the poorest, least educated people in the country. Up until very recently, poverty was presumed to be more important than literacy in this regard, but new studies suggest the opposite. In a landmark examination of the behavior of illiterate and barely literate voters in Spain, Mercedes Vilanova found that those citizens either stayed away from the electoral process completely or, if they voted, did so without understanding what they were doing. The lower their literacy level, the less able potential voters were to put matters in historical context or to express their emotions and opinions, not only about the votes they were casting but also about every other aspect of life. The completely illiterate were in the most advanced stage of social isolation, living "in passive indifference" to the world around them, unlikely to have relationships with neighbors or co-workers.[9]

As we come closer to one main reason for voter apathy, we also approach the important link between the literate base of a language and the fulfilling of a citizen's civic role in society. A new definition of literacy, encompassing both these matters, has been cogently expressed by the legal scholar James Boyd White: "Literacy is not merely the capacity to understand the conceptual content of writings and utterances but the ability to participate fully in a set of social and intellectual practices."[10]

It was to just that sort of participatory audience literacy that Thomas Jefferson appealed, but today's politicians shy from conflicts in which truth might be sufficient antagonist to error, contending, in effect, that the electorate is no longer literate enough to judge such conflicts, and acting accordingly. Of course, no politician wants to say that he or she is speaking to illiterates, so politicians frequently cite the growing disparateness of the population as reason to speak only in simple language and only about easily understood concepts. It is true that today's electorate shares no common background, no common educational level, and no common literature, but what speakers erroneously assume is that because of this disparateness, they have no choice but to appeal to the most common level of audience interest—instincts. Even speakers prepared by background, training, and desire to aim higher or to argue in Jeffersonian terms often feel compelled to aim lower in these ways. In 1970 Michael Osborn, a professor of rhetoric, ran for Congress and lost; in 1985, looking back, he summed up his audiences' predilections and what they forced him to do:

> What my listeners required was that their enemies be clearly identified, and they wanted moral accountability resolved quickly and easily. They needed a clearly defined image of me which they could identify, and if being fair meant that I had to appear wishy-washy, they would prefer that I be more emphatic than fair. . . . By the final weeks of my campaign I had developed a more concrete, compact, stripped-down mode of utterance.[11]

Imperatives to the politicians such as those emanating from audiences derive in large measure from a source that was largely irrelevant in Jefferson's time but has become a major element in the communications between political speakers and hearers in our own time: the media, in particular, television.

When the Federalists substituted representative for direct democracy, they still expected that issues affecting the public would be fully debated and that citizens would continue to be interested in them. The Federalists did not anticipate that intermediaries such as television would enter and alter such debates. When the television era began, prognosticators said that within a few years the medium would transform politics by allowing more people to participate in the political process. It has done precisely the opposite. Television's influence, according to the exhaustive research of George Gerbner and his associates, narrows the diversity of opinion available to potential voters, celebrates the mainstream and moderation above new ideas, and cultivates consumer values at the expense of political views that might oppose such values. It was nearly inevitable that television would have this effect on politics, Gerbner writes, since television must attract a very wide audience to deliver to advertisers and it can "afford even less than most politicians to project austerity, to denigrate popular bread-and-butter issues, or to urge saving instead of spending for goods, services and security."[12]

If the medium is not the message, it is certainly a venue in which the dominant mentality—the marketing mentality—is coming to affect deeply the content and type of messages conveyed and the manner in which message-appeals are voiced. A searching, complex study of the political scene, the speakers, and their messages, the media say, require an audience that will sit still for, and will respond by generating high ratings for, that sort of coverage. Lacking such an audience, the media argue, the news must be reduced in scope and thoughtfulness, which regrettably further reduces the sophistication of the audience.

The marketing mentality in news, as it affects what most Americans learn about politics and politicians, is exacerbated by television news' structural biases. A handful of these biases are now taken for granted, but they should be understood as distortions and as elements that constrict debate and articulate discourse. The first is the tendency of television news to squash unshapely square pegs of reality to make them fit into the medium's round holes of form, content, and salability. One frequently used pigeon hole is so all-encompassing that most people are unaware of its existence: a constant cycle of stories that oscillate between threats and reassurances. This pattern defines how action in the public arena is generally reported to the audience by the mass media, especially by television: A threat is announced and identified; it is escalated to crisis proportions partly by news media attention; politicians respond to the attention and the threat by actions or words that work through the crisis to a resolution; and people are reassured—until they are again alarmed by reports of the next threat. During the more than forty years of Cold War, Murray Edelman points out, successive American administrations raised the threat that the Soviet Union was ahead of the United States in various military technologies and capabilities—while at the same time reassuring Americans that our own armed forces could meet the threat; similarly, and over an even longer period of time, the FBI has stressed the rising incidence of crime and in its next breath the Bureau's ability to stop crime.[13] Our response to the chaos in Somalia—a response, most agree, stimulated by videotape of the starving population—is a stark example of threat-and-reassurance drama. Part of the Clinton Administration's difficulties in foreign policy is failure to master this threat-reassurance form; the Administration has perceived the crises and made the threats, but in regard to Bosnia, North Korea, and Haiti has not followed through to resolutions that reassure the audience.

The threat-and-reassurance story pattern is most visible in the eagerness of the intermediaries to view politics as a dramatic clash of individuals and in the thrill with which journalists respond to the most easily conveyed facet of that clash, the election campaign. To report the electoral process as no more than a horse race is to eviscerate, almost to obliterate, debate. In today's television news, the daily, familiar crisis of an undecided horse race is played to the hilt, then on election night is seemingly resolved—at least for the time being—by the vote of the people.

It is not truly resolved, Murray Edelman contends, "because elections are implicitly a message about the *limits* of power" that reinforce the common person's feelings of powerlessness. Tens of millions of voters and nonvoters alike sense an unbridgeable gulf between the the active politicians—the only people who seem to be able to affect anything—and themselves, an electorate relegated to spectatorship. The chief reminders of the public's passive role are the newsmakers themselves, in conspiratorial conjunction with the media who cover them. News stories that evoke the high status of officials, their access to information that the rest of us do not have, and their negotiations with one another, Murray Edelman contends, are also "narratives about the exclusion of the rest of the populace from that special world."[14]

By the very heat of their spotlights, the media adversely affect the audience by changing the type and complexity of the material that is debated in front of it. Some matters that might be more adequately considered by elected representatives behind closed doors, where positions can be argued and compromises reached, are pushed into the public eye. In the glare of the spotlight, positions of would-be compromisers frequently harden and simplify, making progress more difficult. This trend feeds into another, the media's constant monitoring of the audience's pulse, which causes politicians and audiences alike to pay undue attention to the momentary fluctuations of that pulse. Politicians are always vulnerable to the vagaries of public opinion; media obsession with it makes politicians more likely to follow poll numbers than their best judgment. We constantly beseech our elected representatives to lead us, but leadership often means championing a position that is not instantly popular. As Edmund Burke pointed out in 1774, "Your representative owes you, not his industry only, but his judgment; and he betrays instead of serving you if he sacrifices it to your opinion."[15]

The betrayal is exacerbated by reporters who ask candidates for instant evaluations of a rival's recent statement to heighten the likelihood of conflict. Tit-for-tat journalism promotes confrontational postures by politicians and provides the media with something easy to report in place of analysis of positions on issues and what those postures might mean for the electorate. Sound bite journalism also forces candidates to expend energy manipulating what is reported, which promotes deception and vagueness. "Public officials face a no-win choice," The political communications analyst Robert Entman suggests. "If they manage the news, they will almost inevitably oversimplify and mislead. But if they do not self-consciously play to the media's biases and limitations, their opponents will; and journalists seeking to hold officials accountable in the only way they can—by quoting those opponents—will inadvertently penalize public servants who fail to manage news skillfully."[16] A detailed proposal presents a big target for an opponent, who can caricature it, then attack the oversimplified version, and with that attack obtain precious air time on the evening news. So candidates in the age of overentertainment have ever more reason to put forth vague proposals and to be deceptive in what they say to audiences about them.

Politics as a continual horse race, the media argue, simply reflects the reality that our representatives are enmeshed in a permanent reelection campaign. This argument avoids the fact that media oil lubricates the gears of that perpetual motion machine and keeps it going when it might be turned off. Horse race journalism damages candidates as well as audiences. A politician continually engaged in saying to the audience whatever is necessary to win the next election has difficulty acting or sounding like a statesman, and media focus on the next election gives the politician no reason to reach for something articulate to offer about an issue. Arguing in the court of public opinion rather than in a more truly deliberative court, the speaker is enabled and encouraged to treat the audience cavalierly and soon comes to believe the audience is deserving of contemptuous treatment.

It has become a modern electoral commonplace that the closer in time to a voting date, the lower the likelihood of debate or even discussion of substantive issues among the candidates. In October 1993 the races for Mayor of New York City, Governor of New Jersey, and such suburban posts as Suffolk County District Attorney disintegrated into personal attacks, accusations, and brouhahas over such secondary matters as whether Louis Farrakhan, a leader of the Nation of Islam, could or should be forbidden to speak in Yankee Stadium. The area's newspapers and television stations lamented the avoidance of debate and discussion of real issues but exacerbated the problem by giving continual prominence to the daily, sometimes hourly attacks and counterattacks of the candidates and their stand-ins. At the last moment the reporters and pundits clucked that no matter who won the elections, the scars produced by such attacks would make it difficult for the winners to govern; on this, at least, they were probably correct. The first job of a politician, the saw goes, is to get elected. Has it become the only job? When the audience is paying only minimal attention and seems to care only about who wins and who loses an election, what incentive has the speaker to treat the audience with respect, or the officeholder to do a good job of governing?

Rational appeals are aimed at publics, emotional appeals at audiences. Apologists contend that in an age of information superhighways, over-entertainment, and euphemisms, appeal to emotion is needed to help audiences find their way through the overwhelming thicket of messages coming at them. Emotional appeals do constitute a particular form of shortcut for audiences, technically known as "heuristic clues." While audience members who are personally involved with a topic tend to respond to the quality of arguments presented about it, those who are relatively uninvolved do not examine arguments closely and instead use heuristic clues to make up their minds. Anthony Pratkanis and Elliot Aronson, who have studied the various types of heuristic clues, summarize the circumstances in which audiences are most vulnerable to them:

> [W]hen we [do] not have *time* to think carefully about an issue, when we are *so overloaded with information* that it becomes impossible to process it fully, or when we believe that the issues at stake are *not very important*. Heuristics are also used when we have *little other knowledge or information* on which to base a decision and when a given heuristic *comes quickly to mind* as we are confronted with a problem.[17]

Heuristic clues are a minor part of everyday speech but are the essence of modern advertising. As with the biases of news media, they have become so familiar that audiences no longer recognize them as distorting or deceptive. For instance, there is the exhortation to buy a product because it is the largest-selling or fastest-growing brand, which is supposed to indicate that all the people who like it cannot be wrong. For a second instance, there are appeals for trust made by an actor long identified with the role of a doctor that he plays on television, who asks the audience to buy the over-the-counter drug he recommends.

Today's mass market advertising believes the audience infinitely malleable, manipulates the audience's emotions, and shows contempt for the audience, in particular for its intelligence. There are few constraints on advertising's ability to twist our willingness to trust, on its appeals to our flagrant self-interest, on its predilection for giving us license, or on the ways it plays on our insufficiencies. "Advertising deals in open sores," according to Jerry della Femina, an agency founder. "Fear. Greed. Anger. Hostility. You name the dwarfs and we play on every one. We play on all the emotions and on all the problems." Pierre Martineau wrote in an advertising insider's textbook that one of advertising's "very definite purposes" is "to help the consumer become articulate about his buying choices, to put words in his mouth which sound convincing, even if they are not the right words."[18]

As political discourse moves ever closer to advertising, it exhibits more of the same ventriloquist tendencies, the same marketing mentality, the same contempt for our intelligence, and plays on the same dwarfs that advertising does. In the 1988 campaign for the presidency, a particular success for this constellation of pandering attributes came from the "Willie Horton" television commercial, which blamed Michael Dukakis for the failures attendant on a program that let convicted murderers out on prison furlough. The commercial was apparently wildly effective in persuading voters to vote against Dukakis and for George Bush, but it was roundly derided for its nasty tone and half-truths. Vice President Bush disavowed it, and so did his campaign consultant, Roger Ailes, who went so far as to threaten lawsuits against those who said that the commercial had been his idea. Its success, however, has been imitated by more and more negative ads, appeals to fear, and similar strategies aimed at the audience's emotions rather than at their ability to reason.

The 1992 presidential campaign featured many "marketing mentality" attempts to control the audience's thought, some of them so much more coercive than persuasive that they raised questions as to whether they were deliberately based on duplicitous techniques well known to motivational and linguistic researchers. For instance, experiments have shown that when people are deliberately warned that the next message may contain misleading information, their resistance to that message is increased. President Bush made use of this "task instruction" technique when he advised a debate audience that when they listened to what candidate Bill Clinton had to say, they should remember to watch their wallets. Another similar "processing" directive used by both candidates appeared to be based on manipulation research, which has learned that evoking visual images can short-circuit an audience's analytic propensities and induce it to substitute a simple picture for the vastly more complex reality. Governor Clinton, for instance, asked campaign audiences to envision a future in which everyone would be covered by universal health care and no one would have to worry about the cost of falling ill. Both candidates also made use of a technique of verbal overkill that derives from a laboratory experiment on the effect of words on memory. In that experiment, groups were shown a film of an automobile accident and then asked questions about it; those people who heard the word "smash" in the questions estimated that the cars were traveling at higher speeds than those whose questions contained the word "bump" or "hit"; a week later, those who heard "smash" recalled seeing broken glass in the film, though there had been none. The charged words had actually altered what they thought they remembered. Candidates are often guilty of using verbal overkill in attempts to make audiences remember issues and opponents precisely as the candidates want them depicted. The Republicans' simplistic characterizing of Democrats as tax-and-spenders and the Democrats' simplistic characterizing of Republicans as trickle-downers are frequently employed instances of the use of this technique.

When politicians put words into audiences' mouths, they do so in the expectation that those words will later be repeated as rallying slogans by whichever of their hearers become willing to help persuade others to vote for the speakers. Consider this classic example:

> The streets of our country are in turmoil. The universities are filled with students, rebelling and rioting. Communists are seeking to destroy our country. Russia is threatening us with her might, and the Republic is in danger. Yes—danger from within and without. We need law and order! Without it our nation cannot survive.[19]

The passage makes irrational, unproved, and undocumented connections between various symptoms, which may not actually be parts of one all-encompassing problem, and insists that the speaker's vague solution will cure those symptoms and the problem. Nonetheless, because this discourse spoke to its audience in what Kenneth Burke identified as the voice within, because it played so well on the dwarfs that della Femina enumerated, and because it used powerful heuristic clues, it was very effective. It stirred people to vote overwhelmingly for the speaker. It is not from the turbulent 1960s in the United States, however, but from a speech made by Adolf Hitler in the fall of 1932, during the last democratic election campaign of the Weimar Republic, which Hitler won. It is considered an example of pure demagogic address.

Demagogic speech is communication that starts from a base of a particular political ideology and focuses only on those problems and solutions which reflect that ideology. Its essential techniques are demonization of the opponent and solidification of the audience by focusing its hate against the enemy. It is the sort of speech we have despised and deplored in the mouths of the Nazis and the Soviet Communists, and in the discourse of the most notorious of American demagogues, Senator Joseph McCarthy. Earlier, I have argued that we have adopted many of the despotic language practices of the Nazi and Soviet regimes. To reach today's audiences, many of our politically active groups and individuals have also, and not entirely unwittingly, borrowed the demagogic tactics of McCarthy.

They do so because those techniques are especially effective when the audience is overloaded with information and entertainment to the point of fragmentation and distraction, and when there is an enabling presence in the form of news media that continually thirst for celebrity and controversy with which to feed that audience.

Today, we remember McCarthy as a fanatic and have forgotten that for a span of half a decade he successfully appealed to a wide spectrum of the American audience. During the 1950 congressional election season, for instance, he was the most requested and heavily booked of all Republican speakers, receiving more invitations to speak than the total for all the other Senators combined.

McCarthy's appeals were fueled by the news media's tacit compliance with him. Whenever McCarthy spoke the newspapers, radio, and television reported his attacks, but then did not unearth facts to refute them or give equal space to those few people of stature who condemned McCarthy. News organizations offered the excuse that he was too newsworthy to ignore. That hands-tied attitude granted McCarthy almost four years during which he was virtually immune from criticism, able to garner reams of publicity, and free to engage almost unchallenged in despotic behavior.[20]

"Well, it's good to get away from Washington and back here in the United States," McCarthy would invariably say upon being introduced to a new audience. Since 1976, most successful presidential candidates have adopted this appeal and run against Washington. McCarthy's basic message was that our once-strong nation was going to the devil because it had been betrayed by elements within our government, that the dirty and unpleasant job of rooting out those elements had to be done, and he would do it to save the nation from ruin. Jimmy Carter, Ronald Reagan, and Bill Clinton have all since used variations of these appeals in their successful presidential campaigns. McCarthy used specious reasoning, guilt by association, exaggeration, and many other techniques reminiscent of the Nazi and Soviet regimes. His charge that liberals were soft on crime and therefore unable to govern echoed Hitler's insistence that law and order would correct all the troubles of the Weimar Republic. McCarthy regularly and deliberately misspoke the name Adlai (Stevenson) as Alger (Hiss), and stigmatized those who in their youth might have flirted with Communism or carried a Party card. When George Bush referred to Michael Dukakis as "a card-carrying member of the ACLU," no less than when Governor Jim Florio of New Jersey referred to his challenger, Christine Whitman, in 1993 as a "card-carrying member of the NRA," McCarthy-type guilt by association tactics were again on display.

Demagogy is a matter not only of political ideology or evil speakers but of fringe-group audiences; it is found most often on the left and right extreme edges of mainstream society, not in the center. Demagogic excess attacks the status quo by violent or coercive rhetoric and occurs when such attacks seem necessary to their makers because other assaults on the status quo are not working. Moreover, the political analyst Steven R. Goldzwig contends, the rhetoric of the demagogue is often an attempt to bring cohesion within audiences that were formerly composed of disparate groups, and a way to bring those groups into a dialogue with the mainstream, a dialogue that they could not previously sustain.[21] McCarthy's started with fringe-groups, but after his first big speech in Wheeling, West Virginia, his constituency enlarged considerably, galvanized by tactics that stressed the audience's common hates. As McCarthy reached for stardom, polls showed him well regarded by those who feared Communists, atheists, and academics. He soon came to be cherished by that even larger fraction of the population who looked askance at people whose views or skin color or national origin were not the same as theirs. Shortly, regular Republicans adopted his rabid anti-Communist appeals as a way to help defeat Democrats, who had been in sole control of national politics for twenty years. In 1952, even though the presidential candidate, Dwight D. Eisenhower, kept his distance from McCarthy, he did not repudiate the Senator and permitted vice presidential candidate Nixon to label the Democrats as the "party of Communism, Korea and Corruption" and their candidate as "Adlai the appeaser," with "a Ph.D. from Dean Acheson's Cowardly College of Communist Containment." Not until after the midterm elections of 1954, in which both houses of Congress swung from Republican to Democratic majorities, was McCarthy censured, and then mostly because his unchecked abuses had become dangerous to all politicians, not because his audience appeal had dimmed.

It is false comfort to believe that since we have left behind reflexive anti-Communism, McCarthy, his demagogic style, and the qualities of the audience he appealed to are also behind us. In many ways that have since come to be considered important, McCarthy was a very successful politician, and success breeds imitation. How many politicians today do as McCarthy did, and pander to the worst in us? How many appeal to what Tocqueville feared, the endeavor to secure the "petty and paltry pleasures" of the self-absorbed individual? How many do what classic demagogues like Hitler did, and tie their divisive appeals to current social problems to divert audience attention from more pressing and more realistic concerns?

We need to be concerned with demagogy and the audiences that permit it, because the media conditions that sustained and magnified Senator McCarthy's power in his time are today more prevalent than they were at the start of the television era. The media are particularly effective in one very disturbing direction: They extend demagogic possibilities and thereby bring the speaker into more intimate, more unchallenged touch with the audience. Rather than brake, filter or exclude outright the demagogue's appeals, today's television, radio and tabloid press repeat the appeals, not least because demagogues are entertaining and frequently charismatic. In this way, fear-based, enemy-identifying, stigmatizing, coercive emotional appeals are routinely condoned, legitimated and passed on to audiences without accompanying analysis that stresses their demagogic character. The great reach of the media is a terrible temptation to a politician who may wish to use persuasion to reach his public but who thrills to the seductive potential of coercion as a sure path to manipulating his audience.

Ronald Reagan, considered the best communicator of recent times, compiled a remarkable presidential record and maintained great popularity with the American public throughout eight years in office. His success as candidate, Governor, and President relied heavily on his ability to communicate to an American populace transformed from a public to an audience. While the particulars of the next few pages refer to Reagan, they are applicable as well to the methods of President Clinton and in all likelihood will be the methods of the next President.

Robert Schmuhl, a presidential communications scholar, calls Reagan's presidency "not only rhetorical but theatrical, with daily performances."[22] Those performances owed a great deal to the practices of advertising and market research, and constituted emotionally coercive rather than rationally persuasive oratory. Reagan's was a rhetoric ideally suited for, and made possible by, the advances in mass media. He conceived of talking to the camera as talking to individuals who were alone or in clusters around television sets in the privacy of their homes, not as speaking to members of the public gathered in a public place.

Reagan's intimate, conversational style was admirably suited to being understood and accepted by a television audience already geared to what Ong calls "oral noetic" ways of acquiring, storing, formulating, and retrieving information. He relied heavily, for instance, on what Frank Dance, following Ong, identifies as speaking strategies that are particularly effective in communicating to audiences who learn in oral noetic ways: the use of praise and vituperation, the misappropriation of history, the painting of ceremonial or cartoonlike characters, the endless reiteration of a few phrases and themes.[23] Reagan told stories instead of explaining policy, spoke about values rather than issues, revealed his feelings rather than his programs, used cinematic imagery language, simplified extremely complex matters, and relied heavily on community-building images. Emotion-based rhetorical strategies of that sort, are ideally suited for television.

Toward the end of his presidency, Reagan acknowledged his acting skills as a key to his success in office. He wondered to David Brinkley, "How you could do this job and not be an actor?" He informed a group in Moscow that acting had prepared him for the presidency by teaching two indispensable lessons, the first: "To grasp and hold a vision, to fix it in your senses—that is the very essence, I believe, of successful leadership." The second: "You get inside a character, a place, and a moment."[24] What Reagan said as President echoed what he had been saying for more than twenty years. "You have to keep pounding away with your message, year after year, because that's the only way it will sink into the collective consciousness. . . . If you have something you believe in deeply, it's worth repeating time and time again until you achieve it." In his autobiography, he wrote of his communications that "I wasn't just making speeches—I was preaching a sermon."[25] A sermon, of course, presumes an audience that does not talk back, does not analyze, and relies heavily on leaps of faith rather than facts.

Before being elected as Governor, Reagan was rousing when at his most apocalyptic, for instance in his 1964 convention speech for Barry Goldwater, which he ended with an image of American children being sent on a forced march into Communist slavery.[26] During his eight years as California Governor, his speeches displayed an "us versus them" axis, with the enemy variously identified as the government, the bureaucracy, rebellious students, and the faculty that coddled them. From 1975 to 1980, while running for the presidency, according to Mary E. Stuckey, he was "giving voice to American dissatisfaction in a simple and emotionally powerful way," one that sought to return the United States and American politics to what Reagan identified as its original values.[27]

He kept repeating his message, but attempted to widen its appeal to ever broader constituencies, as in the now famous speech in which he accepted the Republican party nomination in 1980. Appeals to the audience's emotions, rather than to its ability for rational analysis, were at the core as he painted himself as the candidate of unity, "ready to build a new consensus with all those across the land who share a community of values embodied in these words: family, work, neighborhood, peace, and freedom." Reagan was in control of definition here, interpreting for the audience what those values were and implying that anyone who did not share them might be un-American. In that latter group Reagan shortly placed President Jimmy Carter, who he said had led the nation so far astray that it was faced with "a disintegrating economy, a weakened defense, and an energy policy based on the sharing of scarcity." In contrast, Reagan offered not a specific program but an emotional "rebirth of the American tradition of leadership," with himself as the true representative of the common man, who would, with him, "pledge to care for the needy, to teach our children the values and the virtues handed down to us by our families, and to have the courage to defend those values and the willingness to sacrifice for them."

Speaking of the 1980 campaign years later, Michael Deaver told Bill Moyers that Reagan never said anything substantive because the audience he wished to reach had no patience for substance. "In a democracy that's interested in where their leaders are going to stand, in what they are going to do on the issues," Deaver said, the taking of a more substantive approach "would have been the right thing to do, but this country isn't interested in it. They want 'feel good' and 'fuzz' and to not be upset about all of this. They want to just sit in their living rooms and be entertained."[28]

The strategy of appealing to the audience's feelings rather than to their intellects or abilities to analyze was reinforced when Reagan won election in a landslide; it carried over into Reagan's communications as President.

In his presidential rhetoric, he confined himself more than any previous President to the ceremonial mode and excluded from his communications the two other kinds of rhetoric originally identified by Aristotle, the deliberative, used in the arena of public debate, and the forensic, used in a court of law.[29] His ceremonial rhetoric had three strains, all of them highly emotional. *Populism*, in which Reagan managed to identify himself with the people and against elites, as when he allied himself with "a special interest group that has too long been neglected . . . men and women who raise our food, patrol our streets, man our mines and factories, teach our children, keep our homes and heal us when we're sick." At its best, populism permitted the audience to feel good about itself and helped it over moments of national loss, as when Reagan spoke after the accident that destroyed the space shuttle *Challenger*. But most of the time this populism was called upon to direct the audience against the enemy, which Reagan identified in speech after speech as "too many unaccountable people in Washington, D.C." In pinpointing this particular enemy, Reagan allowed his audience to project its frustrated rage on a single scapegoat, thereby to avoid dealing with the complex causes of their problems and with complex issues. Reagan's discourse was also keyed to his conception of a *civil religion*, based on the idea that the United States was a chosen land and Americans a chosen people. Often in his discourse, Reagan was factually wrong, but that seemed not to matter to audiences who were not geared to analysis. Because his contentions were presented in emotionally charged language, it was difficult for an audience to disagree with what he said. In Reagan's famous characterization of the Soviet Union as "the evil empire," not only is the enemy identified, and its opposite, the United States, presented as the sole repository of good in the world, but the phrase also functions as a catechism that excludes and stigmatizes anyone who disagrees with the categorization of the Soviet Union as an evil empire. Reagan's third strain was frequent invocation of *national security*. Lyndon Johnson had expanded national security discourse to justify escalation in Vietnam, Richard Nixon had done so in an attempt to deflect attention from the Watergate scandal, and Jimmy Carter in trying to focus attention on the perceived need for a national energy policy. Reagan used national security as an umbrella for all sorts of matters, ranging from the raid against Libya to the "war" on drugs to trade imbalances with Japan, with primary emphasis on an expanded definition of where the United States' strategic interest lay.

A complete meshing of all three rhetoric strands came in Reagan's speech after the Grenada operation:

> In these last few days, I've been more sure than I've ever been that we Americans of today will keep freedom and maintain peace. I've been made to feel that by the magnificent spirit of our young men and women in uniform and by something here in our Nation's Capital. In this city, where political strife is so much a part of our lives, I've seen Democratic leaders in the Congress join their Republican colleagues, send a message to the world that we're all Americans before we're anything else, and when our country is threatened, we stand shoulder to shoulder in support of our . . . Armed Forces.[30]

In this address, Reagan deliberately appropriated something quite usual (rather than unusual) in the history of the United States: the refusal of Congressional leaders to question a military operation while it is in progress, turned it into an affirmation of his actions and of his lifelong beliefs—and did so in a way that stigmatized any possible opposition or questioning of his actions as unpatriotic. In technical terms, his was a "refutative epideictic," in which criticism of himself or his policies was treated as criticism of the country. This refutative epideictic was often and more nakedly on view in his press conferences, interviews with journalists, and momentary exchanges during photo opportunities or walks to the helicopter. Out of 4,715 legitimate questions put to Reagan in such circumstances, Mary Stuckey found that Reagan had answered 960 of them directly; the remainder of his responses consisted of delays, evasions, deflections, avoidances by means of attempts to discredit the opposition, or the telling of personal stories—in other words, refusals to make direct answers. Reagan not only set the agenda for the nation, Stuckey writes, but also decreased the media's "control over the dissemination of the news and increased the ability of the White House to command the kind of coverage he desired."[31]

Unwilling to discuss, unwilling to provide real proof for his contentions in the form of facts, unwilling to take the opposition's position into any consideration, while at the same time working hard to control the agenda before the audience, Reagan all but closed the door on the era in which Presidents believed that, as Jefferson wrote, the truth had nothing to fear from error or opposition, and in which Presidents regularly participated in the public debate, and opened the door onto another era, in which

Presidents promulgate their views in emotionally compelling ways to television audiences and routinely avoid the possibilities of debate.

When on the issue of health care reform President Clinton appeared unwilling to enter into real discussion with opponents, unwilling to provide real proof for his contentions, while at the same time working hard to control the agenda before the public—and nonetheless was unable to convert his agenda into law—the failure of his rhetorical patterns, as well as the failure of his particular vision of reform, were openly on view. However, the rhetoric's failure has been little noted, perhaps because coercive, emotional appeals are now routinely accepted as part of mainstream political discourse. For coercion to have become a principal weapon in the rhetorical arsenal of Presidents and other high-ranking government officials, where it was heretofore considered as the outrageous excess of demagogues, is a sign that democracy itself is under fire.

When the concept of democracy was first elucidated in ancient Greece, Aristotle had no problem suggesting that orators adopt strongly persuasive (if not coercive) rhetorical techniques to communicate their messages more effectively, because he assumed that the other equally necessary elements of a debate-based democracy—the forum as a place for discussion and the requirement that issues be discussed before being resolved—were already in place and were the givens of the system. When democracy became the principle of governance in Parliamentary England and in the nascent United States of America, it did so in an era when reason was celebrated and democracy understood as an expression of rationality. In the modern era this "epistemological" conception of democracy as a system based in reason and discourse has been so scraped away from our political system that what remains is only an outer shell, which we know as the electoral process. The philosopher James F. Bohman, following Habermas, describes what happens when the epistemological basis of a society is leached away: "Democracy then has to do with the expression of desire rather than knowledge, with the will rather than reason," and it becomes either "a mere legal procedure, reducible to the counting of votes in majority rule" or "a way of aggregating individual preferences," such as choosing what brand of material goods to consume.[32]

As has been shown in the last few chapters, there is a great deal of evidence that democracy in the United States is grossly subject to the marketing mentality and perilously close to being reduced to the counting of votes at election time. Also, and to our dismay, we are confronted with evidence that as Eastern Europe throws off the shackles of communism its various countries and regions are lurching more toward the democracy of the marketplace, the expressing of desires for goods, than toward the participatory democracy based on rationality and the deliberative process. Historians in the next century may legitimately wonder whether the diminished and distorted version of governance known as *marketplace democracy* grew stronger in direct proportion to the degree to which *deliberative, participatory democracy* weakened.

These days, because the speaker has so little incentive to opt for persuasion instead of coercion, the canceling out of the effects of coercive speech and the fomenting of change that will foster debate and deliberative, participatory democracy must come from the other elements of the communicative mix, the media and the members of the public. There *are* ways to accomplish this. Since we exist more than ever before in an age of publicity, that which is not reported and repeated by the media can have little power. The media's control over the nascent demagogue's access to the means of publicity, exercised more vigorously, can relegate many such appeals to fringe status. Similarly, the media's power to critique can be more readily and finely brought to bear on all coercive address. At the moment, as it did in McCarthy's time, too much speech that is harmful to the body politic slips through the filter of the mediators, because the news media are still trying to maintain the fiction of objectivity. Objective reporting is not only impossible, but in the context of serving the public it is also irresponsible, for to repeat but not to evaluate a political appeal is to legitimate and condone that appeal. The media must take as their task to educate in depth rather than to inform in brief or—as many television broadcasts, magazines, and newspapers now do—to entertain us with political gossip. The key to better media participation in the political process is the fact that broadcasting licenses and access to broadcasting bands are awarded and regulated by the government and are known to be the source of large profits for the entities that purchase them. In return for lucrative licenses, the electronic media at least can be required by the government to devote more hours of programming to information and analysis. Interactive programming, which requires the use of similarly regulated telephone lines, can also be pressed into use for mandated voter education as part of the license holder's cost of doing business. Candidates' or representatives' positions on issues; their voting records; how they are rated by the various liberal or conservative or environmental or health care conscious groups; their campaign funding; and other relevant material about them could all be made available without charge to members of the public through the electronic media, perhaps on one of the several hundred new cable channels that will shortly become available.

If the media would champion debating prowess with the same vigor and enthusiasm as they bring to celebrating prowess on the ballfields, the level of discourse would surely rise. If the media would highlight and present debatable issues such as health care or tax reform with the same vigor and enthusiasm as they bring to highlighting the controversies inherent in the O. J. Simpson case, the level of public understanding of the issues would soar.

The countering of the coercive speaker, the championing of debate, and the changing of the system, though, cannot be left to the media to handle. In the final reckoning, it is individuals who must alter the system and attempt to bring back the "public" aspects of being an audience. For all of us, this means a change from being passive listeners to active ones.

There must be increased vigilance on the part of individuals, the kind of vigilance that exposes and dismisses excessively coercive and emotional appeals. Because Americans now grow up seeing and hearing thousands and thousands of advertising ploys, which are patently coercive and emotional, we have developed skills that help us reject the vast preponderance of them. As studies of advertising's efficacy frequently show, more of these appeals get through to us than we care to admit, but we do have some proficiency. However, we have not yet learned to apply the same skeptical skills to materials that we do not mentally categorize as advertising—to the emotion-based appeals of politicians, which so often come to us, as do the commercials, through the television set.

An example of what audiences need to do has emerged, of all places, from the former Soviet Union. In the time just prior to the collapse of the Communist regime, according to a recent study, people there became steadily more vigilant and more openly willing to distrust what they heard and saw on television, especially the news from state-controlled sources. According to Oleg Manaev, the "distrusters" constituted a "disagreeing audience" who in their skepticism were the true vanguard of a democratic future. Manaev conducted his research in Byelorussia between 1984 and

1988, and its most interesting findings were those that dashed his precon-
ceptions. He expected the "disagreers" to be the young, the good students,
the ideologically oriented, but he learned that his guesses were wrong. The
disagreers were not the university students but somewhat older subjects
who had been out in the real world and were able to perceive the difference
between things as portrayed and things as they actually were. The disagreers were not the ideologically rigid but the pragmatists, not the good
students who passively accepted what was beamed at them but those who
constantly challenged what they were taught. The only expected element
that was confirmed: Disagreers had larger libraries than the conformers—
disagreers were people who read and, possibly in consequence, thought.
Manaev concluded, "Availability of a disagreeing audience (or, more
exactly, an audience of different agreements) is not dysfunctional—it
characterizes the freedom and openness of the society."[33]

In the modern era, the philosopher Jürgen Habermas has attempted to
find a new understanding of democracy by examining what he calls its "communicative bases," and his work has relevance for a disagreeing audience
that would again become a true public.[34] In Habermas's view, all societies
are the products of social constructions of reality that are made manifest to
its members through the process of communication. Whether the society
consists of a bunch of hunters sitting around a campfire or a much larger
and more sophisticated group, the defining communications come principally from those who are active in leading the society, and those communications can be either genuine and truthful or nongenuine. The nongenuine are those that reveal the speaker's undue concern with pragmatic
or strategic considerations. In genuine democratic political debate, the participants suspend strategic considerations in order to question, argue, and
eventually construct the background consensus for any proposed action. A
member of the public can determine whether a political communication is
or is not genuine, Habermas holds, by putting what is said to four tests:

1. Is it *understandable?* That is: comprehensible, free from confusion or
   obfuscation?
2. Is it *true?* That is: congruent with reality as the speaker understands
   reality?
3. Is the speech *truthful?* That is: Does it reflect the genuine and sin-
   cere intentions of the participants?

4. Is the speech *appropriate?* That is: suitable to and reflective of the general interests of the participants?

If all these conditions are met, there is the possibility of having a true debate, carried out in a manner that will assure that the final solution to a problem, once reached, will (as much as any solution can) satisfy most of the participants and those whom they represent. However, when any one of Habermas's conditions is *not* met, there is no debate. Instead, the audience is subjected to systematically distorted communication—speeches and writings in which strategic considerations are primary and predominant. In the absence of genuine communications and debate, the audience is immersed against its will in a situation where propaganda prevails, the news media's abilities to evaluate that propaganda are continually sabotaged, and public opinion is routinely subsumed and subverted to the politician's goals. Moreover, when the Habermasian conditions are *not* met, politicians who wish to communicate in a genuine way find themselves less able to do so and routinely lose out to the propagandists, who have no intention of speaking the truth.

We, the audience of the United States, are today subjected to enormous amounts of propagandistic communications. As White House officials have done in every recent presidential administration, press officers and other advisers spend a large percentage of their waking hours attempting to control, precisely word, and put interpretive spin on what is said officially and unofficially by members of the administration—evidence of the substantial predominance of strategic considerations in those communications. The same strategic considerations are also primary for those opposed to White House policies. Businesses of all sizes spend time and energy crafting what they will say to the public about their activities, and many also pay advertising and public relations agencies to perform that task for them. Innumerable self-help tomes and magazine articles coach individuals on strategically controlling and exerting calculated influence in their personal communications. At all levels of society, Habermas argues, the communicative uses of language, those that have to do with producing understanding, are being displaced by strategic uses, those that urge a target audience to do what the communicator wants them to do. In other words, the marketing mentality is pushing out all attempts at communication that enable an audience to understand and is substituting communication that attempts to move an audience to agree and to obey. In so doing, the commodification of politics seriously threatens democracy itself.

A member of the public wishing to transform the system must therefore do more than become a disagreer with the status quo; he or she must move from private feelings to public action. In the United States, this means speaking up, in one way or another, and using the frequently noted exquisite sensitivity of political officeholders and candidates to openly expressed pressure. Disagreement or encouragement might take the form of letting a candidate know that you will not consider voting for him or her unless the candidate takes part in certain debates, provides more information about positions on the issues, and so on. Organized campaigns of letter-writing, phone calls, telegrams, and faxes have proved remarkably effective in spurring action from politicians. Were the average American voter—or potential voter who has been turned off from voting or otherwise excluded from the system—to devote the time each week he or she spends complaining about the status quo to taking active part in altering it, either through organizations established for that purpose or by personally making his or her concerns known, the great American audience would travel a long way toward reestablishing itself as a true public.

Some evidence that audiences can and do become publics comes from two enduring features of the American scene: the actions of juries and the actions of community boards. People who sit on juries regularly tell stories of how a dozen people from a variety of backgrounds, educational levels, and inclinations have set aside preconceived notions, used their intelligence and gifts for analysis, and applied themselves to serious deliberation and discussion about the matters before them. Frequently, in jury rooms, persuasion based on facts and common sense sways those who were initially opposed to the other side's view, or who had been undecided. When the citizen acts as though he or she is a member of a large jury, obliged to listen carefully to others' viewpoints and to arrive jointly at a decision, the citizen enlarges the likelihood of acting in a public responsible manner and diminishes the possibility that he or she will be easily manipulated by coercive, emotional, or demagogic appeals.

Community boards, too, are venues in which audiences can and sometimes do become publics. Of course there are boards where petty tyrants hold sway or where the in-group uses procedural rules to maneuver around those who might object to their agenda, but after recently attending meetings at several community boards in Manhattan, I have been impressed by the willingness of the board members to consider citizen complaints and suggestions carefully and to make compromises in order to accommodate the members of the public who have voiced complaints or suggestions. In one recent meeting, because residents and business owners expressed their concerns, a bus route was altered, as were the timing of a street repair and the allocation of community resources. That happened, the leadership later told me, because those citizens bothered to attend the meeting. Had those citizens not moved themselves from passive to active, the plans would have been put into effect as originally constituted by city agencies and might later have produced howls from affected residents, who would claim to never have been consulted about things of importance to them. At this board meeting, the leadership went so far as to ask residents who had attended the meeting to come back again, even at times when their concerns were not uppermost on the agenda, and to volunteer for committees.

It is, of course, a long leap from juries of twelve and from local community boards to the governance of cities, states, and the country, but the same active, articulate participation and presence of mind that galvanize citizens in the small venues must be brought to bear in the larger ones if today's passive audiences are ever again to constitute a public engaged in its own governance.

Conclusion:

TOWARD A REVOLT
OF THE ARTICULATE ELITE

Articulateness is learned, not inherited. This means its decline has to do with inadequacies and wrong turns in the learning process, but is also means that such declines are capable of being reversed.

In the previous chapters the decline of articulate behavior has been documented as of momentous social and cultural importance. Because articulate behavior is fundamental to the democratic system, its decline is of greater significance to the future of the country than other cultural indicators, such as the widely noted changes in sexual behavior. The chapters to this point have also traced the decline to three interlocking cultural causes that influence and exacerbate each other.

One is the shift away from the use of the full, literate-based language and toward a culture of secondary orality that derives its literacy from television, popular music, telephone conversations, and the like. The speech forms, the vocabulary, and some of the thought processes of this secondarily oral culture are more reminiscent of cultures without a written language than they are of cultures that possess vocabularies in the hundreds of thousands of words. In secondarily oral cultures people become unable to sing the songs of complex argument because they no longer know the words and are reduced to humming simple melodies.

A second cause of the decline is a dearth of articulate models of behavior and of sponsorship for articulate behavior. The lack of good models and good speech in the speech community in which infants first learn their language is exacerbated by the absence of articulate parents from the home during most hours of the day. It is further deepened by the scarcity of articulate teachers, by the teaching methods in schools devoted more to social than to academic purposes, and by the countervailing presence of inarticulate models in the popular culture. Our pantheon now denigrates the eloquent and glamorizes rather inarticulate athletes, movie heroes, and actors who cannot intelligently speak for themselves. Those attitudes become crystallized into entertainment industry products that reinforce stereotypes of dumb but honest heroes and glib but evil villains. Celebration of the antiarticulate has colonized today's public sphere, which is now largely defined by the absence of fine political oratory and by the presence of overly loquacious but shallow presidents, governors, and mayors. Belligerent and banal political officeholders' attempts at expression are repeated and magnified by an uncritical press, which also short-circuits debate by goading those in the political arena to assume more and more confrontational roles and postures.

As the marketing mentality takes over endeavors in mass culture and politics, commodification pushes out all objectives other than selling the product to the largest number of consumers. Mistakenly assuming that a lower target means a broader audience, those who aim low in creating television entertainment, news programs, and political candidacies dissipate their time and energy in the titillation of a large audience and have no creative energy or incentive to address such secondary objectives for their products as the championing or modeling of articulate behavior. Marketing's affinity for propaganda and polemic speech, whose goal is always to drown out opposing viewpoints, may succeed in capsizing what is left of political discourse, as well as killing off all true debate.

What will happen if these trends continue unchecked? Several dystopian visions referred to earlier in this book may provide some clues to the inarticulate future.

In the 1830s, Tocqueville wrote that if Americans should someday be reduced to occupying themselves only with their own personal and material affairs, and were not also able to deal with matters of public importance, they would feel the loss as a vast void in their lives and "would be incredibly unhappy."[1] Moreover, he wrote, if Americans gave up the public interest to pursue individualistic, material gain, in consequence they would soon be ruled by the unscrupulous powerful who would keep them in perpetual emotional and intellectual childhood. Americans' pursuit of individualistic, material gain is well noted, as is the understanding that we have largely given up the public interest. We have not accepted the concomitant that Tocqueville foresaw: the degree to which these matters go hand in glove with an audience kept in perpetual emotional and intellectual dependency. As politicians determine more and more of our agenda, as they manipulate us with appeals to emotion and make it difficult for us to analyze and critique, we lose more and more touch with our own governance and with control of our own lives. Tocqueville's vision helps us see that infantilizing tactics by our rulers prevent us from being personally concerned with the public interest and from debating the issues among ourselves, and thereby influencing those who seek to represent us, and that such tactics must be actively opposed. His notion also implies that were we to turn our minds more to the public's business and less to personal gain, we would be forced into those modes of thought that constitute more advanced articulate behavior of the sort necessary to dealing with the public business.

Closer to the present, there is Orwell's doublespeak dystopia of *Nineteen Eighty-Four* and its counterpart in Horkheimer's contemporaneous essay about *The Eclipse of Reason*. Orwell's ultimate vision is encapsulated in his book's final image, a boot stomping on a human face, but in the body of his book he ascribes more power to words and thought manipulation than he does to the use of brute force. By black example, Orwell demonstrates the potential results of narrowing language by outlawing certain words, as well as by the processes of reification and ideological capture. Horkheimer's example and ultimate image has to do with the death of Socrates. Horkheimer maintains that Socrates was made to drink hemlock by the community elders because he subjected the most thoroughly accepted ideas of the community to the critique of reason, thereby paving the way for alternative views of individual and social life that could undermine the status quo. Orwell and Horkheimer too provide clues to an inarticulate future. It will be one in which diversity in language and opinion will be curtailed, and in which critical analysis of anything will be decried by the powerful elites as well as by the masses. The denigration of critical analysis will leave unchallenged all products or ideas promulgated by the government, the ruling majority, or the purveyors of entertainments. The determination of truth through mental investigation and conversation is a process usually forbidden in any totalitarian country, and it would be the sin of sins in such an inarticulate future, but it is obviously of the essence for an articulate future.

Third, there is the vision of Marshall McLuhan, intended at the time he wrote, in the 1960s, as a positive vision of a global village that would solve humanity's communication problems, but which can now be understood as a vision with a rather dark side. In the feel-good 1960s, the idea of the global village and its sponsorship of primordial and tribal feelings was welcome, because it was an antidote to a prior nonexpressive climate. Ignored at the time was McLuhan's associated prediction that the ascendancy of the global village would eclipse the few centuries of literacy; today, when literacy is in real danger of being obscured if not eclipsed, such prospects are real and frightening. McLuhan made it clear that "primordial and tribal feelings" frames of mind would ultimately replace literacy in the general population. Such primacy of feelings would render future citizens unduly dependent for their ideas and language on the output of mass politics and the products of mass culture. Feelings would no longer be just one part of our mental life but would be relied on exclusively to negotiate our daily existence, and we would pay less or no attention to logic, rationality, and other written-word–based analytic guides for our actions. McLuhan's inarticulate dystopia would mean the spilling over of talk show television programming into all of life—an endless celebration of the feelings of the inchoate, with the pop psychologist and the talk show host or hostess as the ultimate authority figures.

Before going into more specific solutions to stem the decline, let us take a moment to consider some further consequences for society if the trends to inarticulateness were to continue unchecked.

The inarticulate society of the future will be like the country of the blind, where the one-eyed man is king and everyone else is subject to the king's whim. The one-eyed kings of such a society will be those who take advantage of the situation, not those who are literate or who seek to change the situation. For the first time in the history of the earth, the inarticulate majority rather than the articulate minority will be of the greatest importance, because its buying power and voting power will make of it the ultimate mass populace, capable of being aimed not only in one single direction (as in Hitler's Germany) but in many different buying directions each day. Inarticulateness will ensure a plentiful supply of future consumers who are unable to cut through the fog of advertising and are very willing to follow the dictates of heroes/spokesmen created through publicity for the express purpose of serving as pitchmen. The intermeshing of Hollywood, the Super Bowl, and Washington will become complete, with heroes/spokesmen moving easily from a role in one arena to a role in another.

Manipulation of the diminished intellectual and analytical capacities of the inarticulate will be the key to wealth and position. Greedy manufacturers or unscrupulous politicians will rub their hands with glee at the prospect of stewardship over the majority, at the thought of having in their thrall generations of endlessly malleable consumers who can be sold products or ideas whose true value will be dubious and transitory. The producer-kings will manufacture silly entertainments, shabby household products, and political candidates without morals, and will be able to sell all of them rather easily to the folks at home, most likely through the agency of cable television.

To twentieth-century totalitarian regimes, as Mao once said, power was what came out of a gun. In a future inarticulate society, power will consist solely of what comes out of a television set, and nothing that exists out of view of a television camera will have much sway over the populace. Television as the source of power will sap the last remaining strength from such institutions as the church and the home, which now rely on interpersonal contact for their influence. In the future, when the father of a family wants to convey something of importance to his child with the most emphasis he can muster, he will make a video recording. In the inarticulate society, schooling will be big business, but it will be machine-intensive, with many computers and television screens, some of them interactive. Teachers will become programmers, not instructors or discussion leaders, and their status will fall commensurately. The content of schooling will consist of vocational training for limited-purpose jobs and taste training for consumption; the ability to analyze, previously considered to be the desired end product of higher education, will become as arcane and little-regarded as knowledge of Latin. Interchanges on the Internet, once predicted as the salvation of literacy, will become steadily reduced to the babble of fan clubs, the expression of feelings, and the trading of insider information on what is or is not currently valuable. As voice-input to computers replaces typing input, there will be even less inclination to use the literate-based language for computer communication, and the computer will no longer be construed as an aid to literacy or to articulate behavior.

The inarticulate society will not be mute; rather, it will be full of noise, music, and conversation and will have very little space in it for silence or for the reflective thought to which silence often gives birth. When not serving as audiences, people will chatter endlessly; those members of society who are habitually quiet will be thought odd and may be ostracized. Words will be everywhere, featured as graphic elements on television and computer screens and in other advertisements, but their variety and resonances will be circumscribed. The ability to speak well will be measured in terms of volubility or quickness, not in terms of whether one has anything germane to say. Secondarily oral products will replace nearly all literate products; history, for instance, will be reduced to comic-book renderings of the past, with commensurate distortion of the facts and with excess visual emphasis. Vocabularies will be condensed until there is very little difference between the written and the spoken language. The types and uses of sentence structures will be reduced. Punctuation will be voluntary. Spelling will be phonetic, with many variations acceptable, and no one standard. Libraries will have more audio-visual materials than books.

The inarticulate member of this society will not be unhappy, except insofar as he or she is unable to purchase or vote for something touted on the television or computer screen as being of particular value. Rather, most people will be quite content with their lives, untroubled by attempts to analyze or critique current events, by intellectually provocative artistic endeavors, or by behaviors that have reference to anything other than what is held in the audience's current memory or in the pictorial files of the computers or television banks. Revolt of the inarticulate masses against the status quo will become increasingly impossible, though changes in rulership may be frequent, since the seizing of power will require only gaining control of the communications apparatus.

As for the literate and the articulate in an inarticulate society, they will exist either in isolation or in small groups that speak only to each other. They may renounce television as though it were an addictive drug that must be avoided, even in small doses, and may surround themselves with books as a defense against the majority. Such pariahs will have very little chance of reaching a broad audience and may give up trying to do so. Instead of missionaries inspired to proselytize the word, the articulate will become monks in hermetic cells.

The only danger to the producer-kings will come from the audiences' love of the new, which may occasionally result in the overthrow of an entrenched politician, a television sitcom, or a breakfast cereal in favor of someone or something newer. Youth who express their rebellion by means of exhibiting new clothes and by possession of the latest recordings and entertainments, youth who view schooling as a waste of valuable leisure time, youth who are always focused on love of the new, youth who feel they have no influence on the political future, will be of inestimable service to kings of the inarticulate society, for they will make the most pliable audience of consumers.

In order for the United States of America to avoid becoming the inarticulate society, we need a coordinated national program to counter inarticulateness and to sponsor and reward articulate behavior. It is a program that cannot be left to the government to organize or operate, though government must play a part in it, that cannot be left to the educational system, though schools and teachers bear a large share of the burden, that cannot be left to producers of culture, though they must be willing to change some of what they do, and that cannot be left only to families, though they, too, must be prime agitators for change. Everyone must take part, and the greatest responsibility for it may fall on each individual as an individual.

In the early days of the republic Alexander Hamilton delineated the concept of the "public good." A program to foster articulate behavior must first canonize such behavior as a public good, as behavior that will benefit the country. Articulate behavior must be understood as essential to full citizen participation in our country's culture and governance, and therefore the responsibility of government, institutions, and individuals.

In many and varied ways, the program must celebrate the word and all that devolves from the word, including literacy, political debate, speech as an art form, conversation as entertainment and as education. It must insist on full literacy, not on that which comes from secondarily oral ways of acquiring the language. It will attempt to establish a climate in which literate and articulate behavior can flourish. That climate will exhort speakers of all sorts—in government, in entertainment venues, in classrooms, in businesses, in families—to aim higher. Discourse that presumes a low audience level of intelligence, vocabulary, and appreciation for words will only exacerbate the decline of those very factors. Aiming higher will not (as many producers and politicians now believe) result in products that go over the heads of members of the public; rather, it will foster products that have the possibility of pulling the audience up to them. There is no intrinsic reason why a President delivering a State of the Union address to Congress, a business group leader exhorting his or her team, a parent discussing the implications of the day's events with children at home, an educator conveying an idea in the classroom, or a talented writer scripting a mainstream motion picture should feel the need to pull rhetorical punches: These are occasions and situations in which the audience can be presumed to be listening with full attention, moments when members of the public expect to strain a bit for comprehension and are eager to be challenged and not coddled.

The program will focus on four specific arenas: the home, the educational system, the entertainment and news media, and the political arena.

Positive challenges to enhance articulate behavior must begin within the family, and they mean much more work for parents who have currently abdicated such efforts to the schools. Children must be encouraged to learn that articulate expression is valued by the parents, is something to which they should aspire, and takes work to accomplish. Though most households have left behind the era in which parents posted a vocabulary word a day on the refrigerator bulletin board for the children to learn, parents must treat the dwelling place as more than a pit stop for refueling family members and must undertake to use the home to champion and reward desirable behavior. Recognizing that certain valuable stimulants to articulate behavior have fallen by the wayside because of the changes that have taken place in family life, we must seek out ways to reintroduce and reinforce those elements.

For the individual parent, this may mean a reconsideration of when and how parents work outside the home, who or what institution will serve as substitute parent when the parents have no economic choices but to work outside the home, and how parents who do not spend enough time at home inculcating good language habits in their children can compensate for this lack of communication. Social recognition of the importance of the linguistically enriched home environment to a future citizen's articulate behavior might appropriately translate into tax credits to enable parents to stay home more and tutor their children, and into low-priced or subsidized access to programs that teach parents how to increase children's articulateness.

As William Fowler's experiments have made clear, training for articulateness enhancement work is of the essence. In early language training, Fowler has concluded, the key factor is what the adults do; when properly trained, adults are able to contribute substantially to the child's development by varying their own vocabulary, syntax, themes, and narratives while speaking to and with the child.[2] Even university-graduate mothers and fathers need such specialized training to know which adult behaviors sponsor and which undercut the child's learning. Such training should be made widely available. The hiring of inarticulate baby-minders, or of those whose language training is not in standard English, must no longer be considered neutral in terms of the inculcation of articulate behavior. Although it would be impractical to sanction employers who hire inadequately trained childminders, employers who hire child-minders with appropriate verbal skills could be rewarded with small tax incentives. The fast-growing elderly population might be readily trained for second careers as articulate behavior tutors to preschool children and remunerated in ways that would not result in lowering their Social Security payments. Voluntary and charitable programs that bring together the elderly and the very young—and there are a good many such programs—can be readily expanded. Social approbation of people who give of their time as articulateness tutors should be equal to that given to those who serve in hospitals.

We have currently ceded too large an amount of space and time in our lives to television, recorded music, and the like. If we are to maintain any semblance of an articulate society, we are going to have to reverse our willingness to be overentertained, and instead relearn to entertain ourselves with our voices and minds. Parental sponsorship of articulate behavior at home must include turning off television sets or imposing strict limitations on children's television viewing time. Aside from countering television's pernicious influence on language use, this will also create more time for conversation. Restoration of the Victorian family situation is not likely or desirable on many counts; it is essential, though, to try to reproduce in some way the atmosphere in which an extended family of several generations by its language usage stimulated the children's abilities, for that stimulus appears to be the single most important element in shaping articulate behavior in the child. Gatherings of adults that purposely include the children, occasions that bring grandparents or other older people into the conversational circle, and parlor games that emphasize literate and articulate behavior are all useful as well as pleasurable. Arrange dinners around discussion topics; invent stories to which each person at the table must contribute; ask children to report on their days, on something good that happened or on something interesting they observed. If television must be watched, then news programs can provide starting points for such discussions. Familial time devoted to articulate pursuits is among the best investments a parent can make in a child's future. In our family we play such word games as Upwords, a board game that builds words and that like Scrabble, provokes occasional forays into dictionaries. To see a child voluntarily delve into a large dictionary to discover whether a word exists and what it means is gratifying to parents. Encouraging reading as entertainment, we also designate certain spaces in our apartment as "reading corners." They have proper light, comfortable seats, and a bit of isolation, which combine to invest them with an aura of privacy, sanctity, and invitation. Other families concerned about articulate behavior read aloud to one another; beyond mutual entertainment, this serves to erase the artificial boundaries between the spoken and the written language, and to encourage the use of more advanced forms of speech that are based on the written word.

The educational system is in need of serious reform in order to gain effectiveness in training children to be articulate. Among the first orders of business ought to be the abolition of teachers' colleges and teaching degrees. Certainly those who would become teachers need to study pedagogical techniques, but the teachers' colleges do not spend enough time or effort on academic subjects and currently produce graduates who are technically but not intellectually qualified to be teachers, especially in fields that depend heavily on literate and articulate endeavor. Graduates of academic programs are likely to be better tutors in articulate behavior, and states ought to take steps to ensure that such graduates can qualify to teach with a minimum of difficulty.

If we accept, as most thinking people do, that the future will require more and better schooling of our children, then there must be a revolution in teaching. Teachers must be better paid in relation to other occupations, so that a college graduate can consider teaching as a career even when other choices are available to him or her. Currently our grade school and high school teacher salaries lag well behind those in Japan, the Netherlands, Germany, and such cities as Hong Kong, Ottawa, and Zürich.[3] Bringing teachers up to the average salary level of, say, engineers in the United States would go a long way toward redressing the imbalance. Such changes would raise the teachers' status, with helpful consequences for student respect toward them and what they teach. We will know our teachers have gained heroic status when an education award ceremony commands equal air time with the Oscars and the Emmys.

To make more money available to pay teachers, the process of teaching needs to be reexamined to determine which aspects, subjects, and chunks of knowledge can be conveyed adequately by means of computers and other technology, and which will benefit the most from the presence of a human teacher in the classroom. Those subjects that require only rote learning or that fit comfortably into the paradigm of "recitative" learning can be done by machines, thus freeing teachers for real interaction with students, of the sort that encourages students to better articulate behavior. It may be that under this new system, if both machines and teachers are properly deployed, a school can get along with fewer (though better-paid and probably better-qualified) teachers.

Since most of a child's competency in language usage is reached before entry into grade school, it is essential for parents to choose among kindergarten experiences for the child based on the institution's ability to inculcate the prerequisites of articulate behavior. That does not mean the forcing of children to read before they are ready, but it does mean the teaching of social interaction and language readiness skills. As Dimitracopolou's experiments show, the ability to take the other person's perspective, as well as verbal agility, is the key to communicative competence. Kindergartens that stress such abilities and competencies—rather than strictly social abilities—are to be preferred. In general, this means more work for the parents in making choices among preschool educational experiences for their children, and more work in monitoring the progress of the children through them. For the state, it may mean more work in certification; currently in New York State, for example, preschools are under the jurisdiction of the Board of Health, not of the

Board of Education; a shift to guidance by the latter might produce standards (among them, teaching the prerequisites for articulate behavior) to which educational institutions for toddlers must adhere. Also, some states, such as Illinois, have historically tried to keep their education budgets low through the dubious stratagem of delaying entry into state-funded grade schools until a child has reached the age of six, by which time many children's language abilities have been permanently fixed at too low a level; if formal schooling were to begin at age five, more children might benefit from in-school articulateness training.

Dozens of techniques have proved useful for the inculcation of language and higher-order-thinking skills (HOTS) in the primary grades. They should be adopted by U.S. schools, most of which now pay too little attention to these matters. Higher-order literacy, not building-block basic training in letters and short words, is what will be required of tomorrow's adults. There is no single best way to teach language, but there is evidence that many types of approaches are useful, the choice depending on the type of students and the general circumstances. In France, which has a higher literacy rate than any other country but Finland, each teacher is permitted to choose his or her own method, providing he or she makes sure that children are able to read by age seven. The most effective method, the French found, includes reading aloud and book play well before children are able to read. In Finland, which for the past hundred years has had the highest literacy rate in the world, the approach that works best is very long hours of schooling.[4]

The "whole language" approach to teaching reading, writing, and oral communication skills, which has been shown to be marvelously effective in Australia and New Zealand, has been only selectively effective in suburbs near New York City, perhaps because American populations are more mobile and do not stay in the same school systems long enough for a gradually phased approach to achieve its great potential. In Toronto, according to Rexford Brown, a school district that had been mostly upper-middle-class and suburban, but which absorbed another town that included Canadians of Jamaican, West Indian, Pakistani, and East Indian heritage, achieved a terrific level of "higher literacy" among all its students by approaches that encouraged natural curiosity. It avoided the pitfall of making the students take standardized tests, but the new Canadians showed by other measures that they had achieved considerable English language competence.[5]

In any program of articulateness training and language enhancement, we need to uphold high standards of language knowledge and usage. A proper standard is one that will help ensure that the vast majority of the population—everyone who graduates from high school—will have mastered the basic mental tools that enable them properly to speak their minds and to evaluate what is being communicated to them. The courage to stake out and define high standards, the creativeness to help children attain them, and the tenacity to maintain such standards in the face of pressure to relax them will be of the essence in guaranteeing good-quality citizenship skills to the next generation.

Classrooms at all levels must be made more Socratic. Several innovative Socratic discussion-based techniques for grade schools and high schools were discussed in earlier chapters, and it is to be hoped that their number will increase. Many critics of our education system have railed about the disappearance of the civics class in which students learned about American history, government, and public issues. The modern substitute is social studies, which is expected to prepare students to assume their responsibilities as citizens and in many areas has not done so. Such social studies programs ought to be pushed again in the direction of civics. One technique is called "scored discussions." A Colorado high school teacher, John Zola, conducts scored discussions with groups in grades seven through twelve, on subjects that have ranged from the Great Depression and the debate over the adoption of the Constitution to the Strategic Defense Initiative and even more current affairs issues. Students are seated in what Zola calls a fishbowl, with the discussants in an inner circle and the observers, including the teacher, in an outer circle. Discussions are kept short and focused, and are meticulously scored:

> The teacher awards positive points for such activities as taking a stand on the issue, presenting factual or research-based information, making a relevant comment, drawing another student into the discussion . . . asking clarifying questions and moving the discussion along. . . . The teacher assigns negative points for distractions, interruptions, monopolizing discussions, personal attacks, and making irrelevant comments.

The "most heinous offense" is monopolizing the conversation. For Zola, one of the pleasures of such discussions "is hearing students excuse themselves for interrupting a group member who is speaking." Nearly all the participants felt they had learned useful information, and what they learned went beyond knowledge of the topic and reached understanding of how to investigate and talk about issues in a civil way.[6]

On the college level, the most promising development has been the Speaking Across the Curriculum (SAC) programs, in which regular academic departments make oral presentation, listening, and structured discussions part of the course requirements.[7] Most of the fifty colleges and universities that have instituted such programs are small or midsize institutions principally devoted to instructing undergraduates and less focused on graduate programs and research grants. Hamline in Minnesota, DePauw in Indiana, Radford in Virginia, and the University of Colorado at Colorado Springs are among the innovators. DePauw's "S" (speaking) program has now been in place for more than ten years and includes seventy-five courses in eighteen academic departments; the "S" courses are mostly junior- and senior-level offerings, for instance in economics, politics, psychology, history, and other liberal arts; students are required to take one or two of these courses and must also demonstrate competency in oral communication in order to be eligible to graduate. A survey taken among alumni of the "S" program reported that they perceived it as critical to later job success; many commented that they wished the speaking requirements for graduation had been stiffer.

At Hamline University, every department now offers "speaking-intensive" courses, and at Radford, the new twist is IVI, interactive video instruction. Computer video disks force students from passive to active involvement with course materials. One such program tutors students in listening skills, among them improved note-taking, listening empathetically, anticipating the speaker's major points, and paraphrasing. The technique has proved highly effective in enabling students to remember and use what they learn.

At the University of Colorado at Colorado Springs, the Center for Excellence in Oral Communications is part of a campuswide effort to raise student competencies in oral communications, writing, mathematics, science, computer skills, and foreign languages. Visiting the program, I found students busy fashioning and critiquing speeches, reviewing their own videotaped performances, and preparing oral communications materials for other courses. All seemed excited by the program and their progress in it. Sherwyn Morreale's emphasis has been on meticulously evaluating students' progress in speech courses, as well as promulgating oral communications across the curriculum. Entering freshmen and transfer students are tested on their oral abilities, then are tracked and assisted in speaking throughout their college years. Morreale identifies eight different "competencies" students must master in their presentations—for instance, the ability to use language appropriate to the audience and occasion—and she also rates speeches for their ethical dimension. In a recent study, her team found that all students gained in communicative competency from taking speech courses, females as much as males, but that "white" and "Asian" students made larger gains than "blacks" and "Hispanics"; accordingly, emphasis is now being placed on working even harder with minority students.[8]

The key in SAC programs has been the ability to push faculty from various disciplines to work together with the communications staff to promote articulate behavior. Every institution that has SAC has previously put in place a "writing-across-the-curriculum" (WAC) program and insists that writing is a basic skill that underlies oral competency. From the evidence amassed thus far, it seems clear that WAC and SAC programs ought to be adopted by every institution of higher learning in the United States.

Beyond classroom work, articulate behavior is best encouraged in high school and college through debating societies and teams. Earlier in this century most elected representatives in this country had been debaters during their school years. Today the percentage of debaters in legislatures has dropped drastically, but still the National Forensic League counts among its prominent former members Presidents and Vice Presidents, Senators, Oscar and Emmy winners, and network news anchors.[9] Currently the National Forensic League has more than 85,000 students on its roster—less than 1 percent of the high school students in the United States. More students must be encouraged to debate. In the course of the 1992 presidential campaign, Vice President Dan Quayle, in an attempt to strike at his opponent in a televised confrontation, Senator Al Gore, did just the opposite. He discouraged debate by charging that it was an upper-class skill taught only at elite schools, such as those Gore had attended. Quayle's charge was untrue and unfair. Ronald P. Stewart, debate coach of the private York Preparatory School in New York City, which in each of the last several years made it into the final round of the New York "mock trial" contest, sponsored by the New York State Bar

Association, pointed out in a letter to a newspaper that public schools, even inner-city schools, both teach and achieve in debating; he reported that York had been defeated in those finals three years in a row, each time by a different New York City public school.[10] High school debaters should be sought after by colleges with the same enthusiasm and promised the same level of scholarships as are dangled in front of high school athletes, if for no better reason than that champion debaters are even more likely than ballplayers to become successful alumni inclined to make future donations to their alma maters.

According to the American Forensic Association, whose eight hundred college professor members teach argumentation and debate, a majority of colleges have debate programs, but they are underemphasized. The perennial national collegiate debate team leaders generally do not come from highly prestigious academic institutions. Rather, the leading teams are those that have strong coaches and are sponsored by institutions with established traditions of valuing debate. In the past few years, Seton Hall University's debate team has reached high national rankings, even though it has been made up of students from varied backgrounds, half of whom never participated in formal debates before entering college. Visiting the campus, I learned that Coach Catherine Zizik considers a debater's critical thinking abilities to be the key to championship-caliber debate. To engage the debate team members in critical thinking, Zizik has stressed preparing for individual debate events, in which students must choose their own topics, research them, and write out their arguments. The 1993–94 academic year's individual-event "persuasions" topics chosen by her team members include drug interaction, racial discrimination, and—the most unusual one—holocaust museum architecture. Debaters also participate in more standard team events, in which they must be able to respond to negative criticism from opponents, overcome it with their own rebuttal arguments, and pose good cross-questions. Memorization capacity is exercised by having to master and recite on cue any of thirteen different ten-minute speeches for and against the issues. Being on the team entails frequent practice and exhausting intercollegiate meets—all the apparatus of competition. "These kids go around with thesauruses and dictionaries in their backpacks," Zizik marveled. They also discover, she says, that debating expands their vocabularies, makes them reach more deeply for metaphors, spurs them to research varied topics, and enables them to write better essays in other courses. Some have changed career directions because of the experience, deciding to go into law, library work, the sciences—in general, to seek more schooling, rather than go directly into workaday jobs. Those career change choices are not simply a result of raised personal confidence, Zizik maintains; rather, they reflect the students' revived curiosity about the world and increased fascination with words and argument.[11]

These debaters are swimming against the predominant cultural current, because in the United States today we mainly celebrate and admire people on a basis that has little to do with articulate behavior. As pointed out earlier, we often celebrate those who are decidedly inarticulate. Though we may have no realistic hope of entirely substituting heroes of eloquence for heroes of the movie screens and of the playing field, we can reasonably plead that our star actors, actresses, and ballplayers, who are our heroes, become models for children in more ways than visiting hospitals. Imagine the positive effects if professional ballplayers and screen stars spent part of their charitable energies taking their young fans with them to museums, libraries, and debate contests. Imagine if the considerable power that Hollywood stars bring to their movies and television programs could be turned to championing more articulate characters and better turns of speech. Imagine if star athletes were to do more than utter simple warnings to stay in school, say, by interesting themselves more directly in particular schools or in affiliative partnerships with outstanding teachers. The modeling and sponsorship of good articulate behavior is essential to reversing the trend toward inarticulateness. Some of it already exists. The current celebration (and financial success) of such thoughtful, articulate interviewers as Bill Moyers and Charlie Rose—and of the generally articulate people they and their staffs choose to interview—demonstrates that such rewards are possible. President Bush's official sponsorship of organizations that embodied the "thousand points of light" he had referred to in his 1988 presidential campaign could be replaced by a new President's celebration of heroes of articulation and literacy.

It is through entertainment and news media products that our attitudes are formed, so these venues are of principal importance to the championing of articulate behavior. Campaigns to decrease drunk driving, to foster safe sex, and to highlight multiculturalism have been embraced by the entertainment producers, who have worked to have these "public good" concepts surface as themes in sitcoms, focal points for segments of news broadcasts, and the like. Such producers could easily substitute themes centered on the need for more and better articulate behavior. For instance, mimicking the popular feature on ABC's evening news, the "Person of the Week" could be a featured speech of the week or clips of a particularly interesting or compelling speaker. A subplot on the soap opera *Days of Our Lives* might involve some perilous plight of an inarticulate character faced with a crisis in which he or she desperately needs to be more articulate. Oprah Winfrey might hire a vocabularist to cook up some delectable words for her talk show; perhaps such a person might shortly enjoy the commercial success that has recently come to Ms. Winfrey's personal chef.

Entertainment and news producing entities will not voluntarily do much to support articulate and literate products over those that they consider to have wider appeal. They must be provided with incentives or compelled to make more "highbrow" products. The key here is the access of broadcasters to the airwaves, which are government-controlled but licensed to the broadcasters for fees. New regulations could require that networks broadcast more news and public affairs programs in exchange for licenses, and that such broadcasts adhere to certain elevated levels of language use without infringing on First Amendment rights. Within networks, correspondents and anchors' word use could be monitored so that they meet certain higher standards of vocabulary and complexity of sentence structure. The use of verbal headlines by anchors could be expressly prohibited.

A notion currently under consideration is a 1 percent tax on the gross revenues of commercial broadcasters to be used for the support of "public" television.[12] While the objective of supporting good programming is laudatory, such a tax would only further encourage commercial networks to relegate cultural and highbrow programming to the ghetto of public television and to continue to avoid producing such programs themselves. The networks' rationalizations in this regard are wrongheaded. Highbrow programming need not be a money-losing venture. There were no intrinsic reasons why such best-selling, revenue-producing programs as Ken Burns's multipart documentary on the Civil War, Bill Moyers's series of conversations with Joseph Campbell, or Dennis Potter's *The Singing Detective* could not have been funded by commercial networks, except that commercial network executives lacked the courage or the foresight to take the risks associated with such ventures. We need to induce or compel the networks to return to the business of broadcasting high culture as well as low. We might, for example, permit the networks tax writeoffs for news or cultural programs that do not achieve high Nielsen ratings. In terms of producing results that are more salutary for articulate endeavors, a 1 percent tax on broadcasters could as well be directed for the benefit of legitimate theater, whose audiences have been dwindling while the costs of producing plays has been rising to the point of pricing the experience of going to the theater out of the range of the broader audience. Because theater generally celebrates the word, more plays and more theaters, accessible to larger groups of people, will help engender a more literate and articulate populace.

In reference to "public broadcasting," we must also encourage corporate sponsors to back programs that have the possibility of being provocative instead of the certainty of being bland. It is far safer for an oil company to pay for the broadcast of a ballet performance than it is to sponsor an experimental drama, and since public broadcasting is so dependent on corporate funding, its programmers habitually prefer bland programs that can be easily funded to those that might ruffle some feathers. We should structure tax deductions for the corporate sponsorship of cultural programming to reflect priorities that emphasize the spoken and written word, and the provocative risk, over ballet and rebroadcasts of BBC productions.

To enhance the articulate and literate nature of American commercial entertainment products like motion pictures and television programs, more control over content must be ceded to the writers. A "Lifetime Current Member" of the Writers Guild of America, I have encountered instances personally, and have been told of myriad others by Guild member friends and colleagues, in which literary references, slightly advanced vocabulary, complexity of character and of narrative, and other "highbrow" components have been crossed out of scripts or vetoed in advance of writing by producers and network executives, on the grounds that they would "turn off" the prospective audience. Scriptwriters, who have very little power in commercial endeavors, have been forced to yield to aim-lower directives; I am convinced that the directives are not only unnecessary but wrongheaded. If literary references and complexities were left in, the end products would be no less popular with audiences and might even prove to be more popular.

Aiming higher in the political arena is also essential to encouraging and sustaining an articulate society, if for no other reason than the populace's inclination to follow and replicate the behavior of its political leaders. Although in the previous chapter I maintained that responsibility for better political discourse lies principally with the electorate, a program for reform must certainly mandate changes for the speakers, both political candidates and elected officials. Presidents should speak less and say more. Giving fewer presidential speeches will ensure that more attention is paid by the public, the media, and the speechmakers to each one that is made. Preparation of those speeches should involve more thought and more elevated language; moreover, the speeches should reflect a President's obligation to educate the public as well as the President's need to lead an audience. Presidential candidates ought to be required to debate the issues with their opponents on a regular basis throughout the primary and election seasons, on pain of losing federal matching funds should they refuse to participate. Strict limits should be imposed on campaign spending for the production and broadcasting of television commercials, in an attempt to prevent the better-heeled candidate's message from overwhelming that of a candidate with an equally important message who has less money available to spread his or her word. The same fairness and truth-in-advertising standards that apply to messages for deodorants, automobiles, and department store merchandise ought to be applied to political advertising, with substantial penalties if boundaries are transgressed.

In legislatures, the seniority system for advancement to committee and party leadership positions ought to be eliminated and replaced with a merit system. If such a new system were, like the British system, to be based in part on the legislator's ability to speak to and for the electorate and its representatives, persuasive political speakers would shortly come to the fore, the general level of debate would be raised, and one of the reasons frequently advanced for term limits would be obviated. Whether or not the seniority system is changed, legislators ought to be evaluated on their participation in debates on issues, and those legislators who do not regularly take part should be subjected to ridicule if not to censure.

The task of encouraging articulate behavior is intertwined with sponsorship of debate. If we are to have a democracy at all, in the sense of a system that involves the public in its own governance, we are going to have to invent ways to reassert the participatory and deliberative elements that were once primary in our democracy.

How and where to begin the process? Perhaps by seeking to instill what the historian Paul Gagnon defines as the quality that citizens in a democracy must demonstrate in order to raise the level of public debate: judgment. For Gagnon, judgment means being able

> . . . to question stereotypes . . . to discern the difference between fact and conjecture . . . to distrust the simple answer and the dismissive explanation . . . to realize that all problems do not have solutions . . . to accept costs and compromises, to honor the interests of others while pursuing their own . . . to speak the truth and do the right things when falsehood and the wrong thing would be more profitable, and generally to restrain appetites and expectation—all the while working to inform themselves on the multiple problems and choices their elected officials confront.[13]

Many of the qualities of mind that Gagnon lists are precisely those essential to good articulate behavior, whether in our legislative representatives or in members of the public.

Daniel Yankelovich, a polling expert, argues that such judgment exists within the public but is improperly measured by polls, especially by instant polls, and that our governing elites "resist most efforts to enhance the quality of public opinion" because it serves their own interests to keep that quality low.[14] Instant polls provide politicians with ammunition to back up preconceived and often wrong decisions. There is no way to outlaw instant polls or to forbid politicians from relying on them as a basis for their own actions, but the need is clear: to enhance the quality of public opinion in order to counter such polls and their influence.

There is also a need for the public to understand that coming to reasoned and mature judgment may be a lengthy process, one that requires thought, reflection, testing of hypotheses against one another, and so on. Yankelovich has researched the steps by which public opinion (and, by implication, all individuals) reaches reasoned judgment on any single issue. In the first stage, there is a dawning awareness of a problem; in the second, the problem takes on greater urgency; in the third, we discover the alternative choices. A fourth stage is characterized by wishful thinking that occurs when people are faced with the realities of costs and tradeoffs, but in the fifth stage people are forced back into weighing the pros and cons of defined alternatives. In the sixth and seventh stages they "clarify fuzzy thinking, reconcile inconsistencies, consider relevant facts and new realities, and grasp the full consequences of choices," after which they can finally make judgments that are morally and emotionally responsible. On issues of overwhelming complexity, such as health care, Yankelovich wrote in 1992, it might take the public as much as ten years to reach the fully mature stages.[15]

Concerned citizens with fully mature judgments on important issues are still staying away in droves from the political process. Some purely practical measures must be taken to improve citizen participation in the processes of government. While this country has an abysmal record of voter participation—at slightly better than 50 percent, we are twentieth out of twenty-one democracies in this regard—when our record is expressed as a percentage of *registered* voters who regularly vote we fare better, ranked eleventh, with 86.8 percent participating.[16] This statistic argues that if we can get people to register, they will at least vote. However, the United States is the only democracy in which the burden of registering is on the individual rather than on the government. Attempts now under way to raise registration by making it easier for people to accomplish ought to have a salutary effect by increasing citizen voting. That, at least, will be a start on further participation.

Many people claim not to vote because they think the candidates unworthy. For the last twenty years, if not more, the cry has been that those who run for public office have not been among the best, the most capable, and the most qualified people in the country. How can we change the system to induce better candidates to run for office, especially for the presidency? James S. Fishkin, who has studied alternatives to the candidate selection system, points out that either our candidates are selected in large primaries by "politically equal but relatively incompetent masses" or chosen by "politically unequal but relatively more competent elites" such as party bosses in back rooms. As an alternative, Fishkin has suggested that the first step in the selection of candidates process be a "deliberative opinion poll." Six hundred randomly selected citizens, constituting a national caucus, would be gathered in a single place for a three-day period of questioning and listening to many potential candidates. At the end of the session, those citizens would vote among themselves; their poll, Fishkin says, would "model what the public *would* think if it had a more adequate chance to think about the questions at issue." Candidates who received high ratings from this citizen group might be able to counter the big leads that early state primary winners usually amass, and that might help us end up with better candidates for the presidency, Fishkin theorizes.[17] Such a caucus was originally scheduled to be held in January 1992 and to be broadcast over public television, but it was called off when only half of the $4 million in funds was raised. Fishkin made a second attempt in Manchester, England, in the spring of 1994, where instead of evaluating presidential candidates, those polled focused on a single current issue.[18]

The issue-oriented approach may be more practical, because the problem lies beyond candidate selection, in the overall matter of citizen opportunity and inclination to take part in the deliberative process. Here again we have a protoype that shows some promise for reforming the system. In September 1993 the Markle Foundation and the Public Agenda Foundation sponsored a more limited and more technologized version of a deliberative poll in San Antonio, under the name Condition Critical. An interactive cable television channel permitted citizens to listen to and then participate in a discussion of health care reform, and afterward to choose from among seven different options for reform. People who did not have interactive cable were able to register their views by mailing in a ballot previously printed in the San Antonio *Express-News.* Just prior to the broadcast, Frank Stanton, former president of CBS, extolled the experiment in a newspaper article:

> "Condition Critical" won't invite exasperated citizens to rail against out-of-touch politicians and greedy special interests. Instead [it will] give you the chance to wrestle with the health-care issue and to consider some less-than-perfect choices. It seeks to engage the public—typical citizens, not experts—in a real talk about how to solve the problem. Consequently, what you see in your homes may differ very much from the clashes that characterize the special-interest debates that take place in Washington.[19]

Key factors were that the discussion was highly structured, that it provided viewers with new information, and that it gave them a chance to reformulate their opinions after digesting the information and questioning others about it. While only four hundred families took part in the interactive discussion, the results were intriguing. Polls taken before, during, and after the discussion showed a similar change to that observed in the electronified poll during the "People's Debate" in the 1992 presidential campaign, reported above previously. In this health care debate, support for initially unpopular ideas such as the HMO approach and rationing increased as the issue was debated and the pros and cons of other approaches were weighed. A telephone poll conducted after the event found that every one of the participants surveyed thought this sort of "electronic town meeting" ought to be convened around other pressing public issues.[20]

The success of this experiment is evidence that participatory democracy is not an outmoded concept and that concerned citizens can become a public capable of helping to choose solutions to vexing problems. The fact that several hundred lay participants could achieve some consensus on a difficult matter and were able to consider seriously and support ideas that were initially unpopular also underscores that the 1994 fiasco in Congress over reforming health care was not a true debate on the issue but was compromised by lobbyist and partisan manipulations.

The Public Agenda Foundation has demonstrated that the processes of informing the public, strategically formulating the questions for them to deliberate, conducting a broad-based discussion, and obtaining a nonbinding vote can be directly applied, and with striking success, to many issues, and perhaps best to those that are local or regional. In the Des Moines area, efforts coordinated through newspapers and television stations culminated in a community vote that spurred local hospitals to foster better allocation of beds, while in the Delaware Valley area (encompassing parts of three states), a similar vote directed the efforts of school boards to change the goals and strategies of their educational system. In the past, the Public Agenda's Keith Melville says, elected officials have by and large ignored the foundation's efforts to educate and poll the public, but there have been signs that the White House and such organizations as the Western Governors Conference are paying more attention to such educative efforts.[21]

There does not always have to be a specific focus to debate in order for the process to be beneficial to the participants and to the community. In Orange County, New York, which is 50 miles north of Manhattan, 125 local residents volunteered to join nine separate groups and attend a series of six "brainstorming" meetings focused on what the community ought to be like in the year 2000. Efforts were directed toward controlling the future growth of the area by attempting to preserve its farmland and water supply while making the area more economically viable. One resident told a reporter, "It's not about reacting to an emergency, something coming down the pike that we don't want. It's an opportunity to decide what we want, where we want it, and how we want it done before it happens." Some participants were fearful of the future, others nostalgic for the past, but, the reporter concluded, "each one had decided that staying home and keeping quiet could be as dangerous as the issues that worry them."[22]

The entrenched power structure, because it benefits from a passive and largely inarticulate populace, wants to maintain the status quo. Politicians in office, entertainment and news media producers, child care system entrepreneurs, and marketers of all sorts of products and services will fight increased articulateness and citizen participation in all aspects of life, fearing that the innovations will result in less power for themselves. The efforts and innovations noted in these pages, which are laudable, will not amount to more than a hill of beans unless they are championed, replicated, and improved upon by more and more individuals throughout the country.

Individuals seeking to raise the level of articulate behavior in the country constitutes the opposite of a revolt of the masses; it is a revolt of the articulate elite, a revolt that has as its goal not the usurpation of power but the uplifting of more of the masses to the elite's own level. Articulate behavior is an elite virtue, but the articulateness I advocate is not exclusive; rather, it seeks to include more and more people in its group. Earlier in this century, George Santayana wrote that in the United States, more than in any other country, "eloquence is a republican art" that could bring the best impulses of the community to fruition and "could be turned to guide or to sanction action, and sometimes could attain, in so doing, a noble elevation."[23]

We need that noble elevation now more than ever, not only in ourselves but in our leaders. But because those who benefit from inarticulateness will view a broadening of the articulate elite as dangerous to them, the task of attaining the goal will inevitably devolve upon individuals. It has been amply demonstrated in the twentieth century that in order for evil to triumph it is necessary only that good men do nothing; certainly in the twenty-first century in order to achieve the triumph of a public good it will be necessary for individuals to do something—to do a great deal, actually, to take responsibility for achieving the goal and to take actions toward it in the many roles we fill every day. To be a member of an elite entails an obligation to lead. As a concerned citizen, as a voter, as a parent, as a teacher, as a consumer of news and entertainment products, as a community-minded neighbor, as a potential leader in group efforts—roles that, regardless of our job or educational background, each of us fills—I have multiple opportunities to instill articulate behavior throughout society.

Many people may read this book, agree with its contentions, and do nothing about addressing the problems it identifies. One of the slogans of the 1960s, now forgotten, was that if you were not part of the solution, you were part of the problem. That reasoning must be reinvoked and applied to this instance. Time is short, the tide of mumbling multitudes rises, and this rising is inimical to our culture, our governance, and our individuality. Each of us must do more than acknowledge that the problem of inarticulateness exists; we must act to reverse the trend by taking greater charge of our children's education, demanding fuller news and more challenging entertainment products, insisting by our votes and other actions that our political leaders raise their level of oratory and participate in true debates, and championing public discussion and debate of issues in all forums. Only if we do so in strength can there be realistic hope that the United States can survive as an articulate society.

NOTES

Introduction: The Crisis in Eloquence

1. Ben Jonson, *Timber, or, Discoveries Made upon Men and Matter*, 1640.
2. From "The Seventh Seal," in *Four Screenplays of Ingmar Bergman*, 1960.
3. October 26, 1991, news conference.
4. Leon Wieseltier, "Total Quality Meaning," *The New Republic*, July 19 and 26, 1993.
5. *New York Times*, January 26, 1994.
6. *New York Times*, June 27, 1993, sec. 3.
7. Peter Carlson, "The Heart of Talkness," *Washington Post*, April 25, 1993.
8. Marshall McLuhan and Quentin Fiore, *The Medium is the Massage*, 1967. McLuhan had earlier written that the medium is the message but amended his words.
9. *Ibid.*
10. Walter J. Ong, *Orality and Literacy: The Technologizing of the Word*, 1982.
11. See Lawrence A. Cremin, *The Transformation of the School: Progressivism in American Education, 1876–1957*, 1961.

Part I. Mastering the Process (Prologue)

1. Lawrence A. Cremin, *Popular Education and Its Discontents*, 1990.
2. William Fowler, *Talking from Infancy*, 1990.

1. Learning to Speak

1. Naomi S. Baron, *Growing Up with Language*, 1992.
2. *Ibid.*
3. Daniel N. Stern, *The Interpersonal World of the Infant*, 1985.
4. M. A. K. Halliday, *Exploration in the Function of Language*, 1973.
5. These psychological experiments are reported in Philip Lieberman, *Uniquely Human: The Evolution of Speech, Thought and Selfless Behavior*, 1991.

6. Catherine Garvey, *Children's Talk*, 1984. In her vocabulary counts, Garvey uses a system that counts each separate form as a distinct word. "Go," "going," and "gone" are counted as three words. Other word-counting systems count these as three forms of one word. See Chapter 4 herein.

7. Willem Vanderburg, *The Growth of Minds and Cultures*, 1985.

8. F. E. X. Dance and C. E. Larson, *The Functions of Human Communication*, 1976.

9. Elaine Slosberg Andersen, *Speaking with Style: The Sociolinguistic Skills of Children*, 1990.

10. Harold Barrett, *Rhetoric and Civility: Human Development, Narcissism, and the Good Audience*, 1991.

11. Andersen, *Speaking With Style*.

12. Steven Pinker, *The Language Instinct*, 1994.

13. Bambi Schieffelin and Eleanor Ochs, "Language Socialization," *Annual Review of Anthropology*, vol. 15, 1988.

14. Fowler, *Talking from Infancy*.

15. *Ibid.*

16. *Ibid.*

17. Maryse H. Richards and Elena Duckett, "The Relationship of Maternal Employment to Early Adolescent Daily Experience With and Without Parents," *Child Development*, Vol. 65, No. 1, February 1994; and Jacquelynne Eccles and Susan Goff Timmer, 1981 study, cited in Pepper Schwartz, "The Silent Family: Together, but Apart," *New York Times*, February 16, 1995.

18. Gordon Wells, "Language, learning and teaching: Helping learners to make knowledge their own," in F. Lowenthal and & F. Vandamme, eds. *Pragmatism and Education*, 1986.

19. Celeste P. Jones and Lauren B. Adamson, "Language Use in Mother-Child and Mother-Child-Sibling Interactions," *Child Development*, April 1987.

20. Lieberman, *Uniquely Human*.

21. Baron, *Growing Up with Language*.

22. Richards and Duckett, "Relationship of Maternal Employment." The subjects of this study, however, were adolescent and pre-adolescent children, and the authors concede that other research has shown that considerably younger children are more strongly affected by the absence of the mother.

23. *Journal of Speech and Hearing*, issues of January through June 1991.

24. Gavriel Salomon, "Television Literacy and Television vs. Literacy," in Richard W. Bailey and Robin Melanie Fosheim, eds., *Literacy for Life: The Demand for Reading and Writing*, 1983; Michael Morgan and Larry Gross, "Television Viewing, IQ and Academic Achievement," Journal of Broadcasting, 24, 1980.

25. Charles H. Wolfgang and Karla Lynn Kelsay, "Problem Students in Class: Disobedient—or Just 'De-Valued,'" *Education Digest*, February 1992.

26. Barrett, *Rhetoric and Civility*.
27. Tamar Liebes and Rivka Ribak, "The Contribution of Family Culture to Political Participation, Political Outlook, and Its Reproduction," *Communications Research*, October 1992.
28. Patrick De Gramont, *Language and the Distortion of Meaning*, 1990.
29. Ionanna Dimitracopolou, *Conversational Competence and Social Development*, 1990.

2. Standard Issue

1. Cited in Deborah Sontag, "Oy Gevalt! New Yawkese an Endangered Dialect?" *New York Times*, February 14, 1993.
2. J. Hector St. John de Crevecoeur, *Letters from an American Farmer*, 1782.
3. Statistics, and the quote from Loma, from Deborah Sontag, "English as a Precious Language," *New York Times*, August 29, 1993. Mary Cuadrado, letter, *New York Times*, January 21, 1993.
4. Canadian study cited in Brian Weinstein, *The Civic Tongue*, 1983.
5. Philip Lieberman, *Uniquely Human*, 1991. Also, this vocal tract configuration does not develop completely in human beings until around the age of three, which may explain why infants and toddlers cannot fashion certain speech sounds until that age.
6. This discussion of memory and eloquence follows that of Francis A. Yates, *The Art of Memory*, 1966.
7. Plato, Phaedrus and Letters VII and VIII, 1973 edition.
8. Walter J. Ong, *Orality and Literacy*, 1982.
9. *Ibid.*
10. A. R. Luriia, *Cognitive Development: Its Cultural and Social Foundations*, 1976.
11. Some instances cited in Weinstein, *Civic Tongue*.
12. Colin Cherry, *On Human Communication*, third edition, 1978.
13. John Earl Joseph, *Eloquence and Power: The Rise of Language Standards and Standard Languages*, 1987.
14. *Ibid.*
15. Charles Carpenter Fries, *American English Grammar*, 1940; idem, *The Structure of English*, 1952.
16. Adams and Jefferson quoted in Lee Pederson, "Language, Culture and the American Heritage," *American Heritage Dictionary*, second college edition, 1985. For a further discussion of the Founding Fathers' spat over the language, see H. L. Mencken, *The American Language*, 1923.
17. Thorstein Veblen, *The Theory of the Leisure Class*, 1899. 1934 edition.
18. Edward Sapir, "The Status of Linguistics as a Science," in *Selected Writings*, 1949; Benjamin Lee Whorf, "Science and Linguistics," in *Language, Thought and Reality*, 1956.

19. Pinker, *Language Instinct*.
20. These examples are collected from various sources. Most are cited in J. Dan Rothwell, *Telling it Like It Isn't*, 1982. Pinker argues that whether the process is inductive or deductive, it is substantially the same thought process, and the difference is inconsequential.
21. Basil Bernstein, *Class, Codes and Control*, Volume I, *Theoretical Studies Towards a Sociology of Language*, 1971.
22. Joseph, *Eloquence and Power*.
23. William Labov, *The Social Stratification of English in New York City*, 1966.
24. William Labov, *Language in the Inner City: Studies in the Black English Vernacular*, 1972.
25. Studies cited in Andersen, *Speaking with Style*.
26. Quoted from "Icon No. 17," published by Milestone/DC, as reported in Mike Sangiacomo, "Milestone hero addresses black-on-black racism issue," *Springfield* (Massachusetts) *Republican*, August 7, 1994.
27. Experiment reported in Rita Kramer, *Ed School Follies*, 1991.
28. Cajun controversy reported in Weinstein, *Civic Tongue*.
29. Andersen, *Speaking with Style*.
30. Ong, *Orality and Literacy*.
31. Darrell Stover, "Boyz Town," *Washington Post*, May 16, 1993.
32. Richard Wesley and Bushwick Bill quoted in Michael Marriott, "Hard-Core Rap Lyrics Stir Black Backlash," *New York Times*, August 15, 1993.
33. Crouch quoted in Lynda Richardson, "A Jazz Critic Stretches His Solos, Not Caring Who Winces in Pain," *New York Times*, August 29, 1993.
34. Various articles in *New York Times, Daily News*, and *New York Post*, May 7–10, 1993, and David Hinckley, "Rap & Rev with Pastor Butts & Preacher Earl," *New York Daily News*, June 3, 1993.
35. This discussion follows that of W. Ross Winterowd, *The Culture and Politics of Literacy*, 1989.
36. *Ibid*.
37. Larry Rivers, *What Did I Do?* 1992.

3. The Unhelpful Schoolhouse

1. Karen de Witt, "S.A.T. Scores Improve for 2nd Consecutive Year," *New York Times*, August 19, 1993, and Christopher Shea, "What's Happened to Writing Skills?" *Chronicle of Higher Education*, February 3, 1993. Starting in 1994–95, the Scholastic Board will raise all applicants' scores so that the median score will again be 500. This action lowers the bridge after the water level has receded.
2. Quoted in Shea, "What's Happened?"
3. Francis Flaherty, "U.S. Decline: A New Clue," *New York Times*, May 30, 1993.

4. Diane Ravitch and Chester E. Finn, *What Do Our 17-Year-Olds Know?* 1987; Jane M. Healy, *Endangered Minds*, 1990.

5. Edwin De Lattre, "The Insiders," in Bailey and Forsheim, eds., *Literacy For Life*, 1983.

6. Dialogue with Meletus condensed from Plato's Apology, in Raphael Demos, ed. *Plato Selections*, 1927.

7. Kenneth Burke, *Philosophy of Literary Form*, 1957.

8. Virginia Woolf, *Orlando*, 1928. "Just as it is useless in handball to strike the ball hard if it is not returned to you, so conversation cannot be pleasant if repartee is lacking." François La Mothe Le Vayer, 1640, quoted in Peter Burke, *The Art of Conversation*, 1993.

9. Burke, *Art of Conversation*.

10. Winston Churchill, schooled during this era, was able to write by dictation, but he insisted on using prominently displayed notes to deliver speeches. See Manfred Weidhorn, *Churchill's Rhetoric*, 1987.

11. James A. Berlin, *Writing Instruction in Nineteenth-Century American Colleges*, 1984.

12. Peter Burke reports that at Oxford in the late 1950s, these rules still included prohibitions against speaking more than five words in a foreign language, talking shop, or mentioning a lady's name. Burke, *Art of Conversation*.

13. Kenneth Cmiel, *Democratic Eloquence*, 1990.

14. *Ibid.*

15. Cited in *ibid.*

16. *Ibid.*, quoted from George Carpenter, Franklin Baker, and Fred Scott, *The Teaching of English in Elementary and Secondary Schools*, 1903.

17. Cremin, *Transformation of the School*; William H. Honan, "Report Says Colleges Are Failing to Educate," *New York Times*, December 5, 1993; and William Celis III, "Study Says Half of Adults in U.S. Lack Reading and Math Abilities," *New York Times*, September 9, 1993.

18. Rexford G. Brown, *Schools of Thought*, 1991.

19. David Perkins, *Smart Schools*, 1992. Emphasis in original.

20. Brown, *Schools of Thought*.

21. National Association of Education Progress, 1981.

22. Frank J. DeAngelo, "Literacy and Cognition: A Developmental Perspective," in Bailey and Forsheim, *Literacy for Life*.

23. Brown, *Schools of Thought*.

24. Paying better salaries permits a school district to choose the best teachers from among the applicants for teaching jobs, but although the school districts that pay the highest teacher salaries often have the highest student test scores, this may be as much due to those districts' upper middle class pool of students as to the effectiveness of the teachers.

25. Rita Kramer, *Ed School Follies*.
26. Studies reported in Thomas Toch, *In the Name of Excellence*, 1991.
27. B. T. Watkins, "Denials of Re-accreditation Rise Sharply Under New Teacher Education Policies," *Chronicle of Higher Education*, October 4, 1989; Toch, *In the Name of Excellence*.
28. John C. Carroll, Peter Davies, and Barry Richman, *The American Heritage Word Frequency Book*, 1971; quotes from Carroll's introductory essay.
29. Donald P. Hayes, "Speaking and Writing: Distinct Patterns of Word Choice," in *Journal of Memory and Language*, October 1988.
30. *Ibid.*, and as quoted in "Baby-Boomer Books Faulted in S.A.T. Drop," *New York Times*, November 3, 1993.
31. John W. Black, Cleavonne S. Stratton, Alan C. Nichols, and Marian Ausherman Chavez, *The Use of Words in Context*, 1985.
32. Black and colleagues did not make or comment upon the comparisons drawn in this paragraph, and the conclusions made are my own, not theirs.
33. Hayes, "Speaking and Writing."
34. Jeanne S. Chall, Vicki A. Jacobs, and Luke E. Baldwin, *The Reading Crisis: Why Poor Children Fall Behind*, 1990.
35. *Ibid.*
36. *Ibid.*
37. Mary Sleator Temperley, "Grammar Rules Weren't Made in Heaven," letter to *New York Times*, February 13, 1993; personal communication, April 16, 1993.
38. Brown, *Schools of Thought*.
39. See for instance, Arnold D. Witherspoon, Carolyn K. Long, and Eugene B. Nickell, "Dropping Out: Relationship of Speaking Anxiety to Self-Esteem, Crime, and Educational Achievement," *Psychological Reports*, October 1991.
40. Stanley Aronowitz, "Mass Culture and the Eclipse of Reason: The Implications for Pedagogy," in Lazare, ed., *American Media and Mass Culture*.
41. Lev Vygotskii, *Thought and Language*, 1986.
42. Michael Cronin and Phillip Glen, "Oral Communication Across the Curriculum in Higher Education: The State of the Art," *Communication Education*, October 1991; A. Vangelisti and J. Daly, "Correlates of Speaking Skills in the United States: A National Assessment," *Communication Education*, 1989; Sherwyn P. Morreale *et al.*, "Assessing Oral Communication Competency in Undergraduate Students," unpublished paper, April 1993.
43. William Douglas, "Expectations About Initial Interaction: An Examination of the Effects of Global Uncertainty," *Human Communication Research*, March 1991.
44. Catherine Zizik, personal communication, December 1993.
45. Sherwyn Morreale, Pamela Shockley-Zalabak, and Penny Whitney, "The Center for Excellence in Oral Communication: Integrating Communication Across the Curriculum," *Communication Education*, January 1993.

46. Michael Purdy, "Introduction," in Deborah Borisoff and Michael Purdy, eds., *Listening in Everyday Life*, 1991.
47. Allan Collins, John Selly Brown, and Susan E. Newman, "Cognitive Apprenticeship," in Lauren B. Resnick, ed., *Knowing, Learning, and Instruction*, 1989.
48. *Ibid.*

Part II. Extracurricular Educators (Prologue)

1. José Ortega y Gasset, *The Revolt of the Masses*, 1985.
2. See Jürgen Habermas, *The Theory of Communicative Action*, Vol. I, *Reason and the Rationalisation of Society*, 1984.
3. See Antonio Gramsci, *Selections from Cultural Writings*, 1985.
4. See Richard Sennett, *The Fall of Public Man: On the Social Psychology of Capitalism*, 1977.

4. The Entertained Culture

1. Quotes from Groening and the fourteen-year-old in John Leland, "Battle for Your Brain," *Newsweek*, October 11, 1993.
2. Figures from Anthony R. Pratkanis and Eliot Aronson, *Age of Propaganda*, 1992; Kathleen Hall Jamieson and Karlyn Kohrs Campbell, *The Interplay of Influence*, 1988; Peter M. Nichols, "Home Video" column, *New York Times*, July 30, 1993. *Newsweek*, August 2, 1993, reports that Nielsen Media Research estimates the average daily viewing time for television as six hours and forty-six minutes.
3. A later Gerbner report summarizing many earler findings is "Women and Minorities on Television," a report to the Screen Actors Guild and the American Federation of Radio and Television Artists, issued in June 1993. See also George Garbner, Larry Gross, Michael Morgan, and Nancy Signorielli, "Charting the Mainstream: Television's Contribution to Political Orientations," in Donald Lazare, ed., *American Media and Mass Culture*, 1987.
4. Betsy Sharkey, "The Secret Rules of Ratings," *New York Times*, August 28, 1994.
5. Quoted in Walter Goodman, "All That Piffle on TV? It's Someone Else's Fault," *New York Times*, February 21, 1993.
6. See Martin Jay, *The Dialectical Imagination: A History of the Frankfurt School and the Institute of Social Research, 1923–1950*, 1973.
7. Robert Evans, *The Kid Stays in the Picture*, 1994.
8. William Goldman, *Adventures in the Screen Trade*, 1983.
9. T. D. Adorno, *The Philosophy of Modern Music*, 1973.
10. Jeffrey Wells, "Blazing Trailers," *Washington Post*, May 23, 1993.

11. Franco Ferraroti, *The End of Conversation*, 1988. On the topic of television as addiction, see also Marie Winn, *The Plug-In Drug: Television, Children and the Family*, 1985.

12. Linda Seger, *Making a Good Script Great*, 1987.

13. Goldman, *Adventures in Screen Trade*.

14. Pierre Martineau, *Motivation in Advertising*, 1957.

15. Statistics reported in "Kiddie TV Packs the Most Punch," an Associated Press story in *New York Post*, January 28, 1993, and Don Feder, "MTV = Mindless TV," *New York Post*, April 22, 1993.

16. Tom Shales, "Saturated with Sex," *New York Post*, September 13, 1993.

17. Elizabeth Kolbert, "Not Only Bochco's Uniforms Are Blue," *New York Times*, July 26, 1993.

5. Transforming the News

1. Shanto Iyengar and Donald F. Kinder, *News That Matters: Television and American Opinion*, 1987.

2. Statistics cited in Jamieson and Campbell, *Interplay of Influence*, and in Robert M. Entman, *Democracy Without Citizens*, 1989.

3. Pamela J. Shoemaker, Caroline Schooler, Wayne A. Danielson, "Involvement with the Media: Recall Versus Recognition of Election Information," *Communication Research*, February 1989. Many other studies echo these conclusions.

4. Anthony R. Pratkanis and Eliot Aronson, *Age of Propaganda: Everyday Use and Abuse of Persuasion*, 1992.

5. Stephen Hess, Brookings Institution, 1981, cited in Kathleen Hall Jamieson, *Eloquence in an Electronic Age*, 1988.

6. Howard Kurtz, "Tabloid Sensationalism Is Thriving on TV News," *Washington Post*, July 4, 1993.

7. Remarks quoted in Verne Gay, "Rather Cutting," *Newsday*, October 1, 1993.

8. I use the word "reluctant" here because I consider myself an alumnus and a fan of CBS News, having worked on a documentary series for the network for three years, 1966–69.

9. Museum of Television and Radio item T81:0518.

10. W. Nelson Francis and Henry Kucera, *Frequency Analysis of English Usage: Lexicon and Grammar*. 1982.

11. The figure here is adjusted to take into account the difference in amount of words of each sample. The AH is based on 5 million words, the Brown on 1 million. The compilers of the Brown sample report that it's "predictability" was high, that is, if an additional million words had been sampled, the word-frequencies in that second million would have been almost precisely the same as in those in the first million. So I have multiplied their number of occurrences by five.

12. MTAR Item T79:0409. It should be noted that the Museum's collection is far from complete; in fact, it is made up principally of donated items, rather than those which have been sought for the collection by the museum's directors or scholars.
13. MTAR Item T81:0519.
14. Francis and Kucera, *Frequency Analysis of English Usage*.
15. MTAR Item T:20355.
16. Hartvig Dahl, *Word Frequencies of Spoken American English*, 1979.
17. E. J. Dionne, Jr., "Clinton's Bully Pulpit," *Washington Post*, November 16, 1993; Anthony Lewis, "Now Be the President," *New York Times*, November 19, 1993.
18. Walter J. Ong, *Rhetoric, Romance and Technology*, 1971.

A Pause for Reflection: What Is Being Lost

1. Max Picard, *The World of Silence*, 1952.
2. *Ibid.*
3. Thomas Merton, *The Seven Storey Mountain*, 1948.
4. You cannot engage a book in dialogue either, as Plato was the first to point out.
5. Malone quoted in John Markoff, "A Phone-Cable Vehicle for the Data Superhighway," *New York Times*, October 14, 1993.
6. Later, Cronkite went even farther, charging that neither television news nor most newspapers were doing their jobs properly. "The trouble at least for some newspapers is that they are being prepared for people who can't read by people who can't write," Cronkite told an audience in 1979. Deirdre Carmody, "Cronkite Faults Papers and TV, Citing Coverage," *New York Times*, April 26, 1979.
7. Statistic for the 1984 campaign for the presidency, compiled by the George Washington University Media Analysis Project, cited in Kathleen Hall Jamieson, *Eloquence in an Electronic Age*, 1988.
8. Mihaly Csikszentmihalyi, "Relax? Relax and Do What?" *New York Times*, August 12, 1993.
9. A perhaps apocryphal story is told in Hollywood about the film distributor who called up a studio head and decreed, "Don't send me no more pictures with people who write with feathers."
10. Jamieson and Campbell, *Interplay of Influence*.
11. Jon Pareles, "Rock to Blues to Country: At the Post Office," *New York Times*, October 9, 1992.

6. Land of the Word

1. Reported in Richard L. Berke, "Unhumbled, Buchanan Backs Bush," *New York Times*, August 18, 1992, and Maralee Schwartz and Kenneth J. Cooper, "Equal Rights Initiative in Iowa Attacked," *Washington Post*, August 23, 1992.
2. All quotes taken from transcript in *New York Times*, October 16, 1992.
3. Michael X. Delli Carpini, Robert D. Holsworth, and Scott Keeter, "'Consumer Journalism' in the Electronic Age: Instant Reaction to the 'People's' Presidential Debate," *The Finish Line* (pamphlet), 1993.
4. Uwe Reinhardt, quoted in Walter Goodman, "Assessing the Candidates' Health-Care Ideas," *New York Times*, October 29, 1992.
5. Kenneth Burke, *The Philosophy of Literary Form*, 1941.
6. Moses Coit Tyler, quoted in Barnet Baskerville, *The People's Voice*, 1979.
7. Quoted in *ibid.*
8. Alexis de Tocqueville, *Democracy in America*, 1838.
9. Joshua I. Miller, *The Rise and Fall of Democracy in Early America, 1630–1789: The Legacy for Contemporary Politics*, 1991.
10. Michael P. Kramer, *Imagining Language in America*, 1992.
11. Baskerville, *People's Voice*.
12. Barrett, *Rhetoric and Civility*.
13. Richard Sennett, *The Fall of Public Man*. 1977.
14. Holbrook quoted in Carl Bode, *The American Lyceum*, 1956.
15. From the 1840 census: Counting potential voters who were white and over age twenty, in Connecticut only one in 574 was deemed illiterate, while in North Carolina, the figure for illiterates was one out of nine. Cited in Bode, *ibid.* However, since voting eligibility was still highly restricted, those figures do not completely reflect the literacy rate of the country or region.
16. Holmes and Emerson quoted in *ibid.*
17. Anti-Federalists had argued against the adoption of the Constitution on just this point: they feared the executive would absorb power and eventually come to resemble a king.
18. Kenneth Cmiel, *Democratic Eloquence: The Fight over Popular Speech in Nineteenth-Century America*, 1990.
19. E. L. Godkin in *The Nation*, quoted in Baskerville, *People's Voice*, and J. G. Holland in *Scribner's Monthly*, quoted in Bode, *American Lyceum*.
20. Sennett, *Fall of Public Man*.
21. Lowell and others cited in Baskerville, *People's Voice*. Italics in original.
22. Joseph C. Gould, *The Chautauqua Movement*, 1961.
23. As printed, e.g., in Louis W. Koenig, *Bryan, a Political Biography*, 1971.
24. Letter to Mary Hulbert, August 25, 1912, quoted in Arthur S. Link, *Wilson: The Road to the White House*, 1947.
25. Quoted in Joseph L. Gardner, *Departing Glory: Theodore Roosevelt as Ex-President*, 1973.

26. Wilson, *Public Papers*.
27. Quoted in Tom Shachtman, *Edith and Woodrow*, 1981.
28. Robert S. Lynd and Helen M. Lynd, *Middletown*, 1929.
29. Gould, *Chautauqua Movement*.
30. Jamieson, *Eloquence in an Electronic Age*.
31. William Safire, *Before the Fall: An Inside View of the Pre-Watergate White House*, 1975.
32. Erving Goffman, *The Presentation of Self in Everyday Life*, 1959; idem, *Behavior in Public Places*, 1963.
33. Sig Mickelson, *The Electric Mirror*, 1972.
34. Samuel Kernell, *Going Public: New Strategies of Presidential Leadership*, 1986.
35. Roderick P. Hart, *The Sound of Leadership: Presidential Communication in the Modern Age*, 1987.

7. Politics and Language

1. Raymond Gozzi, Jr., *New Words and a Changing American Culture*, 1990. Henry Kucera, "The Mathematics of Language," in *The American Heritage Dictionary*, Second College Edition, 1985.
2. Kucera, "Mathematics."
3. Gozzi, *New Words*.
4. *Ibid*.
5. Hannah Arendt, *On Revolution*, 1963.
6. Murray Edelman, *Constructing the Political Spectacle*, 1988.
7. Gozzi, *New Words*.
8. Kenneth G. Wilson, *Van Winkle's Return*, 1987.
9. Various articles in Reinhold Aman, ed., *The Best of "Maledicta,"* 1987.
10. Vivian de Klerk, "Expletives: Men Only?" in *Communications Monographs*, vol. 58, June 1991.
11. Dominic A. Infante, Teresa A. Chandler, and Jill E. Rudd, "Test of an Argumentative Skill Deficiency Model of Interspousal Violence," in *Communications Monographs*, vol. 56, June 1989.
12. Irving Lewis Allen, *The Language of Ethnic Conflict*, 1983.
13. Cmiel, *Democratic Eloquence*.
14. Anita L. Vangelisti, Mark L. Knapp, and John A. Daly, "Conversational Narcissism," *Communications Monographs*, December 1990.
15. H. L. Mencken, *The American Language* (originally pub. 1919–23), revised and abridged ed., 1977.
16. This section on the language usages of the Nazi and Soviet regimes follows that in John Wesley Young, *Totalitarian Language*, 1991.
17. Foucault, quoted by Martha Cooper, "Ethical Dimensions of Political Advocacy from a Postmodern Perspective," in Robert E. Denton, Jr., ed., *Ethical*

Dimensions of Political Communications, 1991. Jacques Ellul, *The Technological Society*, 1964.

18. Cited in Young, *Totalitarian Language*.
19. Cited in *ibid.*
20. *Ibid.*
21. Max Horkheimer, *The Eclipse of Reason*, 1947. Italics in original.
22. Young, *Totalitarian Language*.
23. Aleksandr Solzhenitsyn, *The Gulag Archipelago*, 1974.
24. Shevchenko quoted in Young, *Totalitarian Language*.
25. F. E. X. Dance, "Ong's Voice: 'I,' The Oral Intellect, You, and Me," lecture, August 5, 1987.
26. George Orwell, *Nineteen Eighty-Four*, 1961 edition. Italics in original.
27. William Lutz, "Introduction" in Lutz, ed., *Beyond Nineteen Eighty-Four, Doublespeak in a Post-Orwellian Age*, 1989.
28. Hugh Rank, *The Pep Talk*, 1984.
29. Hugh Rank, "The Teacher-Heal-Thyself Myth," in Rank, ed., *Language and Public Policy*, 1974.
30. William Lutz, "Notes Toward a Definition of Doublespeak," in Lutz, *Beyond Nineteen Eighty-Four*.
31. The case is cogently analyzed in Richard O'Mara, "A Terrorist Is a Guerrilla Is a Freedom Fighter," *The Quill*, October 1990.
32. Kathleen Hall Jamieson, "The Cunning Rhetor, The Complicitous Audience, The Conned Censor, and The Critic," *Communications Monographs*, vol. 57, March 1990.
33. Richard Ohrmann, "Worldthink," in Lutz, ed., *Beyond Nineteen Eighty-Four*.
34. Greenspan, 1981 quote, cited in Lutz, "Notes." A dozen years later, now as Chairman of the Federal Reserve Board, Greenspan continued to perplex. At a February 22, 1994, congressional hearing, he said, "When the Federal Reserve tightens reserve market conditions, it is not surprising to see some upward movement in long-term rates as an aspect of the process that counters the imbalances tending to surface in the expansionary phase of the business cycle."
35. Orwell, "Politics and the English Language," in *The Orwell Reader*, 1956.
36. Danet, "Language in the Legal Process," *Law and Society Review*, Spring 1980.
37. Charles Weingartner, "What Do We Know?" in Lutz, ed., *Beyond Nineteen Eighty-Four*.
38. See, e.g., Jürgen Habermas, *Toward a Rational Society*, 1971.
39. Susan Chira, "A Scholar's Convictions Keep Her Pushing the Power of Words," *New York Times*, November 15, 1992.
40. David Gonzalez, "What's the Problem with 'Hispanic'? Just Ask a Latino," *New York Times*, November 15, 1992.

41. Steven Pinker, "The Game of the Name," *New York Times*, April 5, 1994.
42. Joe Klein, "City of Euphemisms," *Newsweek*, February 22, 1993.
43. George Vecsey, "Unseeded, Not Uncheered," *New York Times*, June 23, 1993.
44. Michael Winerip, "What's Humor to One Brings Pain to Another," *New York Times*, June 6, 1993.
45. Patrick de Gramont, *Language and the Distortion of Meaning*, 1990.

8. "We, the Audience of the United States"

1. Marsha L. Vanderford, "Vilification and Social Movements," *Quarterly Journal of Speech*, May 1989.
2. Michael Huspek and Kathleen E. Kendall, "On Withholding Political Voice," *Quarterly Journal of Speech*, February 1991; F. Christopher Arterton, *Teledemocracy: Can Technology Protect Democracy?* 1987.
3. Stanley A. Deetz, *Democracy in an Age of Corporate Colonization*, 1992.
4. Press release, April 16, 1993. Voter turnout has declined by more than 20 percent in the last two decades, the committee has found. American turnout is 25 percent lower than in Canada or the United Kingdom, 35 percent lower than in many states in continental Europe, and 40 percent lower than in Sweden, Italy, or Austria. See also James S. Fishkin, *Democracy and Deliberation*, 1991, and David Glass, Peveril Squire, and Raymond Wolfinger, "Voter Turnout: An International Comparison," *Public Opinion*, December–January 1984.
5. Tocqueville, *Democracy in America*.
6. Gladstone quoted in Baskerville, *People's Voice*; Kenneth Burke, *A Rhetoric of Motives*, 1950.
7. Barrett, *Rhetoric and Civility*.
8. Michigan studies, Entman, *Democracy Without Citizens*; Markle study reported in Michael Oreskes, "Study Finds Astonishing Indifference to Elections," *New York Times*, May 6, 1990.
9. Mercedes Vilanova, "Anarchism, Political Participation, and Illiteracy in Barcelona Between 1934 and 1936," *American Historical Review*, February 1992.
10. James Boyd White, "The Invisible Discourse of the Law," in Bailey and Fosheim, eds. *Literacy for Life*.
11. Quoted in Jamieson, "Cunning Rhetor."
12. Gerbner *et al.*, "Charting the Mainstream."
13. Murray Edelman, *Constructing the Political Spectacle*, 1988.
14. *Ibid.* Emphasis in original.
15. Speech to the Electors of Bristol, November 3, 1774.
16. Entman, *Democracy Without Citizens*. I disagree with his contention that the media can only quote a politician's critics back at him. Analysis is always

possible, but to produce it takes time that broadcast journalists avow they do not have or are not willing to devote to the task.

17. Pratkanis and Aronson, *Age of Propaganda*. Emphasis in original.

18. Della Femina quoted in William Meyer, *The Image Makers*, 1984; Martineau, *Motivation in Advertising*.

19. *The Speeches of Adolf Hitler*, April 1922–August 1939, 1969.

20. See Barrett, *Rhetoric and Civility*; Baskerville, *People's Voice*; Edelman, *Constructing Political Spectacle*; Jamieson and Campbell, *Interplay of Influence*; and David H. Bennett, *The Party of Fear*, 1988.

21. Steven R. Goldzwig, "A Social Movement Perspective on Demagoguery: Achieving Symbolic Realignment," *Communication Studies*, Fall 1989.

22. Robert Schmuhl, *Statecraft and Stagecraft: American Political Life in the Age of Personality*, 1990.

23. F. E. X. Dance, "Ong's Voice: 'I,' The Oral Intellect, You, and Me," lecture, August 5, 1987.

24. Cited in J. Jeffery Auer, "Acting Like a President," in Michael Weiler and W. Barnet Pearce, ed., *Reagan and Public Discourse in America*, 1992.

25. Ronald Reagan, *Speaking My Mind: Selected Speeches*, 1989; Reagan, *An American Life*, 1990.

26. Mary E. Stuckey, *Getting Into the Game: The Pre-Presidential Rhetoric of Ronald Reagan*, 1989.

27. Stuckey, *ibid.*

28. Deaver quoted in Michael Weiler and W. Barnett Pearce, "Ceremonial Discourse," in Weiler and Pearce, *Reagan and Public Discourse*.

29. *Ibid.*

30. Ronald Reagan, *Public Papers*, vol. II, (1983), 1985.

31. Mary E. Stuckey, *Playing the Game: The Presidential Rhetoric of Ronald Reagan*, 1990.

32. James F. Bohman, "Participating in Enlightenment," in Marcelo Dascal and Ora Gruengard, eds., *Knowledge and Politics*, 1989.

33. Oleg Manaev, "The Disagreeing Audience," *Communications Research*, February 1991.

34. Habermas's views are expressed in many works, among them, *Towards a Rational Society*, 1971; *Legitimation Crisis*, 1975; and *Theory of Communicative Action*, 1981–87. This section is also indebted to Bohman, "Participating in Enlightenment," and to Martha Cooper, "Ethical Dimensions."

Conclusion: Toward a Revolt of the Articulate Elite

1. Tocqueville, *Democracy in America*.

2. Fowler, *Talking from Infancy*.

3. Teacher salary figures from American Federation of Teachers' study, cited in William Celis III, "Teachers in U.S. Trail Those Elsewhere in Pay," *New York Times*, August 18, 1993.

4. Alan Riding, "France: A Method of Teaching That Produces Readers," and Anita Peltonen, "Finland: A Free School System with Very Few Cracks," *New York Times*, December 9, 1993.

5. Joseph Berger, "Fighting over Reading," *New York Times*, November 17, 1993; Rexford G. Brown, *Schools of Thought*.

6. John Zola, "Scored Discussions," *Social Education*, February 1992.

7. For this section, I am indebted to voluminous materials sent to me by Dr. Michael Cronin at Radford University, Dr. Robert O. Weiss at DePauw University, Dr. Patricia R. Palmerton at Hamline University, and Dr. Sherwyn Morreale at University of Colorado, Colorado Springs, who are among the leaders in the SAC movement.

8. Materials from The Center for Oral Excellence, University of Colorado at Colorado Springs, February 1993.

9. Letters and materials from American Forensic Association and National Forensic League, February 1993.

10. Ronald P. Stewart, "Best Debaters Come from Public Schools," letter, *New York Times*, October 16, 1992.

11. Catherine Zizik, personal communication, December 1993.

12. Alvin H. Perlmutter, "The 1% Solution," *New York Times*, December 29, 1994.

13. Paul Gagnon, "Why Study History?" *Atlantic Monthly*, November 1988.

14. Daniel Yankelovich, *Coming to Public Judgment*, 1991.

15. *Ibid.*, and Daniel Yankelovich, "How Public Opinion Really Works," *Fortune*, October 19, 1992.

16. Glass *et al.*, "Voter Turnout."

17. James S. Fishkin, *Democracy and Deliberation: New Directions for Democratic Reform*, 1991. Emphasis in original.

18. John Darnton, "American in London to Test 'Deliberative' Polling," *New York Times*, September 21, 1993.

19. Frank Stanton, "Test TV town meetings," *San Antonio Express-News*, September 1, 1993.

20. Don Finley, "San Antonians Chime in on Health-care Proposals," *San Antonio Express-News*, September 2, 1993; and *idem*, "Taking Citizens Seriously," *America's Agenda*, Fall 1993.

21. Supplement to Des Moines newspapers, November 1982; and supplement to News-Journal papers, Wilmington, Delaware, May 6, 1985. Melville, personal communication, November 1993.

22. Charles Strum, "Town Meeting's Agenda: Way of Life," *New York Times*, October 22, 1993.

23. George Santayana, *Character and Opinion in the United States*, 1955.

BIBLIOGRAPHY

Adler, Mortimer J. *The Paideia Proposal: An Educational Manifesto*. New York: Macmillan, 1982.

Adorno, Theodor D. *The Philosophy of Modern Music*. New York: Seabury Press, 1973.

Allen, Irving Lewis. *The Language of Ethnic Conflict*. New York: Columbia University Press, 1983.

Aman, Reinhold, ed. *The Best of* Maledicta. Philadelphia: Running Press, 1987.

Andersen, Elaine Slosberg. *Speaking with Style: The Sociolinguistic Skills of Children*. London: Routledge, 1990.

Arendt, Hannah. *On Revolution*. Penguin Books, 1977 edition Hammond & Worth, Eng. 1963.

Aristotle. *Rhetorica ad Alexandrum*. Trans. W. S. Hett and H. Rackman. Loeb Classical Library Volume XVI. Cambridge: Harvard University Press, 1983.

Arterton, Christopher. *Teledemocracy: Can Technology Protect Democracy?* Newbury Park, Calif.: Sage, 1987.

Bailey, Richard W., and Robin Melanie Fosheim, eds. *Literacy for Life: The Demand for Reading and Writing*. New York: Modern Language Association of America, 1983.

Baron, Naomi S. *Growing Up with Language: How Children Learn to Talk*. Reading, Mass.: Addison-Wesley, 1992.

Barrett, Harold *Rhetoric and Civility: Human Development, Narcissism, and the Good Audience*. Albany: State University Press of New York, 1991.

Baskerville, Barnet, ed. *The People's Voice: The Orator in American Society*. Lexington: University of Kentucky Press, 1979.

Bennett, David H. *The Party of Fear*. Chapel Hill: University of North Carolina Press, 1988.

Bergman, Ingmar. *Four Screenplays of Ingmar Bergman*. Trans. Lars Malmstrom and David Kushner. New York: Simon & Schuster, 1960.

Berlin, James A. *Writing Instruction in Nineteenth-century American Colleges*. Carbondale: Southern Illinois University Press, 1984.

Bernstein, Basil. *Class, Codes and Control*. Vol. I: *Theoretical Studies Towards a Sociology of Language*. London: Routledge & Kegan Paul, 1971.

Black, John W.; Cleavonne S. Stratton; Alan C. Nichols; and Marian Ausherman Chavez. *The Use of Words in Context: The Vocabulary of College Students*. New York: Plenum Press, 1985.

Bode, Carl. *The American Lyceum: Town Meeting of the Mind*. New York: Oxford University Press, 1956.

Bohman, James F. "Participating in enlightenment: Habermas's cognitivist interpretation of democracy." In Marcelo Dascal and Ora Gruengard, eds. *Knowledge and Politics: Case Studies in the Relationship Between Epistemology and Political Philosophy*. Boulder, Colo.: Westview Press, 1989.

Boorstin, Daniel. *The Image: A Guide to Pseudo-events in America*. New York: Harper, 1962.

Borisoff, Deborah, and Michael Purdy, eds. *Listening in everyday life, a personal and professional approach*. Lanham, Md.: University Press of America, 1991.

Brown, Rexford. *Schools of Thought: How the Politics of Literacy Shape Thinking in the Classroom*. San Francisco: Jossey-Bass, 1991.

Burke, Kenneth. *Philosophy of Literary Form, Studies in Symbolic Action*. New York: Vantage Books, 1957.

———. *A Rhetoric of Motives*. New York: Prentice-Hall, 1950.

Burke, Peter. *The Art of Conversation*. Ithaca, N.Y.: Cornell University Press, 1993.

Carroll, John B.; Peter Davies; and Barry Richman. *The American Heritage Word Frequency Book*. Boston: Houghton-Mifflin, 1971.

Chall, Jeanne S.; Vicki A. Jacobs; and Luke E. Baldwin. *The Reading Crisis: Why Poor Children Fall Behind*. Cambridge: Harvard University Press, 1990.

Cherry, Colin. *On Human Communication*. Cambridge: MIT Press, 1977.

Chomsky, Noam. *Language and Mind* New York: Harcourt Brace Jovanovich, 1972.

Cialdini, Robert B. *Influence: How and Why People Agree to Things*. New York: Morrow, 1984.

Cmiel, Kenneth. *Democratic Eloquence: The Fight Over Popular Speech in Nineteenth-century America*. New York: Morrow, 1990.

Cremin, Lawrence A. *The Transformation of the School: Progressivism in American Education, 1876–1957*. New York: Knopf, 1961.

———. *Popular Education and Its Discontents*. New York: Harper & Row, 1990.

Cronin, Michael, and Philip Glenn. "Oral communication across the curriculum in higher education: The state of the art." *Communication Education*, vol. 40, no. 4, October 1991.

Dahl, Hartvig. *Word Frequencies of Spoken American English*. Essex, Conn.: Verbatim, 1979.

Dance, F. E. X. "Ong's voice: 'I,' the oral intellect, you, and we." Lecture, August 5, 1987.

————, and C. E. Larson. *The Functions of Human Communication: A Theoretical Approach*. New York: Holt, Rinehart & Winston, 1976.

Danet, Brenda. "Language in the legal process." *Law and Society Review*, Spring 1980.

Deetz, Stanley A. *Democracy in an Age of Corporate Colonization*. Albany: State University of New York Press, 1992.

De Gramont, Patrick. *Language and the Distortion of Meaning*. New York: New York University Press, 1990.

Delli Carpini, Michael X.; Robert D. Holsworth; and Scott Keeper. "Consumer journalism in the electronic age: Instant reaction to the 'people's' presidential debate." In *The Finish Line: Covering the Campaign's Final Days*. New York: Columbia University, 1993.

Denton, Robert E., Jr., ed. *Ethical Dimensions of Political Communication*. New York: Praeger, 1991.

DeWitt, Jean; Mary Bozik; Ellen Hay; Judith Litterst; C. Sue Strohkirch; and Karolyn Yocum. "Oral communication competency and teacher certification in the U.S.: Reality and recommendations." *Communication Education*, vol. 40, no. 2, April 1991.

Dimitracopolou, Ionanna. *Conversational Competence and Social Development*. Cambridge: Cambridge University Press, 1990.

Douglas, William. "Expectations about initial interaction: An examination of the effects of global uncertainty." *Human Communication Research*, vol. 17, no. 3, March 1991.

Edelman, Murray. *Constructing the Political Spectacle*. Chicago: University of Chicago Press, 1988.

Ellul, Jacques. *The Technological Society*. Trans. John Wilkinson. New York: Knopf, 1964.

Entman, Robert M. *Democracy Without Citizens: Media and the Decay of American Politics*. New York: Oxford University Press, 1989.

Evans, Robert. *The Kid Stays in the Picture*. New York: Hyperion, 1994.

Ferraroti, Franco. *The End of Conversation: The Impact of Mass Media on Modern Society*. New York: Greenwood Press, 1988.

Fishkin, James S. *Democracy and Deliberation: New Directions for Democratic Reform*. New Haven: Yale University Press, 1991.

Foucault, Michel. *The Archaeology of Knowledge*. Trans. Sheridan Smith. London: Tavistock, 1972.

————. *Discipline and Punish: The Birth of the Prison*. Trans. Alan Sheridan. New York: Pantheon, 1977.

————. *Language, Counter-memory, Practice: Selected Essays and Interviews*. Trans. Donald F. Bouchard and Sherry Simon. Ithaca, N.Y.: Cornell University Press, 1977.

Fowler, William. *Talking from Infancy*. Cambridge: Brookline Books, 1990.

Francis, W. Nelson, and Henry Kucera. *Frequency Analysis of English Usage: Lexicon and Grammar*. Boston: Houghton-Mifflin, 1982.

Fries, Charles Carpenter. *American English Grammar*. New York: Appleton-Century-Crofts, 1940.

————. *The Structure of English*. New York: Harcourt Brace, 1952.

Gagnon, Paul. "Why study history?" *Atlantic Monthly*, November 1988.

Gardner, Joseph L. *Departing Glory: Theodore Roosevelt as Ex-President*. New York: Scribner's, 1973.

Garvey, Catherine. *Children's Talk*. Cambridge: Harvard University Press, 1984.

Gerbner, George. *Women and Minorities on Television: A Report to the Screen Actors Guild and the American Federation of Radio and Television Artists*. Privately printed, June 15, 1993.

Glass, David; Peveril Squire; and Raymond Wolfinger. "Voter turn-out: An international comparison." *Public Opinion*, December–January 1984.

Goffman, Erving. *The Presentation of Self in Everyday Life*. Garden City: Doubleday, 1959.

————. *Behavior in Public Places*. Glencoe, Ill.: Free Press, 1963.

————. *Relations in Public*. New York: Basic Books, 1971.

Goldfarb, Jeffrey C. *The Cynical Society: The Culture of Politics and the Politics of Culture in American Life*. Chicago: University of Chicago Press, 1991.

Goldman, William. *Adventures in the Screen Trade: A Personal View of Hollywood and Screenwriting*. New York: Warner Books, 1983.

Goldzwig, Steven R. "A social movement perspective on demagoguery: Achieving symbolic realignment." *Communication Studies*, vol. 40, no. 3, Fall 1989.

Gould, Joseph E. *The Chautauqua Movement: An Episode in the Continuing American Revolution*. Albany: State University of New York Press, 1961.

Gozzi, Raymond, Jr. *New Words and a Changing American Culture*. Columbia: University of South Carolina Press, 1990.

Gramsci, Antonio. *Selections from Cultural Writings*. Ed. David Forgacs and Geoffrey Nowell-Smith. Trans. William Boelhower. Cambridge: Harvard University Press, 1985.

Habermas, Jürgen. *The Theory of Communicative Action*. Vol. 1: *Reason and Rationalization of Society*. Vol. 2: *Lifeworld and System: A Critique of Functionalist Reason*. Trans. Thomas McCarthy. Boston: Beacon Press, 1981, 1987.

————. *Legitimation Crisis*. Trans. Thomas McCarthy. Boston: Beacon Press, 1975.

————. *Towards a Rational Society*. Translated by J. J. Shapiro. Boston: Beacon Press, 1970.

Halliday, Michael A. K. *Explorations in the Function of Language*. London: Edward Arnold, 1973.

Hart, Roderick P. *The Sound of Leadership: Presidential Communication in the Modern Age*. Chicago: University of Chicago Press, 1987.

Hayes, Donald P. "Speaking and writing: Distinct patterns of word choice." *Journal of Memory and Language*, vol. 27, October 1988.

Healy, Jane. *Endangered Minds: Why Our Children Don't Think*. New York: Simon & Schuster, 1990.

Hess, Stephen. *The Washington Reporter*. Washington: Brookings, 1981.

Horkheimer, Max. *The Eclipse of Reason*. New York: Oxford University Press, 1947.

———, and Theodor Adorno. *Dialectic of Enlightenment*. New York: Seabury Press, 1972.

Huspek, Michael, and Kathleen E. Kendall. "On withholding political voice." *Quarterly Journal of Speech*, vol. 77, no. 1, February 1991.

Infante, Dominic A.; Teresa A. Chandler; and Jill E. Rudd. "Test of an argumentative skill deficiency model of interspousal violence." *Communications Monographs*, vol. 56, June 1989.

Iyengar, Shanto, and Donald F. Kinder. *News That Matters: Television and American Opinion*. Chicago: University of Chicago Press, 1987.

Jamieson, Kathleen Hall. *Eloquence in an Electronic age: The Transformation of Political Speechmaking*. New York: Oxford University Press, 1988.

———. "The cunning rhetor, the complicitous audience, the conned censor, and the critic." *Communications Monographs*, vol. 57, no. 2, March 1990.

———, and Karlyn Kohrs Campbell. *The Interplay of Influence: Mass Media and Their Publics in News, Advertising, Politics*. Belmont, Calif.: Wadsworth, 1988.

Jay, Martin. *The Dialectical Imagination: A History of the Frankfurt School and the Institute of Social Research, 1923–1950*. Boston: Little, Brown, 1973.

Jones, Celeste P., and Lauren B. Adamson. "Language use in mother–child and mother–child–sibling interactions." *Child Development*, vol. 58, no. 2, April 1987.

Joseph, John Earl. *Eloquence and Power: The Rise of Language Standards and Standard Languages*. London: Frances Pinter, 1987.

Kernell, Samuel. *Going Public: New Strategies of Presidential Leadership*. Washington, D.C. CQ Press. 1986.

Klein, Joe. "City of euphemisms." *Newsweek*, February 22, 1993.

Klerk, Vivian de. Expletives: Men Only? *Communications Monographs*, vol. 58, no. 3, June 1991.

Koenig, Louis W. *Bryan: A Political Biography of William Jennings Bryan*. New York: Putnam's, 1971.

Kramer, Michael P. *Imagining Language in America: From the Revolution to the Civil War*. Princeton, N.J.: Princeton University Press, 1992.

Kramer, Rita. *Ed School Follies: The Miseducation of America's Teachers*. New York: Free Press, 1991.

Kucera, Henry. "The mathematics of language." In *The American Heritage Dictionary*. Boston: Houghton-Mifflin, 1985.

Labov, William. *Language in the Inner City: Studies in the Black English Vernacular*. Philadelphia: University of Pennsylvania Press, 1972.

————. *The Social Stratification of English in New York City*. Washington: Center for Applied Linguistics, 1966.

Lazare, Donald, ed. *American Media and Mass Culture: Left Perspectives*. Berkeley: University of California Press, 1987.

Leland, John. "The battle for your brain." *Newsweek*, October 11, 1993.

Lieberman, Philip. *Uniquely Human: The Evolution of Speech, Thought and Self-less Behavior*. Cambridge: Harvard University Press, 1991.

Liebes, Tamar, and Rivka Riebak. "The contribution of family culture to political participation, political outlook, and its reproduction." *Communications Research*, vol. 19, no. 5, October 1992.

Link, Arthur S. *Wilson: The Road to the White House*. Princeton, N.J.: Princeton University Press, 1947.

Luriia, A. R. *Cognitive Development: Its Cultural and Social Foundations*. Trans. Martin Lopez-Morillas and Lynn Solataroff. Cambridge: Harvard University Press, 1976.

Lutz, William, ed. *Beyond Ninteen-Eighty Four: Doublespeak in a Post-Orwellian Age*. Urbana, Ill.: National Council of Teachers of English, 1989.

Lynd, Robert S., and Helen M. Lynd. *Middletown: A Study of Modern American Culture*. New York: Harcourt Brace, 1929.

Manaev, Oleg. "The disagreeing audience." *Communications Research*, vol. 18, no. 1, February 1991.

Martineau, Pierre. *Motivation in Advertising*. New York: McGraw-Hill, 1957.

McLuhan, Marshall, and Quentin Fiore. *The Medium Is the Massage*. New York: Bantam, 1967.

Mencken, H. L. *The American Language* (1919–23). One-volume abridged ed. New York: Knopf, 1977.

Merton, Thomas. *The Seven Storey Mountain*. New York: Harcourt, Brace, 1948.

Meyer, William. *The Image Makers*. New York: Times Books, 1984.

Mickelson, Sig. *The Electric Mirror: Politics in an Age of Television*. New York; Dodd, Mead, 1972.

Miller, Joshua I. *The Rise and Fall of Democracy in Early America, 1630–1789: The Legacy for Contemporary Politics*. University Park: Pennsylvania State University Press, 1991.

Morgan, Michael, and Larry Gross. "Television viewing, IQ and academic achievement," *Journal of Broadcasting*, vol. 24, 1980.

Morreale, Sherwyn; Pamela Shockley-Zalabak; and Penny Whitney. "The Center for Excellence in Oral Communication: Integrating communication across the curriculum." *Communication Education*, vol. 42, no. 1, January 1993.

Morreale, Sherwyn; M. Hackman; P. Shockley-Zalabak; and A. Gomez. "An innovative approach to teaching oral communication: The Center for Excellence in Oral Communication." *Education*, vol. 112, 1991.

O'Keefe, Daniel J. *Persuasion: Theory and Research*. Newbury Park, Calif.: Sage Publications, 1990.

O'Mara, Richard. "A terrorist is a guerilla is a freedom fighter." *The Quill*, vol. 78, no. 8, October 1990.

Ong. Walter J. *Orality and Literacy: The Technologizing of the Word*. London: Routledge, 1982.

————. *Interfaces of the Word: Studies in the Evolution of Consciousness and Culture*. Ithaca, N.Y.: Cornell University Press, 1977.

————. *Rhetoric, Romance, and Technology: Studies in the Interaction of Expression and Culture*. Ithaca, N.Y.: Cornell University Press, 1971.

Ortega y Gasset, Jose. *The Revolt of the Masses*. Trans. Anthony Kerrigan. Notre Dame, Ind.: University of Notre Dame Press, 1985.

Orwell, George. *Nineteen Eighty-four* (1948). New York: New American Library, 1961 edition.

————. "Politics and the English language." In *The Orwell reader*. New York: Harcourt Brace, 1956.

Pederson, Lee. "Language, culture and The American Heritage." In *The American Heritage dictionary*. Boston: Houghton-Mifflin, 1985.

Perkins, David. *Smart Schools: From Training Memories to Educating Minds*. New York: Free Press, 1992.

Picard, Max. *The World of Silence*. Trans. Stanley Godman. Chicago: Henry Regnery, 1952.

Pinker, Steven. *The Language Instinct: How the Mind Creates Language*. New York: Morrow, 1994.

Plato. *Phaedrus and Letters VII and VIII*. Trans. Walter Hamilton. New York: Viking Penguin, 1973.

————. *Plato's Apology and Other Selections*. Ed. Raphael Demos. New York: Scribner's, 1927.

Postman, Neil. *Technopoly: The Surrender of Culture to Technology*. New York: Knopf, 1992.

Pratkanis, Anthony R., and Elliot Aronson. *Age of Propaganda: Everyday Use and Abuse of Persuasion*. New York: W. H. Freeman, 1992.

Rank, Hugh. *The Pep Talk: How to Analyze Political Language*. Park Forest, Ill.: Counterpropaganda Press, 1984.

————, ed. *Language and Public Policy*. Urbana, Ill.: National Council of Teachers of English, 1974.

Ravitch, Diane, and Chester E. Finn, Jr. *What Do Our 17-year-olds Know? A Report on the First National Assessment of History and Literature*. New York: Harper & Row, 1987.

Reagan, Ronald. *An American Life*. New York: Simon & Schuster, 1990.

————. *Speaking My Mind: Selected Speeches*. New York: Simon & Schuster, 1989.

Resnick, Lauren A., ed. *Knowing, Learning and Instruction: Essays in Honor of Robert Glaser*. Hillsdale, N.J.: Lawrence J. Erlbaum, 1989.

Richards, Maryse H., and Elena Duckett. "The Relationship of Maternal Employment to Early Adolescent Daily Experience With and Without Parents." *Child Development*, Vol. 65, No. 1, February 1994.

Ritter, Kurt, and David Henry. *Ronald Reagan, the Great Communicator*. Westport, Conn.: Greenwood Press, 1992.

Rivers, Larry. *What Did I Do? The Unauthorized Autobiography of Larry Rivers*. New York: Harper Collins, 1992.

Rothwell, J. Dan *Telling It Like It Isn't: Language Misuse and Malpractice*. New York: Prentice-Hall, 1982.

Safire, William. *Before the Fall: An Inside View of the Pre-Watergate White House*. New York: Random House, 1975.

Santayana, George. *Character and opinion in the United States*. New York: Braziller, 1955.

Sapir, Edward. "The status of linguistics as a science." In David G. Mandelbaum, ed., *Selected Writings of Edward Sapir on Language, Culture and Personality*. Berkeley: University of California Press, 1949.

Schieffelin, Bambi, and Elinor Ochs. "Language socialization." In *Annual Review of Anthropology*, vol. 5, 1988.

Schmidt, Rosemarie, and Joseph F. Kess. *Television Advertising and Televangelism*. Amsterdam: J. Benjamins Pub. Co., 1986.

Schmuhl, Robert. *Statecraft and Stagecraft: Americal Political Life in the Age of Personality*. Notre Dame, Ind.: University of Notre Dame Press, 1990.

Seger, Linda. *Making a Good Script Great*. New York: Dodd, Mead, 1987.

Sennett, Richard. *The Fall of Public Man: On the Social Psychology of Capitalism*. New York: Knopf, 1977.

Shachtman, Tom. *Edith and Woodrow: A Presidential Romance*. New York: Putnam's, 1981.

Shoemaker, Pamela J.; Carolina Schooler; and Wayne A. Danielson. "Involvement with the media: Recall versus recognition of election information." *Communications Research*, vol. 16, no. 1, February 1989.

Solzhenitsyn, Aleksander I. *The Gulag Archipelago, 1918–1956: An Experiment in Literary Investigation*. Trans. Thomas P. Whitney. New York: Harper & Row, 1974.

Stern, Daniel N. *The Interpersonal World of the Infant*. New York: Basic Books, 1985.

Stuckey, Mary E. *Playing the Game: The Presidential Rhetoric of Ronald Reagan*. New York: Praeger, 1990.

———. *Getting into the Game: The Pre-presidential Rhetoric of Ronald Reagan*. New York: Praeger, 1989.

Toch, Thomas. *In the Name of Excellence: The Struggle to Reform the Nation's Schools*. New York: Oxford University Press, 1991.

Tocqueville, Alexis Charles Henri Maurice Clerel de. *Democracy in America*. Trans. Henry Reeve. New York: Adlard & Saunders, 1838.

Vanderburg, Willem. *The Growth of Minds and Cultures: A Unified Theory of the Structure of Human Experience*. Toronto: University of Toronto Press, 1985.

Vanderford, Marsha L. "Vilification and social movements: A case study of pro-life and pro-choice rhetoric." *Quarterly Journal of Speech*, vol. 75, no. 2, May 1989.

Vangelisti, Anita L.; Mark L. Knapp; and John A. Daly. "Conversational narcissism." *Communications Monographs*, vol. 57, no. 6, December 1990.

Vangelisti, Anita L., and John A. Daly. "Correlates of speaking skills in the United States: A national assessment." *Communication Education*, vol. 38, 1989.

Veblen, Thorstein. *Theory of the leisure class* (1899). New York: Random House, 1934 edition.

Vilanova, Mercedes. "Anarchism, political participation and illiteracy in Barcelona, 1934–1936." *American Historical Review*, vol. 91, no. 1, February 1992.

Vygotskii, Lev S. *Thought and Language*. Trans. A. Kozulin. Cambridge: MIT Press, 1986.

Weiler, Michael, and W. Barnett Pearce, eds. *Reagan and Public Discourse in America*. Tuscaloosa: University of Alabama Press, 1992.

Weinstein, Brian. *The Civic Tongue: Political Consequences of Language Choices*. London: Longmans, 1983.

Wells, Gordon. "Language, learning and teaching: Helping learners to make knowledge their own." In F. Lowenthal and F. Vandamme, eds., *Pragmatism and Education*. New York: Plenum Press, 1986.

Whorf, Benjamin Lee. "Science and linguistics." In John B. Carroll, ed., *Language, Thought and Reality: The Selected Writings of Benjamin Lee Whorf*. Cambridge: Technology Press of MIT, 1956.

Wieseltier, Leon. "Total quality meaning." *New Republic*, July 19 and 26, 1993.

Wilson, Kenneth G. *Van Winkle's Return: Change in American English, 1966–1986*. Hanover, N.H.: University Press of New England, 1987.

Winterowd, W. Ross. *The Culture and Politics of Literacy*. New York: Oxford University Press, 1989.

Witherspoon, Arnold D.; Carolyn K. Long; and Eugenie B. Nickell. "Dropping out: Relationship of speaking anxiety to self-esteem, crime, and educational achievement." *Psychological Reports*, vol. 69, 1991.

Wolfgang, Charles H., and Karla Lynn Kelsay. "Problem students in class: Disobedient—or just 'de-valued'?" *The Education Digest*, February 1992.

INDEX

Adams, John, 48
Adorno, Theodor, 9, 105, 106
Agassiz, Louis, 162
AH. See *American Heritage Word Frequency Book*
Ailes, Roger, 219
Allen, Irving Lewis, 182–83
Amadeus, 104
Aman, Reinhold, 181
American Forensic Association, 250
American Heritage Word Frequency Book, 81, 121–22, 124, 134
American National Council of Teachers of English, 192
America's Most Wanted, 119
Analysis
  competence in, 77–78
  effect of denigration, 237–38
  as skill, 91–92
  of vocabulary diminution, 83–85
Andersen, Elaine Slosberg, 21–24, 56
Arendt, Hannah, 179
Aristotle, 42, 151, 161
Aronowitz, Stanley, 88
Aronson, Elliot, 116, 218
Articulate behavior
  decline of, 76–87, 95–98, 235–38
  education for and components of, 65, 248–49
  effect of television news on, 118–19
  elements in mastery of, 14–15
  as elite virtue, 259–60
  factors influencing child's, 31
  impact on teaching of, 72–73
  inadequate, 5–6
  models to teach adult, 156

of movie villains, 111
nonexclusivity of, 259
as product of learning, 11, 13
proposals to encourage, 241–43, 249–59
relation to intelligence, 52
of talk-show hosts, 141
Articulate expression
  circumstances for, 2–4
  correlation with achievement, 88
  effect of confrontational discourse, 180
  encouragement of, 242
  during U.S. Civil War, 164
Audiences
  losses with inarticulateness, 143–52
  mass, 100–101
  Reagan's appeal to, 223–28
  response to heuristic clue, 217–20

Babytalk, or Motherese, 22–24
The Barefoot Contessa, 105
Barney, 32–33
Baron, Naomi S., 17–18, 28–29
Barrett, Harold, 22, 34–35, 161, 210
Baskerville, Barnet, 160–61
Beavis and Butt-head, 99–100, 144
Berlin, James A., 72
Bernstein, Basil, 51–52
Bernstein, Leonard, 104
Berra, Yogi, 7
Black, John W., 83
Black English Vernacular (BEV), 53–55
Bochco, Steven, 113–14
Bode, Carl, 162
Bohman, James F., 228

Oral culture
  communication strategies, 57
  languages of, 43–46, 60
  primary and secondary, 10–11, 24–25,
    57–59, 140–41, 235
Oral knowing
  of information and knowledge, 191
  Nazi and Soviet devices, 191–92
Oral languages
  Cajun as, 56
  in-group speech, 59–60
Oral noetic devices, 186–92, 224
Oral societies, 57
  differences from literate societies,
    10–11, 81
Oratory, political, 157–62, 172
  See also Speech, political
Ortega y Gasset, José, 9
Orwell, George, 9, 192, 197, 237
Osborn, Michael, 213

Paradise Lost, 111
Perkins, David, 76
Perot, Ross, 153, 154, 156
Phatic speech, 59–60
Picard, Max, 145
Pictures to tell stories, 107–8
Pinker, Steven, 23–24, 50
Pius XI (pope), 187
Poetic Justice, 143–44
Political correctness, 199
Political discourse, 218–20
Politics
  change in content and process of
    American, 165–66
  Civil War citizen involvement, 164
  effect of commodification on, 156–57
  factors influencing participation,
    207–8
  influence of television on, 214–17
  new language uses, 192–93
  proposal for candidate selection,
    256–57
Povich, Maury, 138–39
Pratkanis, Anthony R., 116, 218
Preacher Earl, 59
Prior, Sandra, 66
Propagandists, 186–87, 232
Public action, 233–34

Public affairs programs, 9
Public Agenda Foundation, 257–58
Public good of articulate behavior, 241
Pulp Fiction, 110
Purdy, Michael, 91

Quayle, Dan, 249
Questioning skills, 91–92

Radio
  effect on audience participation,
    170–71
  effect on Chautauqua attendance, 171
  effect on political discourse, 172
  use for political purposes, 171–72
Rank, Hugh, 193, 194–95
Rap culture, 57–59
Raphael, Sally Jessy, 139
Rather, Dan, 118–19
Ravitch, Diane, 67
Reagan, Ronald
  language of avoidance, 193
  rhetoric and philosophy of, 223–28
Recitation, 72, 77–78
Redpath, James, 166
Reification, 204–5, 237
Rhetoric
  changes in study of, 73
  of demagogue, 220–23
  elements of classical, 157, 162
  in elite curriculum, 71–72
Rhetoric, political
  modern, 157–62
  in support of policy, 175
Rhetorical sensitivity, 22, 35
Ribak, Rivka, 35–36
Rivers, Joan, 137
Rivers, Larry, 60
Robertson, Pat, 153–54
Robin Hood, 105
Roosevelt, Franklin D., 172
Roosevelt, Theodore, 168–70
Roosevelt Center for the Study of
  American Policy, 208
Runyon, Marvin, 151–52

SAC programs. *See* Speaking Across the
  Curriculum (SAC) programs